Geert Brône, Kurt Feyaerts, Tony Veale (Eds.)
Cognitive Linguistics and Humor Research

Applications of Cognitive Linguistics

Editors
Gitte Kristiansen
Francisco J. Ruiz de Mendoza Ibáñez

Honorary Editor
René Dirven

Volume 15

Geert Brône, Kurt Feyaerts, Tony Veale (Eds.)
Cognitive Linguistics and Humor Research

—

ISBN 978-3-11-055397-0
e-ISBN (PDF) 978-3-11-034634-3
e-ISBN (ePUB) 978-3-11-039503-7

Library of Congress Cataloging-in-Publication Data
A CIP catalog record for this book has been applied for at the Library of Congress.

Bibliographic information published by the Deutsche Nationalbibliothek
The Deutsche Nationalbibliothek lists this publication in the Deutsche Nationalbibliografie; detailed bibliographic data are available on the Internet at http://dnb.dnb.de.

The publisher, together with the authors and editors, has taken great pains to ensure that all information presented in this work (programs, applications, amounts, dosages, etc.) reflects the standard of knowledge at the time of publication. Despite careful manuscript preparation and proof correction, errors can nevertheless occur. Authors, editors and publisher disclaim all responsibility and for any errors or omissions or liability for the results obtained from use of the information, or parts thereof, contained in this work.

The citation of registered names, trade names, trademarks, etc. in this work does not imply, even in the absence of a specific statement, that such names are exempt from laws and regulations protecting trademarks etc. and therefore free for general use.

© 2017 Walter de Gruyter GmbH, Berlin/Boston
Dieser Band ist text- und seitenidentisch mit der 2015 erschienenen gebundenen Ausgabe.
Typesetting: RoyalStandard, Hong Kong
Printing and binding: CPI books GmbH, Leck
♾ Printed on acid-free paper
Printed in Germany

www.degruyter.com

Table of contents

Tony Veale, Geert Brône and Kurt Feyaerts
1 **Humour as the *killer-app* of language** —— 1

Eleni Antonopoulou, Kiki Nikiforidou and Villy Tsakona
2 **Construction grammar and discoursal incongruity** —— 13

Benjamin Bergen and Kim Binsted
3 **Embodied grammar and humor** —— 49

Tony Veale
4 **The humour of exceptional cases: Jokes as compressed thought experiments** —— 69

Salvatore Attardo
5 **Humorous Metaphors** —— 91

Ralph Müller
6 **A metaphorical perspective on humour** —— 111

Rachel Giora, Ofer Fein, Nurit Kotler and Noa Shuval
7 **Know hope: Metaphor, optimal innovation and pleasure** —— 129

Gregory A. Bryant and Raymond W. Gibbs Jr.
8 **Behavioral complexities in ironic humor** —— 147

Seana Coulson
9 **Frame-shifting and frame semantics: Joke comprehension on the space structuring model** —— 167

Margherita Dore
10 **Metaphor, humour and characterisation in the TV comedy programme Friends** —— 191

Kurt Feyaerts, Geert Brône and Robin De Ceukelaire
11 **The Art of Teasing** —— 215

Index —— 243

Tony Veale, Geert Brône and Kurt Feyaerts
1 Humour as the *killer-app* of language
A view from Cognitive Linguistics

Language is the ultimate "*killer app*" of the human mind. No other application of human cognition is so flexible, so extensible or so richly-featured, and none does a better job of showing off the diverse functionality of its underlying hardware. The refrain "there's an app for that" is commonplace in our everyday discussions of what our technologies can and should do for us. But language is no less a technology than our software, and has long given us the refrain "there's a word for that". Language, like a universal computer, allows for its own extension and adaptation to the contexts of its use. It allows us to invent words that give solid form to inchoate concepts or newly-birthed and still-unsettled ideas. As Goethe famously put it, words are most useful precisely when our ideas fail us. But language does more than paper over the cracks in our conceptual edifices. Humorous language actively seeks out these cracks, makes them evident to all, and proposes a means of filling the gaps that, if not always entirely practical, is nonetheless entertaining and thought-provoking (Fauconnier 1994; Coulson, this volume; Bergen and Binsted, this volume; Veale 2012; Veale, Feyaerts and Forceville et al. 2013). If language is the ultimate killer-app of the mind, it can often seem that humour – as a powerful conceptual, communicative and social application – is the killer-app of language, in the deepest and most subversive sense of "killer" (Giora 2003; Giora et al., this volume; Feyaerts and Oben 2014).

Language has a unifying power, one that allows us to condense a complex swirl of feelings and ideas into a single, highly evocative word or phrase. It allows us to construct a unified front around cognitive phenomena that are related but far from unified. This power, if unchecked by careful introspection and empirical analysis, can make essentialists of us all. Simplicity comes from having a single convenient word for a complex of related ideas, but simplicity also promotes over-simplification. As the philosopher Ludwig Wittgenstein put it, we are too often bewitched by language, beguiled into thinking that a certain concept – such as KNOWLEDGE – is simple and uniform and uncomplicated – because language has furnished us with a single, simple word like "know". Because we know how to use a word like "know", we tell ourselves that we must also know how to understand the underlying concept of KNOWLEDGE. Much the same dilemma presents itself when we aim to study humour from a linguistic, cognitive or computational perspective. The ease with which we use words like "humour" or "wit" or "joke" beguiles us into viewing HUMOUR as an essentially uniform concept: though it may take on diverse forms in language, we are bewitched into thinking that there is a single coherent deep-structure that gives rise to them all. But this need not be the case: just as Wittgenstein and a generation of cognitive psychologists after him (e.g. Rosch 1978) have shown, we frequently use words like "game" or "fake" that give an unearned impression of simplicity to complex ideas that lack both sharp boundaries and an essentialist, easy-to-define core. As cognitively-minded researchers of HUMOUR, we must admit the same complexity in the study of whatever it is that the word "humour" denotes.

In this regard, the field of Cognitive Linguistics (CL) is ideally positioned to support the study of humour in language (see Brône, Feyaerts and Veale 2006; Brône 2008, 2010, 2012; Feyaerts 2013 for similar arguments). CL acknowledges that, as the killer-app of the mind, language can leverage many diverse aspects of human cognition to explore, shape and communicate our feelings, beliefs and ideas. Likewise, there is no crevice in language into which humour cannot force a wedge. Our jokes and witticisms can exploit the highest structural levels of language, from discourse and genre conventions to narrative forms, down through sentence structures, word-order conventions, agreement constraints, all the way down to morphology, spelling, pronunciation and stress patterns (cf. Attardo 1994, 2001; Ritchie 2004; Raskin 2008; Aarons 2011; Ruiz Gurillo and Alvarado 2013; Dynel 2013; Antonopoulou, Nikiforidou and Tsakona, this volume). There is no automatic process in language that, with sufficient cleverness, humour cannot force us to de-automatize. Humour can wrest control back from the most autonomous of linguistic processes, and force these processes to bring arbitrary aspects of world knowledge or the vagaries of a specific context to bear on their otherwise scripted behaviours. All humour is subversive, and linguistic humour subverts utterly the idea that any part of our linguistic apparatus has any real autonomy (Giora 2003; Giora et al. 2004, this volume).

The wide-ranging CL perspective is much-needed for the study of humorous language, as the need to appear sober and scientific in the study of what many consider to be a frivolous subject has driven many young researchers into the arms of the two least attractive aspects of the scientific enterprise: essentialism and reductionism. All too often, interesting theories on humour are reduced to the closest thing they have to an essentialist core, to yield a snappy label or phrase that fails to accommodate many of the interesting nuances that the underlying theories have to offer. It is as though a humour theory can gain no traction if it cannot be reduced to a pithy two-word oxymoron, whether *incongruity resolution, appropriate incongruity, relevant inappropriateness, benign violation, mutual vulnerability,* or any other pairing of opposites one cares to mention. These are convenient labels to be sure, and convey some flavor of the theories they attach too, but they can also do more harm than good for the study of humour. Humour theorists would do well to distance themselves from these labels. Victor Raskin, for instance, has always shown a wily reluctance to accept the label of *incongruity resolution* for the theory *Semantic Script Theory of Humour* (SSTH, Raskin 1985) and for its evolution into the *General Theory of Verbal Humour* (GTVH, Attardo and Raskin 1991; Attardo 1994, 2001). This reluctance seems odd when one considers that both the SSTH and GTVH give a key role to incongruity resolution, but this reluctance seems more sensible than odd when one considers that their creators consider these theories to offer much more than *just* incongruity resolution.

By providing a broad foundation of cognitive mechanisms into which one can anchor a study of humour, CL offers a way out of the essentialist trap. Humorous language need not hinge on a single cognitive mechanism, but can avail of them all. Ideas like *incongruity resolution, appropriate incongruity, relevant inappropriateness* and *benign violation* are all still useful in a CL account of humour, but they no longer have to serve as enigmatic ciphers for an otherwise ineffable quality or poorly-understood process. Instead, they can serve as convenient short-hands for the complex of interactions between cognitive mechanisms that ultimately give them their meanings. This is the true meaning of Goethe's maxim about words and ideas: words and labels are IOUs when we are temporarily out of cash, or scaffoldings for conceptual buildings that are yet to be completed. Just as Wittgenstein described philosophy as a ladder that one kicks away when one reaches the understanding at the top, our convenient labels in humour research are designed to be cashed out, to be replaced by real cognitive understanding. The papers that comprise this volume each show researchers at different levels on their individual ladders. None is anywhere near reaching the top and kicking away either their ladders or their convenient labels, but each uses CL to climb their ladder, rung by rung. We ask you to judge for yourselves the progress they are making toward their goal, and the relative merits of the different ladders.

Given the focus of this volume on the application of concepts and tools from the broad field of CL, including classical notions such as metaphors, frames, mental spaces, conceptual integration, conceptual salience and grammatical constructions, to a wide range of phenomena that can be subsumed under the category HUMOUR, we do not primarily aim at an extensive review of the literature in humour research (see e.g. Raskin 2008, Martin 2007 for excellent reviews of the literature, and Brône, Feyaerts and Veale (2006), Brône and Feyaerts (2004) and Brône (2010) for a critical review of the position of CL vis-à-vis linguistic humour theories). Rather, the volume is intended as a collection of papers that explore the explanatory potential of the cognitive mechanisms that have played a central role in the field of CL. In this sense, this collection aims to cater for a broad public, including cognitive linguists interested in the empirical elasticity and 'valorization potential' of their conceptual apparatus, cognitive scientists interested in the phenomenon of humour as the playground for the fluid conceptual system and humour researchers seeking additional analytical tools.

Outline of this volume

This volume consists of a total of 10 chapters, divided into four thematic sections, covering a variety of methodological and theoretical issues. The first section deals with the largely unexplored humorous potential of grammar, and the possibility to exploit the semantics and pragmatics of grammatical constructions for humorous purposes (Antonopoulou, Nikiforidou and Tsakona; Bergen and Binsted). The second section focuses on the classical CL notions of metaphor and figure/ground organization, which have been frequently linked to humour and creativity, but whose internal relationship requires further scrutiny (Veale; Attardo; Müller). The third section approaches humour from an experimental point-of-view, in an attempt to empirically substantiate key concepts that were introduced in the literature, as e.g. frame-shifting, optimal innovation and multimodal signaling of irony and humour (Giora, Fein, Kotler and Shuval; Bryant and Gibbs; Coulson). The fourth and final section includes two chapters that present corpus-based investigations of interactional humour, using concepts and insights from CL, such as staged communicative acts, conceptual blending and metaphor (Dore; Feyaerts, Bröne and De Ceuckelaire). In what follows, we present a brief outline of the individual chapters.

In their chapter, *Eleni Antonopoulou, Kiki Nikiforidou* and *Villy Tsakona* investigate whether linguistic phenomena involving the realization of humorous incongruity may be systematically analyzed along the lines of construction grammar (cf. Bergen and Binsted, this volume). Starting point is the observation that although most construction-based analyses have focused on sentence-level phenomena (at best encompassing bi-clausal constructions such as conditionals), the framework may in principle be extended to cover larger pieces of discourse. The authors take up the challenge to analyze discourse-based instances of humorous incongruity as residing in constructional properties, and thus integrated in a theory of grammar. Accordingly, this paper focuses on linguistic units which emerge through their conventional association with specific discourse patterns or contexts, giving rise to humorous incongruity. In their corpus-based study, the authors also explore how conventional discourse patterns from a specific genre may be exploited in a different genre, so as to achieve a humorous effect. It is shown that the combination of discourse patterns originating in different genres does not necessarily result in the creation of a new genre, nor in the transformation of an existing one, but rather creates a unique *discourse space*, which is accessible to, and aims at amusing those readers who are familiar with the conventions of the genres involved. Construction grammar, defined as a usage-based model aiming to account for all types of linguistic knowledge, is argued to be the most adequate approach to provide cognitive grounding and a rigorous methodology for the analysis of large-scale patterns by recognizing that these patterns, just like sentence-level constructions, also consist of less and more fixed parts, of formal/schematic and substantive/lexical material.

Starting from a general theoretical perspective, *Benjamin Bergen* and *Kim Binsted* argue that of all modern language theories, those that go under the rubric of Cognitive Linguistics come closest to providing analytical and theoretical tools for studying the use of language for humorous purposes. The applicability of Cognitive Linguistics to humour derives from its emphasis on the embodiment of language – how it is used by humans with particular sorts of brains and bodies, with particular physical and social goals in specific physical and social contexts. The authors argue that an emphasis on the embodiment of language benefits an account of its role in humour for two reasons. First, the nature of the language used for humour is strongly influenced by the particular social contexts in which it is used and the social purposes it serves. Second, extralinguistic cognitive systems play an important role in processing humorous language. Humour makes use of constructional pragmatics and mental imagery, as well as metaphor and frames. Embodied (construction) grammars elucidate how language is used to produce and understand humour. Humour constitutes a domain of actual language use in which constructional pragmatics and mental imagery are not only obvious, but essential to the function of the language. Constructional pragmatics is acquired through exposure to language in particular social and discourse contexts, and as such, knowledge of them is strongly shaped by the individual's particular experiential history. Similarly, the importance of imagery to the meaningfulness and effectiveness of linguistic humour emphasizes the role that components of the human cognitive system other than strictly grammatical capacities play in human linguistic behavior. Together, the importance of constructional pragmatics and mental imagery evident in humorous language testify to the importance of the individual human experience to language use.

In his contribution, *Tony Veale* embarks on an intriguing exercise of comparing the similarity between humour and thought experiments (or *Gedanken* experiments). The basis for this comparison is the observation of both activities as powerful cognitive abilities, through which human beings – in domains as different as scientific discourse and social intercourse – may explore and even influence category boundaries. Both activities aim at exposing and surpassing the limitations and inconsistencies of received wisdom and habitual thinking, thus bringing about alternative conceptual perspectives and/or previously unarticulated instincts, intuitions and emotions. In both activities, imagination plays a crucial role as it encourages us to occasionally explore our minds as a mental laboratory. Ultimately, Tony Veale argues that many jokes can be described in terms of humorous thought experiments, in which the models under revision are genre conventions, taboos and social norms (cf. Antonopoulou, Nikiforidou and Tsakona, this volume). Conversely, many thought experiments can be interpreted as philosophical jokes, in which the subversive logic of humour is used to induce a contradiction in an opponent's theory. With regard to humour theories, Veale argues that this *Gedanken*-based subversion view of humour is complementary to the juxtaposition view as embodied in mechanisms like bisociation, script switching and frame shifting. According to Veale, the subversion view explains how and why new categories are created from old, thus explaining (rather than just describing) the creativity inherent in both joke production and joke understanding.

Why are some metaphors humorous and others not? How can we define the category of 'humorous metaphors'? In his contribution, *Salvatore Attardo* problematizes this very concept arguing that at most it can be used as an umbrella term for at least three different phenomena: (1) metaphors that are funny in and of themselves, (2) metaphors that describe a referent that is inherently funny, and (3) failed metaphors. Any account of humorous metaphors which has attempted to define such an overarching category presents itself as a variant of the so-called 'distance theory', in which invariably some sort of threshold of 'semantic distance' between the two domains involved in a metaphorical mapping is postulated. This threshold is supposed to represent the norm, beyond which a metaphorical mapping gets overstretched and is therefore perceived as humorous. Problematic about these approaches, however, is the lack of any operationalization or quantification of this threshold. At best, Attardo argues, humorous metaphors may share a family resemblance, but it does not seem possible or even desirable to reduce the idea of 'humorous metaphor' to a unique category. In this paper, Attardo presents an alternative, not necessarily antagonistic approach, which is grounded in recent accounts of the incongruity-resolution approach in humour research.

Ralph Müller bases his contribution on the longstanding belief that there is a conceptual similarity between metaphor and humour. Yet, unlike previous studies in this domain, he also focuses on the fact that humorous experiences are often described in terms of metaphorical mappings. In this respect, Müller points out that not only theoretical terms such as 'superiority', 'degradation' and 'incongruity' are of metaphorical origin, but that even basic experiences such as 'comic relief' or various kinds of laughter are often construed metaphorically. The paper addresses three major aspects of this link between metaphor and humour, the first of which offers a general overview of the rich literature on this topic. The second part investigates metaphorical mappings that describe humour in German and demonstrates that evaluation of humour and reasoning about its functions is strongly influenced by metaphors. A final aspect of the interplay between both phenomena concerns the question whether metaphors have a particular affinity to humour or vice versa.

In their contribution on creative metaphoric language use *Rachel Giora, Ofer Fein, Nurit Kotler* and *Noa Shuval* pursue two goals, the first of which is to demonstrate what processes are involved in language comprehension. The authors discuss a series of experiments in support of the Graded Salience Hypothesis (Giora 1997, 2003), from which can be concluded that less-salient interpretations are processed slower than salient ones, regardless of figurativeness. With respect to coherence, accordingly, it is shown that metaphoric and literal interpretations of utterances are not equally coherent. Only novel metaphor is viewed as hampering coherence, as predicted by the Graded Salience Hypothesis. Second, Giora and her colleagues provide experimental support for the Optimal Innovation Hypothesis according to which optimally innovative rather than metaphoric interpretations account for pleasurability. Accordingly, it is not figurativeness such as metaphor that induces pleasure, as would be expected from traditional views of 'poetic' language, but rather optimal innovativeness. It is only novel metaphor that is viewed as likable; familiar metaphors are just as pleasing as their familiar literal interpretations. What is likable about optimal innovativeness, it is argued, is the recognition of the salient in the novel.

In their contribution, *Gregory A. Bryant* and *Raymond W. Gibbs Jr.* investigate when and how we judge what someone says as being humorous by considering contemporary empirical research on irony and laughter. It is argued that through its highly complex and varied nature, (humour in) irony cannot be reduced to a single cognitive or affective process. On the background of explanatory broad principles and mechanisms, identified and described in theoretical accounts such as humour studies and cognitive linguistics, Bryant and Gibbs suggest additional methods and principles need to be included in the investigation of both the processing and appreciation of ironic humorous speech via laughter. From their review of contemporary research on laughter, tone of voice, and ironic meaning, Bryant and Gibbs Jr. conclude that the appreciation and signaling of humorous situations through laughter depends on so many complex factors that no simple theory can adequately explain the diversity of the phenomenon. It appears that speakers employ a variety of contrastive strategies to mark their ironic or humorous intent. These strategies are essentially multimodal as they are not restricted to the linguistic channel of expression but also include bodily actions as different ways to enact ironic humour as a 'staged communicative act'. In order to achieve this research goal, Bryant and Gibbs Jr. call for more behavioral, corpus-based studies, in which on the basis of different parameters the multimodal dimension of humorous-ironic conversation can be investigated.

In her contribution, Seana Coulson presents the space structuring model, first developed in Coulson (2000) as an integration of ideas from mental spaces theory, conceptual blending theory and cognitive grammar. According to this model, linguistic and non-linguistic elements in the discourse context selectively activate structures from background knowledge in the form of frames, which are distributed in different mental spaces and connected for the purpose of local meaning construction. The role of knowledge in long-term memory in this sense is primarily "one of constraining the topology of the mappings and completing unfilled slots in frames at different levels" (Coulson 2000: 159). In contrast to more traditional frame-based models (including to some extent the SSTH and GTVH), the space structuring model has a somewhat more flexible view in the sense that frames need not be explicitly tied to contextually available elements. Rather, frames are argued to serve to constrain the construction of cognitive models in specific discourse situations. Jokes and other forms of nonce sense provide prime examples of the type of flexible meaning construction covered by the space structuring model, as they often require a sudden and radical reorganization of the cognitive model of the message-level representation. This reorganization process, referred to as frame-shifting in the work by Coulson and colleagues, is obviously a much-debated phenomenon in humour research as well, better known by the term script-switching as it was coined by Raskin (1985).

After the theoretical introduction into the space structuring model, Coulson discusses a series of experiments, using different methodological paradigms, that demonstrate the psychological reality of frame-shifting. The complex relation between word meaning and contextual information in punch line jokes produces the hypothesis that frame-shifting requires a higher cognitive processing load than cases that do not force such a reconfiguration. This hypothesis was tested using self-paced reading (Coulson and Kutas 1998), the analysis of event-related brain potentials (ERP, Coulson and Kutas 2001) and eye-tracking (Coulson et al. 2006). The tests using these three experimental paradigms all confirm the basic hypothesis: reading times, brain wave patterns and gaze behaviour of test subjects are all indicative of the processing complexity of frame-shifting in one-line jokes. In addition the ERP experiment shows neural indices of the frame-shifting process after the final word of the joke has been processes, and the eye-movement data reveal that the higher processing cost is related to higher-level processing. In a following section, Coulson devotes specific attention to the neural substrate of frame-shifting, using a series of experiments that provide insights into the brain regions involved in the cognitive processing of jokes and puns. These experiments (reported in Coulson and Wu 2005, Coulson and Severens 2007) reveal a particular importance of the left hemisphere for pun comprehension (linked to the retrieval of word meaning), whereas narrative jokes draw more strongly on the right hemisphere (linked to frame semantic information). In a last section of the chapter, Coulson discusses the theoretical implications of phenomena like frame-shifting for frame-based models. She concludes that a model based on dynamic internal imagery and schematized simulation will be better equipped to account for the specific demands of joke comprehension.

In line with the contributions by Müller and Attardo (this volume), the study by *Margherita Dore* also sheds light on the often debated relationship between metaphor and humour. In her contribution, Dore focuses on metaphors taken from the first series of the American sitcom *Friends*. In her approach, Dore demonstrates both advantages and limitations of analyzing humorous metaphors through the application of three theoretical frameworks: Conceptual Metaphor Theory (CMT), Blending Theory (BT) and the Generalized Theory of Verbal Humour (GTVH). CMT is shown to help understand the conceptual metaphors underlying series of verbal metaphorical expressions and expressing conventional ways of experiencing and making sense of the world around us. Accordingly, CMT demonstrates how novel metaphors can be easily processed as they rely on the conceptual metaphors which are part of the common ground among the interlocutors. However, it can only deal with metaphorical conceptualizations based on a unidirectional cross-domain mapping. In contrast, BT appears useful in handling complex metaphors as it takes into account the flexible dynamic nature of (humorous) meaning construction in interaction. BT turns out to be better equipped to explain the way in which central inferences are produced while speaking or writing in the context and situation of a specific usage event. Concerning the GTVH, Dore argues that it enriches the linguistic analysis of each metaphorical expression through its focus on both script oppositions and the targets involved. The combination of these theories appeals once again for a well-balanced, non-restrictive approach to a phenomenon as multifaceted as humour.

In their paper, *Kurt Feyaerts, Geert Brône* and *Robin De Ceukelaire* present an empirical analysis of the phenomenon of humorous teasing as it occurs in four American sitcoms of the nineties: The Nanny, Friends, Married with Children and Spin City. The general aim of this study is to gain a better insight in the socio-semantic characteristics of humour involving teasing as a multi-layered and multi-perspectival phenomenon. On the basis of a corpus of 402 teasing sequences, the authors identify five parameters, the combination of which results in an integrated annotation grid. The application of this analytical model allows for a nuanced typological description of teasing as a prototypically structured category of interactional humour. Compared to existing studies of teasing, this corpus-based approach allows for an encompassing, more fine-grained analysis of teasing as an intersubjective process of meaning coordination, in which both cognitive-semantic and social aspects are taken into account. Beyond the scope of this paper, the authors expect this annotation grid to be a valuable starting point for a similar analysis of teasing as it occurs in spontaneous everyday interactions.

References

Aarons, Debra. 2011. *Jokes and the Linguistic Mind*. New York: Routledge.
Attardo, Salvatore. 1994. *Linguistic Theories of Humor*. Berlin/New York: Mouton de Gruyter.
  2001. *Humorous Texts: A Semantic and Pragmatic Analysis*. Berlin/New York: Mouton de Gruyter.
Attardo, Salvatore and Viktor Raskin. 1991. Script theory revis(it)ed: joke similarity and joke representation model. *Humor: International Journal of Humor Research* 4(3–4): 293–347.
Brône, Geert. 2008. Hyper- and misunderstanding in interactional humor. *Journal of Pragmatics* 40–12: 2027–2061.
Brône, Geert. 2010. *Bedeutungskonstitution in verbalem Humor. Ein kognitiv-linguistischer und diskurssemantischer Ansatz*. Frankfurt/ Berlin: Peter Lang.
Brône, Geert. 2012. Cognitive linguistic approaches to irony and humor. In: Hans-Jörg Schmid and Dirk Geeraerts (eds.), *Handbook of Cognitive Pragmatics*, 463–504. Berlin: Mouton de Gruyter.
Brône, Geert and Kurt Feyaerts. 2004. Assessing the SSTH and GTVH: A view from Cognitive Linguistics. *Humor: International Journal of Humor Research* 17–4: 361–372.
Geert Brône, Kurt Feyaerts and Tony Veale (eds.). 2006. Guest edition of a special issue of *Humor: International Journal of Humor Research* on the theme "Cognitive Linguistic Approaches to Humor" (19–3: 203–360). Berlin/New York: Mouton de Gruyter.
Coulson, Seana. 2000. *Semantic Leaps. Frame-Shifting and Conceptual Blending in Meaning Construction*. Cambridge: Cambridge University Press.
Coulson, Seana and Marta Kutas. 1998. Frame-shifting and sentential integration. UCSD Cognitive Science Technical Report 98–03.

Coulson, Seana. 2001. Getting it: Human event-related brain response to jokes in good and poor comprehenders. *Neuroscience Letters* 316: 71–74.
Coulson, Seana and Els Severens. 2007. Hemispheric asymmetry and pun comprehension: When cowboys have sore calves. *Brain & Language* 100: 172–187.
Coulson, Seana and Ying Choon Wu. 2005. Right Hemisphere Activation of Joke-Related Information: An Event-Related Brain Potential Study. *Journal of Cognitive Neuroscience* 17: 494–506.
Coulson, Seana, Thomas P. Urbach and Marta Kutas. 2006. Looking back: Joke comprehension and the space structuring model. *Humor: International Journal of Humor Research* 19–3: 229–250.
Dynel, Marta (ed.). 2013. *Developments in Linguistic Humour Theory*. Amsterdam: John Benjamins.
Fauconnier, Gilles. 1994. *Mental Spaces: Aspects of Meaning Construction in Natural Language*. Cambridge, M.A.: MIT Press.
Feyaerts, Kurt. 2013. Tackling the Complexity of Spontaneous Humorous Interaction: An Integrated Classroom-modeled Corpus Approach. In: Leonor Ruiz-Gurillo, M. Belén Alvarado-Ortega (eds.), *Irony and Humor: from pragmatics to discourse*, 243–268. Amsterdam: John Benjamins.
Feyaerts, Kurt and Bert Oben. 2014. Tracing down schadenfreude in spontaneous interaction. Evidence from corpus linguistics. In: Wilco W. van Dijk, Jaap Ouwerkerk (eds.), *Schadenfreude: Understanding Pleasure at the Misfortune of Others*, 275–291. Cambridge: Cambridge University Press.
Giora, Rachel. 1997. Understanding figurative and literal language: The graded salience hypothesis. *Cognitive Linguistics* 7: 183–206.
Giora, Rachel. 2003. *On our Mind: Salience, Context and Figurative Language*. New York: Oxford University Press.
Giora, Rachel, Ofer Fein, Ann Kronrod, Idit Elnatan, Noa Shuval and Adi Zur. 2004. Weapons of mass distraction: Optimal innovation and pleasure ratings. *Metaphor and Symbol* 19: 115–141.
Martin, Rod A. 2007. *The Psychology of Humor. An Integrative Approach*. New York: Elsevier Academic Press.
Raskin, Viktor. 1985. *Semantic Mechanisms of Humor*. Dordrecht: Reidel.
Raskin, Viktor (ed.). 2008. *The Primer of Humor Research*. Berlin/New York: Mouton de Gruyter.
Ritchie, Graeme. 2004. *The Linguistic Analysis of Jokes*. London/New York: Routledge.
Rosch, Eleanor. 1978. Principles of Categorization. In Eleanor Rosch and Barbara B. Lloyd (eds), *Cognition and Categorization*, 27–48. Hillsdale: Lawrence Erlbaum.
Ruiz Gurillo, Leonor and M. Belén Alvarado Ortega (eds.). 2013. *Irony and Humor: From pragmatics to discourse*. Amsterdam: John Benjamins.
Veale, Tony. 2012. *Exploding the Creativity Myth: The Computational Foundations of Linguistic Creativity*. London: Bloomsbury Academic.
Veale, Tony, Kurt Feyaerts and Charles Forceville. 2013. E Unis Pluribum: Using Mental Agility to Achieve Creative Duality in Word, Image and Sound. In Veale, Tony, Kurt Feyaerts and Charles Forceville (eds.), *Creativity and the Agile Mind: A Multidisciplinary Approach to a Multifaceted Phenomenon*, 37–58. Berlin/New York: Mouton de Gruyter.

Eleni Antonopoulou, Kiki Nikiforidou and Villy Tsakona
2 Construction grammar and discoursal incongruity

1 Introduction: Theoretical background

In a cognitive linguistic framework (Langacker 1987, 1991, 2001, 2008), "any aspect of a usage event, or even a sequence of usage events in a discourse, is capable of emerging as a linguistic unit, should it be a recurrent commonality" (Langacker 2001: 146). The repeated occurrence of the same or similar linguistic material in similar, specifiable circumstances results in the progressive entrenchment of different types of linguistic units "including those pertaining to pragmatics and discourse" (Langacker 2001: 147). This paper focuses on linguistic units emerging through their association to specific discourse patterns or contexts; in such cases, the necessary (for the humorous interpretation) incongruity resides precisely in such conventional discoursal associations.

The analysis is conducted in terms of Construction Grammar, whose cognitive underpinning is precisely the conventional pairing of form and meaning (including pragmatic and discoursal meaning). These pairings result in "constructions" of diverse sorts, specific properties of which can be shown to be responsible for their humorous interpretation. As stated repeatedly (Coulson 2005; Brône, Feyaerts and Veale 2006; Brône and Vandaele 2009), embedding humor analysis in well-studied, cognitive instances of creative language use, such as metaphor, metonymy, blending, prototypes, etc, has been a desideratum of (at least cognitively-oriented) humor research. On the other hand, humor research may further serve to test the explanatory power of such cognitive mechanisms and, therefore, present substantial challenges to the paradigm as a whole. As a cognitive usage-based approach, Construction Grammar (CxG) supports an integrated approach to humor analysis, in which information about the discoursal/textual/register characteristics associated with a particular form can be represented in the meaning pole of the corresponding construction. The dichotomy between semantics and pragmatics is rejected and information about topicality, focus, register, genre etc. is represented in constructions alongside purely semantic information (Goldberg 1995: 7, 2006; Fried and Östman 2004). "Meaning" in CxG stands for "all the *conventionalized* aspects of a construction's function, which may include not only properties of the situation described by the utterance, but also properties of the discourse in which the utterance is found...and of the pragmatic situation of the interlocutors" (Croft and Cruse 2004: 258).

Discoursally-based humorous incongruity, as well as the humorous coherence of whole texts can be seen, therefore, as residing in constructional properties, and thus integrated in a theory of grammar. An additional tenet of CxG, relevant to the analysis of our data, is the recognition of varying degrees of fixedness in constructions. In fact, the need to recognize fixed, substantive constructions alongside the (traditionally recognized) formal or schematic ones, as well as a continuum between the two, has been a founding premise of all constructional approaches. A substantive construction has all its elements fixed, e.g., the expression *It takes one to know one* which is completely fixed (cf. **It took one to know one*). A formal or schematic construction, on the other hand, is a grammatical pattern which is lexically empty, e.g., the subject-predicate construction: any word fitting the required function can be inserted in the appropriate slot of the pattern (Fillmore, Kay and O' Connor 1988; Croft and Cruse 2004). CxG recognizes a continuum between the substantive and the schematic, which ranges from morphemes and monomorphemic words, to complex and compound words, to completely substantive/lexically-filled idioms, to (semi)substantive patterns (*blow one's nose*), to (semi)schematic idioms (*the Xer, the Yer*),[1] to regular grammatical patterns requiring specific subsets of lexical material (e.g., a set of verbs fitting the ditransitive pattern), to completely schematic patterns (the subject-predicate construction).

Although most construction-based analyses have focused on sentence-level phenomena (at best encompassing bi-clausal constructions such as conditionals), the need to extend construction grammar to cover larger pieces of discourse has been noted in the literature. Östman, for instance, notes that certain discourse patterns represent conventionalizations of specific linguistic properties, a characteristic which places them on an equal footing with the conventionalized patterns known as 'grammar'. It stands to reason that "Construction Grammar methodology can be fruitfully extended to account for discourse phenomena" (Östman 2005: 125; see also Östman and Trousdale 2013).[2] In Östman's terms, a

---

[1] It is obviously the semi-schematic/substantive patterns that are theoretically challenging for the generative theories and have originally motivated all constructional approaches.

[2] In the available CxG manual (Fillmore and Kay 1993) regularities associated with larger structures are explicitly excluded from the set of grammatical constructions. However, as noted by Östman (2005: 129), the role of discourse factors in understanding has been recognized very early in the frame semantics literature. In the words of Fillmore (1982: 117 cited in Östman 2005: 129), "knowing that a text is, say, an obituary, a proposal of marriage, a business contract, or a folktale, provides knowledge about how to interpret particular passages in it, how to expect the text to develop, and how to know when it is finished. It is frequently the case that such expectations combine with the actual material of the text to lead to the text's correct interpretation. And once again this is accomplished by having in mind an abstract structure of expectations which brings with it roles, purposes, natural or conventionalized sequences of event types, and all the rest of the apparatus we wish to associate with the notion of 'frame'".

discourse construction specifically represents a conventionalized association of a particular text type (such as argumentative, descriptive, narrative, etc.) with a particular genre (for example recipes, obituaries, fairy tales). In the same line, the supra-clause size of horoscopes and scholarly commentaries, discussed here, can be accommodated in a constructional approach which, at the same time, focuses on the lexical, thematic as well as purely formal features that jointly constitute the relevant text types.

Constructions with identifiable discourse properties can therefore be seen as typical of specific *genres*, in the understanding of genres as social constructs negotiated among the members of specific communities and embedded in their discursive practices. In functional terms, texts belonging to the same genre exhibit similarities in their content, form, and function, thus enabling speakers to enact specific communicative practices (Swales 1990, 2009; Van Leeuwen 2005: 122–123, 127–128; Bhatia 2007). Although genres may initially appear to be static and classificatory constructs, they have been shown to be dynamic ones, in the sense that they allow for innovation and creativity, hence they are subject to manipulation and, eventually, change. As Bhatia (2007: 113) suggests, "[w]ithin generic boundaries, experienced users of genre often manage to exercise considerable freedom to manipulate generic conventions to respond to novel situations, to mix [...] 'private intentions' with socially recognized communicative purposes, and even to produce new forms of discourse". In what follows, we intend to investigate how conventional discoursal patterns coming from a specific genre are exploited in a different one, so as to create a humorous effect. The combination of discourse patterns originating in different genres may not necessarily result in the creation of a new genre or in the transformation of an existing one, but rather create a unique *discourse space* (Langacker 2008: 466) which is accessible to, and aims at amusing, those readers who are familiar with the conventions of the genres involved.

In what follows, we will first consider the extent to which CxG research has addressed the issue of constructions characterized through their discourse properties and suggest an extension of established CxG methodology.

2 Discourse-based constructions: The state of the art

An early attempt to incorporate (in CxG) constructions identified on the basis of their discourse-functional or information-structural value is attested in Croft and Cruse (2004: 242–243) and exemplified through clefts and pseudo-clefts (using

Prince's 1978 functionalist analysis) and topicalising constructions (using Birner and Ward's 1998 research on preposing, postposing and argument reversal). Institutionalized or register-specific discourse (such as recipes analysed in Halliday and Matthiessen 1999, or headlines in Feyaerts 2006) is also accounted for in terms of constructions in Östman (2005) who demonstrates the importance of incorporating holistic, discourse-level frames "akin to genres" (Östman 2005: 126) and proposes specific ways of representing discourse related information within the existing CxG formalization (Östman 2005: 135). In the same line, Nikiforidou (2010, 2012) develops a constructional approach to the analysis of free indirect style, a mode of speech and thought representation licensed only by narrative and associated with very specific genres.

Moreover, discourse-based constructions have been identified before, under different names and within different theoretical frameworks. Indirect speech acts, for one, are, in present terms, semi-schematic constructions (Stefanowitsch 2003), as are also various expressions analyzed as conventionalized implicatures, formal idioms, blended conventionalised formulations, etc. (Moon 1998; Kay 2006).³ In such cases "the lexis is routinely varied without any apparent limits, while the frame or syntagmatic structure and pragmatic/discoursal intention remain fixed" (Moon 1998: 158). Patterns characterizing genres, traditionally identified within conversation analysis and discourse analysis, can be considered also semi-schematic constructions, while to the extent that close lexical lists or fixed expressions of various length are identified within these patterns, the latter constitute the substantive part of the larger constructions.

The discourse patterns we investigate here are typically characterized by both substantive (lexical) elements and by more schematic (productive) features, which may be either grammatical/structural or thematic. The recognition of thematic regularities as constructional features clearly represents an extension of established CxG methodology, albeit a well-justified one, since such features are part of the conventional makeup of the pattern. What brings them together is the fact that they are characterized by their conventionality. In line with much recent work on idiomaticity, phraseology and construction analysis (Nunberg, Sag and Wasow 1994; Cowie 1998; Moon 1998; Bybee 2006; Feyaerts 2006;

---

3 Moon (1998: 158–161) includes formal idioms of the type analyzed in Fillmore, Kay and O' Connor (1988) in the category she calls "free realizations" along with: (a) identical rhetorical questions conjoined for emphasis pre-empting the addressee's agreement (*Am I right or am I right?*), (b) rhetorical/pseudo-questions produced in answer to questions considered unnecessary (*Is the Pope Catholic?*) and interpreted as hints, (c) blended types (*Is a bear Catholic?*). In all she identifies instances of creative formulations and points out that the frame is consistent and the interest lies in the variation (i.e. the substantive part).

Langlotz 2006; Penttillä 2007), we deem that conventionality is the most important, in fact necessary, feature for assigning idiomatic/constructional status.[4] We argue that all the examples here are sufficiently entrenched (Langacker 1987: 57–64, 1991; Goldberg 2006) to be considered conventional linguistic units. That entrenchment (and therefore conventionality) is a matter of degree does not come as a surprise to any cognitive linguist. Given that the conventionality is in this case discourse-based, we may in fact expect some variation in judgments (presumably reflecting the varying entrenchment in particular contexts – and this we discuss with respect to specific examples). But this is an expected and totally natural result in any usage-based theory and in a theory, such as CxG, that accommodates continua of all kinds. The constructional/idiomatic character of such examples lies precisely in their conventional association to established discourse patterns or contexts (which they automatically recall), and should not be missed just because they may on occasion be grammatically straightforward and/or semantically compositional. Our data differ as to the extent they represent genre-specific discourse. Writing conventions for academic research, for instance, are well established and the genre in question immediately identifiable. Classroom discourse is clearly institutionalized as is the discourse associated with the Alcoholics Anonymous, while horoscopes also represent a specific genre, with its own formal and thematic conventions. Such data we discuss in section 4.

However, discoursally-motivated patterns further include certain substantive or semi-substantive expressions which become arguably formulaic within particular discourse types or settings (e.g., interpersonal, couple talk). It is only within such settings and because of their conventional association with them, that these expressions carry certain meanings and/or implicatures.[5] It is these latter cases which highlight yet another aspect of the constructional approach (indeed, of any cognitive linguistic approach), namely the fact that it is usage-based: "facts about the actual use of linguistic expressions such as frequencies and individual patterns that are fully compositional are recorded alongside

---

4 Fillmore, Kay, and O'Connor's (1988) "encoding idioms", Nunberg, Sag, and Wasow's (1994) "idiomatically combining expressions" and Bybee's (2006) "prefabs" are co-extensive categories of expressions defined solely on the basis of conventionality.
5 We may think of such cases, as an extension of the category of idiomatic expressions termed by Fillmore, Kay and O'Connor (1988) "idioms with a pragmatic point". These are expressions which are constrained to be used in certain contexts, e.g., *once upon a time* (fairy tales), *good morning, hey, take care,* etc. (standard ways for opening or closing conversations). Although identified early, idioms with a pragmatic point have not been much explored. What we suggest here is that by realizing that often the pragmatic point is discoursal in nature and triggered within particular settings, we can extend the constructional approach to phenomena that have been hitherto excluded from grammatical analysis.

more traditional linguistic generalizations" (Goldberg 2006: 45). What emerges from such data is the need to refine the frequency parameter so as to reflect frequency within particular discourse types or settings. This allows clearer insights into the actual usage of certain expressions and the prototypical structure of the corresponding category, which may be obscured from simple, discourse-independent counts in general corpora. Section 5 deals with this latter type, while in section 3 below, we focus on the humorous exploitation of discourse patterns within alternative frameworks, juxtaposing them to our own proposal, before we embark on the analysis of our data.

3 Humorous exploitation of discourse patterns

Recycling and recontextualisation for humorous purposes can apply freely in the case of sequences with fixed positions and typically conventionalized, salient meanings attacking conventional use while at the same time keeping the canonical pattern intact. The playful recycling of the relevant, (otherwise) completely fixed formulae, such as the core sequences of telephone call openings, for instance, has been shown to aim at challenging linguistic conventions (Antonopoulou and Sifianou 2003). One point at which the proposed analysis differs from those of different frameworks is the status of these expressions and their relation to the rest of the lexicogrammar of a language.

In discussing the notorious 'doctor wife's joke', Simpson (2003: 35) shows that its humor originates in an opposition between 'discursive units', since it is a departure from the formula of service encounters. The relevant trigger here is the first utterance of the character in the joke described as speaking with a 'bronchial' voice: "Is the doctor in?" This introduces the service encounter setting (as Simpson points out) and gives rise to the first script (patient-doctor) which will then be opposed by the second one (the lover script) activated by the response of the doctor's "young and pretty wife" "No, come right in". Simpson (2003: 36) notes: "the discursive shift [from a public to a private domain] suggested here is predicated upon a culturally driven formula". In Simpson's understanding, discoursal units are juxtaposed to cognitive ones. Within a cognitive framework, there is no cognitive-discoursal incompatibility. In fact, we are drawing attention to the importance of subsuming interactional aspects of discourse to cognitively oriented studies (Brône, Feyaerts and Veale 2006: 211). In Langacker's terms (2008: 457), although discourse is often considered a separate topic, "requiring different methods and descriptive constructs, the contrast with lower levels is at most a matter of degree". In cognitive grammar, discourse is understood as the "very basis for language structure and [...] thus essential for understanding grammar" (Langacker 2008: 457). Conventional patterns of language engendered through recursive occurrence of similar usage events involve all the specific level characteristics of utterances, along with the expression's full conceptual understanding (Langacker 2008: 457–458).

In short, since discourse units signal *conceptual* domains, they have *ipso facto* cognitive status. As already mentioned in section 1, from a Cognitive Linguistics perspective (Langacker 2001: 143), lexical structures of whatever length are "instructions to modify a certain discourse state", allowing for a unified treatment of discourse expectations (Emmott 1997: 270–271). This is precisely the approach taken here where the focus is on conventional units of language linked with specific discoursal properties; in humorous discourse, these may in turn lead to socio-cultural incongruities treated as a side effect of yet another type of constructional property.

In fact, the type of data we examine here can be seen as instances of "encoding idioms" first discussed in Fillmore, Kay and O'Connor 1988 (see also Croft and Cruse 2004; Bybee 2006). These are expressions, which although interpretable by the (syntactic and semantic) rules of the language, they are still idiomatic as associating a particular form with a meaning (e.g., *answer the door, bright red*, etc.). In the same way, the interpretation of the expressions and passages we discuss relies on ordinary rules of semantic composition, but the discoursal setting or context may a) create conventional expectations as to the lexical items used or the way of presentation and/or b) conventionally constrain the possible interpretations or strongly prime some of these as opposed to others. Interaction offers a good opportunity for testing conventional expectations, because it builds on pre-existing (explicit or implicit) context and shapes subsequent turns. We are thus interested in conventionalised linguistic units carrying with them prospective and retrospective suppositions (Langacker 2008: 460).

The following examples instantiate the humorous exploitation of both texts belonging to well described genres, such as those of classroom discourse, and texts which may have not achieved genre status but have salient discoursally identifiable characteristics. The latter we propose to also accommodate in the theory on a par with the former. We actually suggest that unless such discoursal features are identified and their status appropriately established, the humorous effect they trigger would have to be accounted for in an ad hoc manner, impoverishing both humor theory and cognitive linguistic theory (of any denomination).

All the examples discussed in section 4 belong to well established genres. The first one (4.1) parodies the conventions of literary editions and is therefore an instance of conflicting frames on the written level. In 4.2 we consider the humorous exploitation of classroom discourse in a filmscript, thus moving to instances of directly represented spoken interaction. Indirectly represented oral discourse is exemplified with cartoon data in 4.3 and 4.4.

4 Genre-based constructions

4.1 Well established genres: Writing conventions of literary editions

Textual properties of constructions may be echoic of the specific discourse type they are commonly linked to, hence giving rise to incongruity if appearing in a text activating an opposed script. They can also be humorously recycled allowing for implicit metalinguistic comments. This is the standard case in allusive incongruous chunks feeding classical parody and satire, where recontextualisation and recycling of clichés is extensive. Consider, in that connection, the following "editor's comments" (appearing as footnotes) which are selected from *The Compleat Works of Wllm Shkspr (Abridged)* (Borgeson, Long and Singer 1994: 2, 9, 13, 16), a work that parodies not only the well-known Shakespearean plays but also the authority and authenticity associated with a scholarly edition:

(1) [2] '*preëminent Shakespearean scholars*'; he's so preeminent, in fact, that he insisted on the fancy umlaut over the second 'e' in 'preëminent.'

(2) [10] *Romeo and Juliet* was first printed in 1597 under the following title: "An excellent conceited Tragedie of Romeo and Juliet. As it hath been often (with great applause) plaid publiquely, by the right honourable the L. of Hudson his seruants." Perhaps Shakespeare is allowed to be 'conceited', being the greatest playwright ever, but that doesn't excuse wearing plaid in publique. It's a fashion felony.

(3) [19] '*Go thither*'; why Benvolio, who is obviously one of Romeo's closest friends, suddenly starts calling him 'thither' is unclear. Samuel Johnson suggests that 'thither' should read 'zither', and that Benvolio is suggesting that Romeo ease his sorrows by practicing his music. A very dumb emendation. Rowe posited that Benvolio is trying to say 'sister,' but has a terrible lisp. That of course doesn't make any sense either, but it's an amusing image.

(4) [27] '*but love*'; 1598 Quarto edition reads 'butt-love.' In Shakespeare's day, slang for 'homosexual.' See also *Titus Andronicus* (III.ii.197) 'rump ranger,' and *Coriolanus* (V.ii.129) 'rear admiral.'

What renders these hilarious (besides the referentially-based incongruities of course) is precisely their echoing salient features associated with this particular genre. The "expectations" (Langacker 2001) associated with this kind of discourse are conventionally available to anyone familiar with such works and consistently (albeit incongruously) fulfilled in the preceding "scholarly" comments. The semi-substantive features of this genre include the references (not necessarily correct and in some cases blatantly wrong) to archaic language (e.g., 2 and 3) and the umlaut comment in 1, which evokes the knowledge available to the informed reader that such works are eminently associated with German scholarship. But even more salient are the constitutive themes (in our terms, the schematic part) of this particular discourse pattern which, although content-based, jointly contribute to its conventional makeup. Such well-entrenched characteristics include for instance (a) the offering of information on first printings or editions (as in 2), (b) alternative interpretations of disputed passages, commonly by (other than the editor) eminent scholars (as in 3), and (c) alternative renderings of the original (as in 4); the latter represents in fact a typical instance of the genre, complete with alternative renderings and interpretations, and references to other Shakespearian works. The schematic layout of the construction includes, however, a purely formal component as well, namely the *template* in which it is conventionally rendered: this is realized by means of the numbered footnotes corresponding to lines in the text and is fully transparent to readers familiar with scholarly editions. As Östman (2005: 132–133) argues with respect to recipes, the expected template (in his words, "the visual, graphic display") plays a more important role in conceptualizing and categorizing recipes as such than, for instance, the instructive text-type they are couched in. In our case, it is at least as important in conventionally signaling the construction as its other substantive and schematic properties.

Frame shifting of this kind is independent of either the type of humorous exploitation intended (or achieved) or the text type in which it may occur. It is interesting that even in the absence of detailed accounts of their typical features (structural or other) the sequences we discuss saliently evoke the corresponding frames, precisely because they are associated with specific discoursal properties. In this respect they are no different from cases discussed in relation to the 'not-completely compositional' nature of language (Langacker 2000; Coulson, Urbach and Kutas 2006: 232–236): the meaning of a complex linguistic expression is often more specific than the meaning of its individual components, and can stem from discourse-level considerations for which psychological validity is claimed (cf. relevant psycholinguistic research in Coulson, Urbach and Kutas 2006). Such sequences are further consistent with findings from corpus linguistic research on lexical priming and collocations (Hoey 2005), where collocations are seen as psychological associations between words, evidenced by their statistically non-random co-occurrence in corpora and, crucially, in specific and specifiable discourses.

4.2 Well established genres: Classroom discourse

In the literature on classroom discourse (Sinclair and Coulthard 1975), the *lesson* appears (predictably) as the largest unit in classroom discourse. *Transactions* are identified as the next smaller discourse units, as phases signaled by recognizable beginnings and ends through *framing moves*, summing up what has preceded, inviting the class to proceed with the next phase, etc. As in various types of structured discourse (e.g., telephone calls), the linguistic elements signaling beginning and end, for instance, belong to a closed list: As McCarthy (1991: 14) points out "there is a fairly limited number of words available in English for framing transactions", such as the teacher's *Now then, Yes, Right, O.K., So*, etc. Moreover, the fact that some people habitually use the same ones (McCarthy 1991: 14) implies that following an original choice, individual speakers (teachers) tend to further stabilize fixed patterns. Within transactions *exchanges* are further identified with 3 *turns*: 'question', 'answer' and 'follow up'.

Exchange structure has been extensively analyzed and received various labels and definitions, from 'opening', 'answering' and 'follow up-evaluation' moves, with 'moves' corresponding to 'turns', to 'initiation', 'response', 'follow-up' (Sinclair and Brazil 1982: 49). Alternatives include 'initiation', 'response/initiation' (allowing for the possibility of the pupil's responding with a question eliciting a further response from the teacher), 'follow-up' gaining over 'evaluation' and a final bipartite distinction between initiation and response resulting in a maximum of 4 structural elements of the following order: I (R/I) R (Coulthard and Brazil 1992: 71–72). The initiating slot is used to elicit or provide information, the responding slot to provide "an appropriate next contribution, an inform if the I was an elicit and an acknowledge if the I was an inform" (Coulthard and Brazil 1992: 73). The importance of these analyses lies in their recognition of the co-existence of structural and semantic criteria for identifying both moves and exchange boundaries in terms of actual linguistic realizations in accurate detail. These patterns can be directly translated in CxG terms as genre-specific schematic constructions.

Besides such long established linguistic signals of sequences which can appear in more than one genre, classroom discourse in particular also involves semi-substantive constructions, partially specified, i.e. drawing their substantive part from fairly closed lists representative of the lexical fields characterizing individual disciplines and subjects taught.

When parodied, classroom discourse is recognized through both schematic and substantive constructions. In the following extract (5) from the script of the Monty Python film *Life of Brian* (1979; *The Internet Movie Database* 2011), for instance, humor couched both in discoursal organization and in the choice of substantive (simple-lexical and complex-syntactic) constructional material is most evident. In terms of setting, the year is about 30 A.D. and Palestine is under Roman occupation. Brian is a young Jew who has joined a revolutionary movement against the Roman conquerors and has been set the assignment to write slogans on the walls against the Romans. He writes *Romanes Eunt Domus*, upon which a centurion turns up and catches him on the act. The dialogue participants are Brian (B) and the Roman centurion (R). The relevant type of move along with the speech acts involved in it are marked in the first part of the exchange at each turn (identification of speech acts rests also on the intonation pattern used):

(5)

R: *What's this then! "Romanes Eunt Domus". People called "Romanes", "they went" "house" in the Nominative?*	INITIATION (attempt to elicit correct answer) consisting of reprimand (negative evaluation of previous performance): interrogative sentence type
B: *It says "Romans go home"*	RESPONSE (answering the question)
R: *No it doesn't.*	EVALUATION consisting of a negative statement.
What's Latin for Roman? [slaps him]	INITIATION (question requesting information)
Come on ... come on...	Exhortation
B: *Romanus!*	RESPONSE providing information
R: *Goes like?*	FOLLOW UP (through question, signaling INITIATION of next exchange)
B: *Er ... annus*	RESPONSE
R: *Vocative plural of "annus" is ... is ...*	FOLLOW UP (elliptic statement with rising intonation signaling question), functions as INITIATION of next exchange

B: *Anni*	RESPONSE
R: *Romani* *[crossing out -es and substituting i,* *flaps B]* *Now what's this "eunt"?*	EVALUATION (through correction) INITIATION
B: *"Go" ... Er...*	RESPONSE
R: *Conjugate the verb "to go"*	FOLLOW-UP (through exhortation)
B: *Ire ... eo, is, it ... imus, itis,* *eunt ...*	RESPONSE
[...]	
R: *So we have ... Romani ite domum.*	FOLLOW-UP (signaling end of FRAMING MOVE)
Do you understand?	
[...]	
R: *Romans go home. This is motion* *towards, isn't it boy?*	INITIATION (new move)
B: *Dative, sir*[6]	RESPONSE
[...]	
R: *Now write it out a hundred times*	FOLLOW-UP (closing up all preceding exchanges through exhortation)
B: *Yes sir*	
R: *And if it isn't done by sunset,* *I'll cut your balls off*	

There is an obvious clash here between the situationally established script according to which the centurion should arrest Brian for 'anti-Roman acts' and the new, opposing one, featuring the centurion concentrating on the form (rather than the content) of the slogan and pushing Brian to rewrite it in proper Latin. The actual language and the way it is used mimic classroom discourse in

---

6 Although we reproduce the original Month Python script, we have to note here that, in latin, the motion towards is signified by accusative, not dative.

detail. Classroom discourse parody is, therefore, effected through the specific constructions exploited for humorous purposes and the climax of the exchange is in the centurion's final order that Brian should write the slogan (correctly) a hundred times. From the very beginning of the extract, the authoritative tone of voice and the (emphatic stress) intonation pattern used by the centurion interact with lexical and structural characteristics of the expressions used in the first turn, so as to switch from a military authority context to the classroom domain. Hence, they create a prospective supposition not only for the next turn of the interlocutor, but also for the audience and what is to follow. Brian's response is completely sensitive to these characteristics, once again not only in terms of content, but also in terms of tone of voice showing intimidation: he is being apologetic. Thus, his utterances involve a retrospective supposition serving to further establish the total switch to a classroom context. Predictably, there is no pupil-initiation – the pupil is in fact totally intimidated and physically punished for grammar mistakes. Unpredictably, the teacher insists on 'other-initiated self-repair' (Schegloff, Jefferson and Sacks 1977) rather than crossing out the slogan and directly getting the 'student' to rewrite it correctly (i.e. enforcing other-repair) – not to mention the situationally consistent expectation that Brian be punished for terrorist activities rather than be forced to consolidate his knowledge of Latin.

The non-reciprocity in the use of the terms of address is predictably also adhered to through use of totally expected semi-substantive expressions: Brian is called *boy* by the irate teacher while he respectfully addresses the centurion as *sir*, which would be in accordance with the situationally established scenario as well. Substantive constructions marked for "Latin grammar at school" are abundant, (e.g., *Vocative plural of "annus"*), plus more general "teaching grammar" ones which are inherited by the "Latin grammar at school" patterns (e.g., *This is motion towards...*, *Conjugate the verb "to go"*), etc. While these are treated as substantive features from a list, it should be obvious that at the same time they are contained in clausal patterns which represent schematic constructions which are still characteristic of the genre. For example, *conjugate* appears as the lexical filler of the directive (ordering) which is an expected speech act by the teacher. Equally characteristic is the unfinished sentence (*This is motion towards...*), waiting for the student to fill in the missing information of which the teacher is already in possession.

Semi-schematic constructions for this discourse type are also frequent in this passage, including, for instance, *So "eunt" is?*, *Goes like?*, featuring explicit boundaries from a list (e.g. initiation of a directive with *So*). Similarly to the unfinished sentences discussed before, the interrogative elliptic clauses used also attempt to elicit information the teacher already has. This time, the teacher's questions actually elicit incorrect responses from the pupil triggering in turn responses by the teacher, such as *Now write it out a hundred times*, also with lexicalized boundaries through items from a fixed drop-list (*Now*) and classroom directives in 'directing moves' (Coulthard and Brazil 1992: 77).

What emerges from the discussion is that this discourse type is characterized by two kinds of semi-schematic material: one, which is supra-clausal, concerns the overall pattern structured by the tripartite sequence; the other, at the level of the clause, has specific pragmatic content, i.e. it corresponds to a very specific type of speech-act, namely a directive which attempts to elicit information known to the speaker. The possible syntactic realisations of this common pragmatics may be therefore treated as belonging to a drop-list, minimally comprising a full interrogative clause, an elliptic statement with a rising intonation pattern (Antonopoulou and Pagoni-Tetlow 2004: 61), or an elliptic question.[7]

4.3 Indirectly represented oral discourse: Genre blending

The following examples from Gary Larson's cartoons (6–7) are instances of absurd/nonsense humor. Less institutionalized discourse is at work here, but genres or specific communities of practice are still identifiable (Eckert and McConnell-Ginet 1998; Wenger 1998). On that basis we wish to claim construction status for specific sequences, identify their most salient properties as contributed by discoursal/textual circumstances characterizing typical members of their respective categories and finally integrate them in the lexicogrammatical system of the language.

---

[7] In Antonopoulou and Nikiforidou (2011), we formalize the discourse constructions of classroom discourse and telephone-call openings using the box notation proposed by Fillmore in the 1980's and further developed in Fried and Östman (2004). Such a representation indeed highlights the parallelism between clause-level constructions and supra-clause patterns in terms of their associating elements of form (of various sizes) with particular meanings, and shows how Fillmorean frames (both cognitive and interactional) are integrated in the description of constructions. In the present paper, however, we focus on the humorous exploitation of such patterns and the analysis of incongruity in terms of constructional properties, hence we defer the reader to the other paper for a formal representation and a detailed discussion of the implications for constructional theory.

(6) Cartoon by Gary Larson

Genre characteristics of horoscopes (of the so called "popular personal horoscope") have been studied from various angles, such as the extensive use made of modal items (Watts 1984 cited in McCarthy and Carter 1994: 103), the high occurrence of idioms evaluating the reader's character, but, what's more to the point, they have been used to show "how vocabulary distribution is crucially dependent on genre and register" (McCarthy and Carter 1994: 113–114). The text contains semi-schematic constructions echoing the genre of horoscopes of the type where signs of the Zodiac are related to personality characteristics (compare "If your sun sign is Aries, you are not much for relaxing", "You are very impatient and impulsive", etc.; *Horoscopofree.com* 2011) and semi-substantive constructions echoing encyclopaedic information on *homo Neanderthalensis* (compare "Neanderthal man had a larger brain capacity than modern man", "Homo erectus was an accomplished tool maker and tool user", "Homo sapiens neanderthalensis had an effective but fairly simple tool kit"; *Washington State University* 2011). Two distinct frames are therefore blended resulting in the presentation of species characteristics as personality ones, with the substantive material (*capacity, tool-making skills*) contributed by physical anthropology and schematic material (second person + predicate) by horoscopes.[8]

A thematically related blending of frames is illustrated in the cartoon image: two Neanderthals are sitting in a cave, while one of them is holding a newspaper and reading aloud the horoscope. The cognitive dissonance caused by the *juxtaposition* of incompatible elements (on the one hand, Neanderthals, the cave, and the club, and, on the other, the newspaper and horoscope reading) invites readers first to recognize the different input spaces of the blend, then to search for connections between such elements, and, eventually, to identify the incongruity on which humor is based (Marín-Arrese 2008: 5–9; Schilperoord and Maes 2009: 221–222). Humor here is produced by lexis and image interaction. In particular, there is a *symmetrical interaction* between language and image: "words and pictures tell the same story, essentially repeating information in different forms of communication" (Nikolajeva and Scott 2000: 225). This interaction is also *complementary* and *enhancing* in the sense that "pictures amplify more fully the meaning of the words, or the words expand the picture so that different information in the two modes of communication produces a more complex dynamic" (Nikolajeva and Scott 2000: 225–226; Van Leeuwen 2005: 229–230; Tsakona 2009: 1177–1179).

In Langacker's (2008: 466) terms, the *current discourse space* required for the interpretation of the cartoon includes, one the one hand, the verbal and pictorial elements evoking previous usage events and, on the other, their combination (and juxtaposition) in the cartoon to produce the anticipated meaning.

---

[8] This perspective evidently converges CxG with blending theory which produces fine-grained representations of semantic content, highlighting the distinct contributions of input spaces to the final interpretation (the blend). The implication is that CxG, which focuses on the linguistic conventions, and blending theory, which focuses on the conceptual content, cannot but profit from looking at each other's results (see also Nikiforidou 2012).

4.4 Indirectly represented oral discourse: Communities of practice

The following example (7) also involves a discoursal frame which is playfully distorted to create cartoon humour:

(7) Cartoon by Gary Larson

At Maneaters Anonymous

The humorous incongruity relies on the immediate and direct recognition of the discoursal frame of the Alcoholics Anonymous (AA) as a community of practice. This recognition, we would like to claim, would be equally possible even without the title underneath (*Maneaters Anonymous*). Where does it stem from? Obviously, from matching the (encoding) idiomaticity of genuine AA discourse with its slightly altered version in the cartoon. It starts with the semi-schematic construction *My name's X* ("*first name*"), the standard formula for the self-introduction of a new member to a group. This is followed by minimal lexical changes from the AA frame: *killing* is substituted for *drinking*, *warden/ tourist* for *beer/whiskey*. These substantive elements appear, however, within lexically and constructionally recognizable combinations or patterns, fully conventional in this type of discourse. Compare: *It [drinking] all started rather innocently... drinking socially, a beer here, a whiskey there, sometimes I'd even stash an extra one....* The information given by the speaker and the order of the presented events, moreover, matches the conventionally expected one in a prototypical AA scene.[9] Separately, each of these is a fully compositional straightforward expression; but together they constitute the conventional idiomaticity of the original AA frame. Alternatively, they are idiomatic to the extent that they evoke their conventional ties to that particular frame. Crucially, as in the previous example, although no strictly lexical material can be possibly associated with the AA frame, the overall schematic pattern is unmistakably AA, hence the caption recycling the culturally specifiable substantive idiom (*Maneaters Anonymous*).

Once again, lexis and image interact for the production of humor in a symmetrical and enhancing way (see also previous example). Maneating animals (bears, lions, tigers, etc.) appear to sit close to each other and look at the speaker who is standing up, narrating his personal story. The picture strongly evokes the frame cartoon readers are expected to possess for the meetings of the Alcoholics Anonymous. The incongruous *replacement* (Schilperoord and Maes 2009: 220) of

---

9 Although "transcripts" of actual AA sessions are not widely available, there is plenty of literature available at the AA website (*Alcoholics Anonymous World Services Inc.* 2010) to suggest some of the recurring themes and ritualized sequences of the sessions. In the following passage from the Jack Alexander article about AA, the themes referred to, for instance, are, first, the need (on the part of the alcoholic) to offer some excuse for his drinking (cf. *It all started rather innocently* in the cartoon), and, second, the hiding of bottles in unlikely places (cf. *sometimes I'd even stash an extra one*): "There is no specious excuse for drinking which the troubleshooters of Alcoholics Anonymous have not heard or used themselves. When one of their prospects hands them a rationalization for getting soused, they match it with half a dozen out of their own experience.... They tell of the eight-ounce bottles of gin hidden behind pictures and in caches from cellar to attic".

human participants speaking about their alcoholism with animals speaking about their eating addictions contributes to the same blending of the two frames evoked by the cartoon text. Thus, the current discourse space, namely the contextual basis for the interpretation of the cartoon, consists of elements belonging to both its text and its image.

Parodic and satirical discourse is standardly accounted for in terms of register clashes (Attardo 1994, 2001; Simpson 2003), as the interaction of canonical structures or sets of regularly co-occurring contextual variables or typical text structures (Emmott 1997: 95), or as discursive shifts (Simpson 2003: 36). Linguistic material echoing 'other voices' is in fact identified not only as crucial to irony but as the basis of most intentional humor in relevance-theoretic accounts (Curcó 1998: 305) and seen as implicitly making a specific type of dissociative comment in the "(joint) construction of discourse worlds based on and relative to the surface level of the actual utterances" (see *layering* in Brône 2008). The interaction of discourse worlds itself is explained in cognitive linguistic terms through mental space theory, Giora's (2002: 12) 'salience-imbalance' plus an extended notion of 'figure-ground' reversal (Brône 2008), polysemy, underspecification (Feyaerts 2006), etc. The relationship between 'elements of lexico-grammar' and 'higher units of discourse organisation' is posited as one of the major requirements for an adequate account of multilayered modes of humorous communication, such as satire (Simpson 2003: 46). The point here is that the recognition of less fixed constructions which are still identifiable in discoursal terms, both semi-schematic (discourse patterns) and semi-substantive (verging on the borders of typical, lexically full idioms) along with any hybrids conflating these two can bridge the gap between grammar and discourse and receive a uniform treatment within an expanded version of CxG, while at the same time elaborating on the creative potential of language through the recycling of well-established, stored units. We are resting throughout on the assumption elaborated in Goldberg (2006) that patterns are stored as constructions even if they are fully compositional and transparent, since there is evidence from psycholinguistic processing that patterns are also stored if they are sufficiently frequent, even when they are fully predictable (Goldberg 2006: 5; see also Langacker 1988; Bybee 1995; Bybee and Hopper 2001; Pinker and Jackendoff 2005).

In the final sections of the analysis, we turn to instances of constructions echoic of discourse settings which either do not constitute well established genres (5.1), or, even if they do recall recognizable genres (5.2), they are rather peripheral; still, the connection between the constructions and the settings, as highly conventional, should be also incorporated in a model of grammar.

5 Conventionality triggered by discourse settings

In section 4 we discussed examples of constructions related to specific genres varying in fixedness in terms of both structure and lexical/substantive material. We will now move a step forward and show that semi-substantive expressions and discourse organization are responsible for also allowing recognition of constructions unrelated to genres but still strongly associated with specific contexts or discourse settings, from which they can be said to derive their most salient (and humorously exploitable) properties. We claim, in other words, that in dialogue (natural or constructed as in the following examples) such constructions evoke specific discourse situations either on their own (the more fixed ones) or in sequence. This, we suggest, is not to be explained away as 'the contribution of context'. The constructions themselves (their semi-schematic part, in particular) can be seen as having an *echoic function*, provided by, and resting on, a conventional link between specific forms and specific contexts in which these forms appear, to the extent that they become bearers of those discoursal properties, through frequent use and consequent entrenchment.

5.1 Conventionality in couple talk

In the context of the preceding comments, we consider the expression *we need to talk*. One example of the usage we have in mind comes from the sitcom *Friends* (see *Crazy for* Friends 2004) where Monica is reporting to her friends that she is extremely worried because her boyfriend has told her they need to talk and "*when someone says 'we need to talk' they wanna break up*". Nobody contests the validity of the implication in the given context, although in their effort to comfort her, her friends suggest that maybe the exact opposite is the case, maybe he wants to propose marriage to her instead. So, the implication of breaking up is evidently not a necessary feature of the expression *we need to talk*. On the other hand, something more generic, like "there is something very serious regarding our relationship that I must tell you" seems to accompany it in the relevant contexts.

The relevant discourse setting in this case may be characterized as "interpersonal" (Kasper 1997), a prominent subtype of which is "couple talk". In this setting, the truncated expression (without the prepositional complements *to NP* and *about/of NP*) appears to qualify as a separate construction characterized by a pragmatic residue of meaning. In support of this analysis, we may observe that (a) the same implicature is not readily available to propositionally equivalent expressions, e.g., *we must talk*, and (b) the implicature is triggered by the fully substantive expression consisting of the first person plural pronoun subject, the modal *need* in present tense (only) and the infinitival complement *to talk*.

In empirically substantiating the discoursally-triggered meaning of the expression, general corpora are not necessarily very helpful. This is because they are typically not rich in oral discourse but also, and more importantly, because they do not differentiate discourse settings. A search in the BNC (2010), for example, yielded only 27 instances of the general construction (*we need to talk* + one or more of the PP complements) and 11 instances of the truncated expression; of these, 4 were cases of definite null complements,[10] where the theme of the talk was omitted as present in the preceding context (as in example (8)). The remaining 7 *we need to talk* instances were all examples that implied that an important turn of the relationship is signaled by the speaker (as in (9), also from BNC 2010):

(8) he met last Monday in a smoke-choked Des Moines, Iowa, hotel conference room. "I know what you can do. You know why I'm here", he said. "**We need to talk**". But as he spoke, an audience that started out polite but skeptical turned hostile. Gore twice deflected questions about whether the global-warming treaty he championed would send jobs overseas and instead served up encomiums about saving [...].

(9) "How about eating something yourself while we talk?" "Talk?" She eyed him askance as she buttered a slice of toast. Henry ate some of the meal in thoughtful silence, then laid down his fork. "**We need to talk**, Leonora. After last night –" "Let's forget last night". "How can we?" His eyebrows shot together in a black bar. "It may be something you can dismiss easily. I can't".

The need to refine the frequency parameter so as to reflect frequency within particular discourse types or settings becomes evident when considering such data. This would allow clearer insights into the actual usage of certain expressions and the prototypical structure of the corresponding category, which may be obscured from simple, discourse-independent counts in general corpora. This would be in line with recent research in cognitive linguistics and corpus analysis (Geeraerts 2005) which highlights the need to take into account "lectal

---

10 In the general (non-interpersonal) interpretation, we expect the *about/of* PP to be omitted if the theme of the talk is already in the consciousness of the interlocutors by having appeared in the preceding situational or verbal context; so, if the prepositional complement is missing, it is a case of a definite null complement, i.e. a complement that can be omitted because it is known and retrievable from the context (Fillmore 1986, Goldberg 2006).

variation" including "all types of language varieties or *lects*: dialects, regiolects, national varieties, registers, styles, idiolects, whatever" (Geeraerts 2005: 168). Discourse settings of the type we refer to here should presumably fall in the scope of linguistically relevant variation. Although semantically annotated corpora, of the kind we would need in order to identify particular discourse settings, are not yet widely available (Stefanowitsch 2006: 2), corpus linguistics research has addressed some of the issues raised by their lack. The type of corpus we would, for instance, like to have for extracting frequency (and hence entrenchment) data within *specific contexts* is not very different from that required in corpus-based work on metaphor and metonymy, where the corpus should ideally distinguish between different source or target (conceptual/ semantic) domains (Semino 2005, 2006; Martin 2006; Partington 2006).[11]

It is for these reasons that recourse to different ways of assessing the psychological reality of the assumed properties of such expressions is necessary. Popular culture products may in fact prove particularly useful in empirically grounding their discourse-specific conventionality precisely because they are often discoursally marked. In this respect, consider the online *Urban Dictionary* (2011), where definitions are contributed by the users, posted, and approved or not (with thumbs up or down votes by other users whose number is recorded). Despite its name, this particular source is obviously not a dictionary as such; the data it provides however are indeed comparable to those provided from answers to questionnaires, and in this sense valuable for a usage-based approach. The answers for the expression *we need to talk* are suggestive of a particular contextual meaning while the fact that it is included as an expression is further suggestive of its constructional, unit-like status. There were 66 definitions in total, and only 6 did not refer exclusively to or at least include the pragmatic implication in question (see definitions in 10, from *Urban Dictionary* 2011):

(10)   *we need to talk* sample definitions
Definition 1: Is your clue that you need to act quick. If you're good you'll be able to dump her before she dumps you.

Definition 2: women's secret code for: haha sonny, you're fucked.
honey, about our relationship, we gotta talk.

Definition 3: Female code for "This relationship is over"
Hunny, we need to talk...

---

11 The validity of simple frequency counts has been contested in several studies (e.g., Stefanowitsch and Gries 2003; Hoffmann 2004) on the basis of obscuring, among other things, genre-specific and speech-event dependant differences.

Definition 4: The 4 words u never wanna hear when u think your relationship is going well.
Girlfriend: *Jason, we need to talk.*
Jason: *(thinking) I'm screwed.*

Definition 5: Read: "Sorry honey, it's over".
My girl called me up and said "we need to talk", and i knew it was over.

Definition 6: The beginning to the portal of oblivion in which the male will be forced into a comma like state due to prior knowledge of the "talk" portal. Commonly the male is subject to female complaining, bitching, whining, sometimes tears. If this happens the male tends to become either aggressive or resembles a deer in headlights. There is no real end to this portal and the male never quite knows the length in which he will be in it, but while inside he knows it's sheer hell. **This is commonly the opening line to a demise of a relationship.**
A. *I've been thinking, and we need to talk...*
B. *(mind): Aw SHIT! (words): Okay honey*

Definition 7: The famous saying by all significant others when there about to break up with you.
Tom...... i think we need to talk

Definition 8: Date speak for "I'm breaking up with you".
"Honey... We need to talk".

Further google data confirm both the constructional status of the expression and the highly entrenched implicature identified above. Consider the example of a blog starting with the question "*Is there any chance in hell the 'we need to talk' line doesn't mean 'I wanna break up with you?'*" (PlentyOfFish Media INC 2008). The difference between such data and those from the *Urban Dictionary* (2011) is that these sites are interactive and the contributors identify themselves.

In the following example (11) also from the sitcom *Friends* (see *Crazy for Friends* 2004), Monica is trying to justify to Rachel her having gone shopping with Julie, Ross' girlfriend (Ross is Monica's brother for whom Rachel has developed a romantic interest). The following exchange between Monica and Rachel is triggered by Rachel's asking Monica in a shocked and reproachful tone *You were with Julie?*:

(11)   M: *Look, When it started I just wanted to be nice to her, because she was my brother's girlfriend and then one thing led to another and before I knew it we were... shopping.*

R: *Oh, my God!*
M: *Wait! We only did it once. It didn't mean anything to me! Rachel, I was thinking of you all the time. Look, I'm sorry, all right? I never meant for you to find out.*
R: *Oh, please! Please! You wanted to get caught.*
M: *That is not true!*
R: *OK. I just need not to be with you right now.*

No institutionalised discourse is alluded to here, yet the constructions responsible for the humorous reversal (one spouse/lover cheating on the other by being sexually involved with a third party vs. one girlfriend cheating on the other by going shopping with a third party) are evidently so closely linked with the scripts containing stereotypical information on how the members of married or sexually involved couples are expected to behave, that they enable the recipient to immediately activate that stereotypical information along with its structure or other discoursal properties.

In discourse analysis terms, the whole extract is a 'transaction' consisting of 3 adjacency pairs in which one of the interlocutors apologizes to the other for having offended her and the other one rejects the apology. On the basis of the information currently available to the audience (at the time of viewing) whereby the participants in the interaction are friends rather than lovers and the 'offense' is going shopping with another girl, no apology is in order and therefore the humorous reversal applies to the chunk as a unit. The first utterance (*When it started...*) is not unique to specific discourse situations, yet within an apology frame it signals the beginning of a description of how the offender was the victim of circumstances (compare the AA text from G. Larson in 4.4 where the tiger starts by claiming *It all started rather innocently*). In the same turn, two more constructions: (a) *one thing led to another* and (b) *and before I knew it* are equally independent of discourse type, but strongly associated with contexts where uncomfortable interpersonal explanations are provided for things having gone out of hand.

The association of such expressions with "typical contexts" needs to be further qualified, since such patterns are not restricted to a particular discourse, genre, or text type; rather, when found in some particular context or discourse setting, they acquire special meaning and/or special formal properties. In general, non-interpersonal contexts, the expression *one thing led to another* functions, for instance, as a conversational gloss-over meaning "to make a long story short" (see example 12 from BNC 2010):

(12) "I did all this research and learned about mud in the Middle East, mud in the South and the different shades", Westman says. *One thing led to another*, and soon she was doing covers for Harper's Bazaar and Vogue.

But in interpersonal settings (Kasper 1997), it gives rise to conventional pragmatics of providing uncomfortable or embarrassing explanations for things having gone out of hand and this association is not necessarily predicted by the compositional semantics of the expression in combination with Gricean (or other) general principles.[12] While the saliency of this implicature is not necessarily reflected in general corpora, it appears to be recognized by definition writers, conventional and otherwise. *COBUILD* (Sinclair 1987), for instance, while neutrally defining the expression as "when you want to emphasize the end of the story and reach it quickly without discussing the details...", illustrates it with an example of the embarrassing variety. Same in the *Oxford Advanced Learner's Dictionary* (Hornby, Wehmeier and Ashby 2000), where the neutral definition is followed by the example *He offered me a ride home one night, and, well, one thing led to another and now we're married*. Authentic, abundant, and hence important data for this construction are also found in the *Urban Dictionary* (2011). While this is a heavily biased venue with many entries relating to couple relationships,[13] still the answers are suggestive of a particular meaning attached to the expression. In (13), we list selectively some of the definitions from the *Urban Dictionary* (2011) which feature high ratings:

(13) *one thing led to another* sample definitions
Definition 1: Mostly used as a substitute to sexual descriptions, it can also serve to shorten or skip over parts of conversations. It allows the listener to fill in the blanks themselves with their imagination
Definition 2: "Well, me and my girlfriend were watching a movie, and..... one thing led to another and now I've got child support for triplets"
Definition 3: phrase used by people to cut out part of a story that is not necessary, so that they can get to the meat of the story
Definition 4: Usually used when people are talking about how they got a guy/girl in the sack

---

[12] As already noted in section 2.4, in the version of CxG we espouse (cf. Goldberg 2006), non-predictability of the semantics-pragmatics is not necessary for assigning constructional status. However, in other versions of the theory (most notably Fillmore 1996; Kay and Fillmore 1999) constructional pragmatics should be non-derivable by rules of composition and general reasoning or politeness principles.
[13] In this respect, the inclusion of the expression as such is also suggestive.

> **Definition 5:** When telling a story, one uses this phrase to leave out all the intricate details of the situation, leaving all the details up to the one listening. Mainly used when bragging to one's friends about one's sexual prowess. See, "yadda yadda yadda"
>
> **Definition 6:** An excuse for why you cheated on your girlfriend/boyfriend or wife/husband/partner/significant other...
>
> **Definition 7:** Most often used by rather sheepish looking men
> *We were just talking and then one thing lead to another...*

Returning to extract (11), it is worth pointing out that the coherence of the whole passage rests on the initial activation and recognition of the "expectation" (Langacker 2001) evoked by the expression *one thing led to another*. The (poorly marked through dots) prosody of *we were... shopping* is an unmistakable signal of embarrassed hesitation before the theme of the offense (shopping) is finally expressed triggering an outraged response by the offended party (*Oh my God!*). In fact, after the hesitation signal, hardly any expectation is stronger than the occurrence of *making love* or *in bed* (or their low register synonym). Being conventionally used as an excuse for cheating and/or a substitute to sexual descriptions, *one thing led to another* carries with it a prospective supposition, as it influences audience expectations about the discourse that is to follow: Monica's apologetic tone combined with the pragmatics of the actual expression in context creates the expectation of the expression being completed by "before we knew it we were ...*in bed*". Hence, Monica's and Rachel's utterances are interpreted as if they were accusations and excuses between lovers. The current discourse space is informed by the conventional implications of these expressions.

The apologizer continues with a construction which is even more substantive than the ones before it: *We only did it once.* We suggest that *only* is a necessary element here, as is also the choice of a numeral from the lowest numbers (preferably one), since the lower the number of occurrences of the offense the more acceptable the apology. In fact, *only* predisposes for *once* to such an extent that the *only once* part of the construction can be seen as constituting a construction on its own right. Hence, although *it* is not referentially ambiguous here, the double activation of *shopping* and *making love* (or something similar to it) is inescapable. Further evidence as to the strong implication of sexual intercourse involved in *we only did it once* is again supplied by the *Urban Dictionary* (2011; see examples (14)–(16)):

(14) Boyfriend: "Honey, I swear I am a virgin!"
Girlfriend: "Well your exfriend says otherwise".
Boyfriend: "Uhhhhhh....Well *we **only did** it **once***"

(15) Girl: I missed my monthly cycle.
Boy: *We **only did** it **once***, i hope you ain't a ma'ma hen.

(16) "im not gay if *I just **did** it **once***"

Still in the light of the apology, *It didn't mean anything to me!* and *I was thinking of you all the time* are also salient triggers of the 'cheating a sexual partner' frame, for which we would like to claim semi-substantive construction status on the basis of this conventional association. The apologizer's last attempt at mitigating the offense and securing absolution (*I never meant for you to find out*) is totally unsuccessful (*Oh, please! Please! You wanted to get caught*). Use of *caught* here suggests *cheating*, but it is only in adult, Freud-informed talk that the whole sentence acquires any meaning at all and these characteristics are sufficient to mark it as a specific semi-substantive construction with a clear pragmatic-discoursal point.

5.2 Conventionality in "teacher telling off pupils" interaction

In the following example (17) also from the same sitcom (*Friends*; see *Crazy for Friends 2004*), a 'teacher–young pupils' setting is activated in the middle of an interaction between a performer (singing and playing the guitar) and two men of her audience in a café who are talking to each other instead of religiously attending the performance:

(17) (performer): *Excuse me! Excuse me! Noisy boys! Is it something you'd like to share with the entire group?*

(one of the 'noisy boys'): *No. No...That's OK.*

(performer): *Oh, come on. If it's important enough to discuss while I'm playing, then I assume it is important enough for everyone else to hear.*

(another member of the audience): *That guy is going home with a note.*

(one of the 'noisy boys' clearing his voice in a terribly embarrassed manner): *I...I...*

(performer): *Could you speak up please.*

In this exchange there are no typical, semi-schematic constructions characterizing the main transactions in a lesson as discussed in 4.2. This is evidently due to the fact that the exchange is peripheral to the main goal of teacher-pupil interaction: the 'teacher' interrupts the process to castigate 'naughty pupils' for being inattentive and therefore preventing themselves and their neighbors from fully benefiting from the lesson. The semi-substantive constructions used, however, introduce the possibility of activating a situationally inappropriate classroom script right from the start, despite the fact that neither repeated use of the first attention getter (*Excuse me!*) nor the semi-substantive third one (*Noisy boys!*) are genre-specific.

The first turn starts with a repeated, loud and emphatic *Excuse me!* which, besides the pragmatic function of apologizing, involves the discoursal presupposition that the act for which the speaker apologizes will follow rather than precede (as *sorry* does). The next construction in the same turn (*Noisy boys!*) is informed prospectively by the authoritative tone of *Excuse me!* which it sustains. Moreover, it retrospectively renders the apology in *Excuse me!* ironic and reframes the interaction as an adult-child one. In the third part of this turn, the established frame is further specified as teacher-naughty pupil interaction, because of the highly entrenched *Is there something you'd like to share with the entire group?*, and reinforces the irony of the utterance. In view of the above (namely prospectively), the audience clearly expects not a positive and genuinely informative answer, but the actual *No. No...That's OK* expressed with hesitation and in an intimidated, apologetic tone, since the interlocutors have already accepted the teacher-pupil frame. The classroom discourse script is also present in the noisy boys' attempt to initiate a possible excuse statement in the last adjacency pair (i.e. in his last turn *I... I...*). *Could you speak up please* is also uttered with the authoritative tone of voice and prosody marking orders rather than suggestions (high fall rather than low rise on *up*) as are all the contributions of the performer-teacher, thus rendering unmistakable the overall power imbalance characteristic of the exchange.

Although such imbalance is also present in settings (communities of practice and genres) other than classroom ones, such as the army and officer-private interactions, it is the classroom scenario which is most strongly invoked here. This is probably due to its reflecting a practice common to all possible recipients. Therefore all semi-substantive constructions related to it are more highly entrenched. The most genre-specific semi-substantive construction here is *going home with a note*, a clear case of an encoding idiom with a pragmatic point, signaling directly 'informing young pupil's parents of his misbehavior'. However, it is the interaction of all the discoursal properties of the constructions in the text taken jointly and as being part of a unit which makes the exchange an instance of classroom parody.

All the constructions identified so far are assumed here to have discourse-based aspects of meanings which are available for humorous exploitation. We consider these aspects particularly salient in the specific contexts examined, as well as characteristic of the typical (although not necessarily all possible) instances of the expressions discussed. In that sense, this research supports the importance for humor of standard CL notions such as salience and prototypicality, which has been addressed by various humor scholars (Brône, Feyaerts and Veale 2006: 216).

6 Conclusions

In earlier work (Antonopoulou and Nikiforidou 2009) we have focused on the contribution of schematic constructions to the formation and the resolution of humorously exploited incongruity, showing how the conventional semantics-pragmatics of such grammatical semi-productive patterns gives rise to script opposition at the level of metalinguistic awareness. In the present paper we focus on the conventional pragmatic-discoursal properties of language chunks typically larger than the clause. We have adopted throughout a construction grammar approach aiming to incorporate all such phenomena in a systematic manner. Our findings are consistent with any cognitive approach (notably Cognitive Grammar) which assigns pragmatic-discoursal properties to particular forms.

To the extent that all the data in this paper are characterized by specific discourse properties, we suggest that they form conventional discourse patterns or constructions in the sense of Östman (2005). Their construction status is established by the recognizable (semi)-substantive and (semi)-schematic features, as well as the more or less institutionalized contexts which they echo. These properties underlie and motivate the conventional aspect of their meaning which is entrenched and salient enough to characterize them as larger-than-the-sentence constructions. Construction grammar may therefore provide cognitive grounding and a rigorous methodology to the analysis of large-scale patterns by recognizing that, just like sentence-level constructions, they also consist of less and more fixed parts, of formal/schematic and substantive/lexical material. This enriched notion of what constitutes *form* –fixed, substantive constructions alongside the (traditionally recognized) formal or schematic ones, as well as a continuum between the two– allows us to identify constructions of whatever size provided their formal characteristics are associated with a definable meaning or context of use.

The identification of "typical contexts" going beyond genres (or registers even) has never been addressed in the relevant CL (or CxG) literature. This is rather ironic in view of the importance of context in a model for which "the primary source of information is the actual use of language in context" (Brône, Feyaerts and Veale 2006: 211) and the availability of the notions of salience and prototypicality which are in fact indigenous to the model. It is only explainable as the result of the common practice of taking the importance of context for granted rather than justifying it through focusing on the specifics of contextually derived information, its structure, its representation within frames/scripts and its relevance to the specifics of linguistic detail. On the other hand, focusing on the discoursal properties of constructions (other than those identified through discourse or text-linguistic analysis) presupposes a recognition of such context-based constructions, only a subset of which can be found in corpus oriented studies (Moon 1998) or other phraseological literature. This is entirely due to their not being present in sufficient abundance in the (necessarily) limited corpora of English available (such as the BNC 2010 we searched), which further means that frequency counts are an inappropriate means of supporting claims as to their status or the prototypical meanings of their respective categories.

It is for these reasons that recourse to different ways of assessing the psychological reality of their assumed properties is necessary. Unsophisticated (actually naïve) definitions (as the ones in the *Urban Dictionary* 2011) constitute a hitherto unexploited, but particularly useful source, along with popular sitcoms. In other words, we consider that popular culture products seem essential in assessing both the status and the properties of such discourse-based constructions.

The present findings are compatible with the functional view of genre as a dynamic social construct which can be manipulated to serve the communicative purposes of its users. Discoursal conventions belonging in different genres can be mixed to create humor, provided that the audience recognizes the original genres and contexts. More specifically, humorous texts of the kind analyzed here constitute useful test cases for the recognition and the interaction of more than one discourse types in a particularly interesting manner: the conventionalized, discourse-based features are brought forward precisely because they are responsible for the incongruity, which, in turn, would not have been detectable if it were not for their high degree of entrenchment, i.e. their salience in the contexts in which they prototypically occur. In multimodal humorous texts in particular (in the present case, cartoons), incongruity is caused not only by discourse-based features, but also by the cartoon image which represents the different frames blended to create a humorous effect. Obviously, we have focused on more or less well-established discourses, including non-conversational ones, which in some cases amount to distinct genres, on the premise that the higher the degree of institutionalization, the clearer the formal specifications and features (cf. legal texts as a limiting case of institutionalized discourse). For these, we have argued that (semi)-schematic characteristics (supra-clausal sequencing, specific presentational templates, clause-level (semi)-schematic constructions) and (semi)-substantive ones (constrained lexical choices) are discernible and can be identified. This said, it is clear that as our analysis goes from more to less institutionalized instances, the semi-schematic features (both supra-clausal and clause-level) are less determined, albeit always present. Crucially, such humorous texts allow for assigning constructional status to substantive expressions which are not necessarily part of well-established discourse, yet they give rise to incongruity because they echo clearly specific contexts (e.g., *one thing led to another and we ended up... shopping* in example (11), section 5.1). Such constructions lie outside the scope of both discourse analysis and conversation analysis and may well escape the notice of corpus linguists due to their insufficient representation in general-purpose corpora.

Construction Grammar, as a usage-based model aiming to account for all linguistic knowledge along the substantive – schematic and the lexis – clause – and beyond continua, is argued here to be the best approach to such data. The conventional discoursal load of such patterns and the contexts evoked by individual expressions are accommodated as the pragmatic-discoursal pole of the relevant constructions. At the same time, CxG can account uniformly for conventional meanings, whether these are associated with words, grammatical-syntactic patterns or discourses.

References

Antonopoulou, Eleni, and Stamatoula Pagoni-Tetlow. 2004. *The Sounds of English: Units and Patterns*. Potters Bar, Herts.: JRT Systems.

Antonopoulou, Eleni, and Maria Sifianou. 2003. Conversational dynamics of humor: The telephone game in Greek. *Journal of Pragmatics* 35(5): 741–769.

Antonopoulou Eleni, and Kiki Nikiforidou. 2009. Deconstructing verbal humour with Construction Grammar. In: Geert Brône and Jeroen Vandaele (eds.), *Cognitive Poetics. Goals, Gains and Gaps*, 289–314. Berlin/New York: Mouton de Gruyter.

Antonopoulou Eleni, and Kiki Nikiforidou. 2011. Construction grammar and conventional discourse: A construction-based approach to discoursal incongruity. *Journal of Pragmatics* 43(10): 2594–2609.

Alcoholics Anonymous World Services Inc. 2010. Alcoholics Anonymous. http://www.aa.org/?Media=PlayFlash

Attardo, Salvatore. 1994. *Linguistic Theories of Humor*. Berlin/New York: Mouton de Gruyter.

Attardo, Salvatore. 2001. *Humorous Texts: A Semantic and Pragmatic Analysis*. Berlin/New York: Mouton de Gruyter.
Bhatia, Vijay K. 2007. The power and politics of genre. In: Teun van Dijk (ed.), *Discourse Studies*, Vol. I, 111–126. London: Sage.
Birner, Betty J., and Gregory Ward. 1998. *Information Status and Noncanonical Word Order in English*. Amsterdam/Philadelphia: John Benjamins.
BNC. 2010. *British National Corpus*. http://www.natcorp.ox.ac.uk
Borgeson, Jess, Adam Long, and Daniel Singer. 1994. *The Compleat Works of Wllm Shkspr (Abridged)*. New York: Applause Books.
Brône, Geert. 2008. Hyper- and misunderstanding in interactional humor. *Journal of Pragmatics* 40(12): 2027–2061.
Brône, Geert, Kurt Feyaerts, and Tony Veale. 2006. Introduction: Cognitive linguistic approaches to humor. *Humor: International Journal of Humor Research* 19(3): 203–228.
Brône, Geert, and Jeroen Vandaele (eds.). 2009. *Cognitive Poetics. Goals, Gains and Gaps*. Berlin/New York: Mouton de Gruyter.
Bybee, Joan. 1995. Regular morphology and the lexicon. *Language and Cognitive Processes* 10(5): 425–455.
Bybee, Joan. 2006. From usage to grammar: The mind's response to repetition. *Language* 82(4): 711–733.
Bybee, Joan, and Paul Hopper (eds.). 2001. *Frequency and the Emergence of Linguistic Structure*. Amsterdam/Philadelphia: John Benjamins.
Coulson, Seana. 2005. Sarcasm and the space structuring model. In: Seana Coulson and Barbara Lewandowska (eds.), *The Literal and the Nonliteral in Language and Thought*, 129–144. Berlin: Peter Lang.
Coulson, Seana, Thomas P. Urbach, and Marta Kutas. 2006. Looking back: Joke comprehension and the space structuring model. *Humor: International Journal of Humor Research* 19(3): 229–250.
Coulthard, Malcolm, and David Brazil. 1992. Exchange structure. In: Malcolm Coulthard (ed.), *Advances in Spoken Discourse Analysis*, 50–78. London: Routledge.
Cowie, Anthony Paul (ed.). 1998. *Phraseology: Theory, Analysis, and Applications*. Oxford: Clarendon Press.
Crazy for Friends. 2004. http://www.livesinabox.com/friends
Croft, William, and Alan Cruse. 2004. *Cognitive Linguistics*. Cambridge: Cambridge University Press.
Curcó, Carmen. 1998. Indirect echoes and verbal humour. In: Villy Rouchota and Andreas Jucker (eds.), *Current Issues in Relevance Theory*, 305–326. Amsterdam/Philadelphia: John Benjamins.
Eckert, Penelope, and Sally McConnell-Ginet. 1998. Communities of practice: Where language, gender and power all live. In: Jennifer Coates (ed.), *Language and Gender: A Reader*, 484–494. Oxford: Blackwell.
Emmott, Catherine. 1997. *Narrative Comprehension: A Discourse Perspective*. Oxford: Oxford University Press.
Feyaerts, Kurt. 2006. Towards a dynamic account of phraseological meaning: Creative variation in headlines and conversational humor. *International Journal of English Studies*. Special issue on *New Advances in Phraseological Research* 6(1): 57–84.
Fillmore, Charles. 1982. Frame semantics. In: The Linguistic Society of Korea (ed.), *Linguistics in the Morning Calm*, 111–137. Seoul: Hanshin.

Fillmore, Charles. 1986. Pragmatically controlled zero anaphora. In: Vassiliki Nikiforidou, Mary Van Clay, Mary Niepokuj and Dedorah Feder (eds.), *Proceedings of the 12th Annual Meeting of the Berkeley Linguistics Society*, 95–107. Berkeley: U. C. Berkeley Linguistics Department.
Fillmore, Charles. 1996. The pragmatics of constructions. In: Dan Isaac Slobin, Julie Gerhardt, Any Kyratzis and Jiansheng Guo (eds.), *Social Interaction, Social Context, and Language. Essays in Honour of Susan Ervin-Tripp*, 53–69. Mahwah, New Jersey: Lawrence Erlbaum Associates.
Fillmore, Charles, and Paul Kay. 1993. *Construction Grammar Coursebook*. University of California, Berkeley.
Fillmore, Charles, Paul Kay, and Mary Catherine O' Connor. 1988. Regularity and idiomaticity in grammatical constructions: The case of *let alone*. *Language* 64(3): 501–538.
Fried, Mirjam, and Jan-Ola Östman. 2004. Construction Grammar: A thumbnail sketch. In: Mirjam Fried and Jan-Ola Östman (eds.), *Construction Grammar in a Cross-Language Perspective*, 11–86. Amsterdam/Philadelphia: John Benjamins.
Geeraerts, Dirk. 2005. Lectal variation and empirical data in Cognitive Linguistics. In: Francisco J. Ruiz de Mendoza Ibañez and M. Sandra Peña Cervel (eds.), *Cognitive Linguistics. Internal Dynamics and Interdisciplinary Interaction*, 163–189. Berlin/New York: Mouton de Gruyter.
Giora, Rachel. 2002. Optimal innovation and pleasure. In: Oliviero Stock, Carlo Strapparava, and Anton Nijholt (eds.), *The April Fool's Day Workshop on Computational Humour: Proceedings of the Twentieth Workshop on Language Technology* (Series TWTL 20), 11–28. UT Service Centrum.
Goldberg, Adele. 1995. *Constructions: A Construction Grammar Approach to Argument Structure*. Chicago: The University of Chicago Press.
Goldberg, Adele. 2006. *Constructions at Work: The Nature of Generalization in Language*. Oxford: Oxford University Press.
Halliday, M.A.K., and Christian Matthiessen. 1999. *Construing Experience through Meaning: A Language-Based Approach to Cognition*. London and New York: Continuum.
Hoey, Michael. 2005. *Lexical Priming: A New Theory of Words and Language*. London/New York: Routledge.
Hoffmann, Sebastian. 2004. Are low-frequency complex prepositions grammaticalized? In: Hans Lindquist and Christian Mair (eds.), *Corpus Approaches to Grammaticalization in English*, 171–210. Amsterdam/Philadelphia: John Benjamins.
Hornby, Albert Sydney, Sally Wehmeier, and Michael Ashby (eds.). 2000. *Oxford Advanced Learner's Dictionary*. Oxford: Oxford University Press.
Horoscopofree.com. 2011. http://www.horoscopofree.com/en/astrology/signfeature
Kasper, Gabriele. 1997. Linguistic etiquette. In: Florian Coulmas (ed.), *Handbook of Sociolinguistics*, 574–585. Oxford: Blackwell.
Kay, Paul. 2006. Pragmatic aspects of grammatical constructions. In: Lawrence R. Horn and Gregory Ward (eds.), *The Handbook of Pragmatics*, 675–700. Oxford: Blackwell Publishing.
Kay, Paul, and Charles Fillmore. 1999. Grammatical constructions and linguistic generalizations: The *what's X doing Y?* construction. *Language* 75(1): 1–33.
Langacker, Ronald W. 1987. *Foundations of Cognitive Grammar*, Vol. 1, *Theoretical Prerequisites*. Stanford: Stanford University Press.
Langacker, Ronald W. 1988. A usage-based model. In: Brigyda Rudzka-Ostyn (ed.), *Topics in Cognitive Linguistics*, 127–161. Amsterdam/Philadelphia: John Benjamins.

Langacker, Ronald W. 1991. *Foundations of Cognitive Grammar*, Vol. 2, *Descriptive Application*. Stanford: Stanford University Press.
Langacker, Ronald W. 2000. *Grammar and Conceptualization*. Berlin/New York: Mouton de Gruyter.
Langacker, Ronald W. 2001. Discourse in Cognitive Grammar. *Cognitive Linguistics* 12(2): 143–188.
Langacker, Ronald W. 2008. *Cognitive Grammar. A Basic Introduction*. Oxford: Oxford University Press.
Langlotz, Andreas. 2006. *Idiomatic Creativity*. Amsterdam/Philadelphia: John Benjamins.
Marín-Arrese, Juana I. 2008. Cognition and culture in political cartoons. *Intercultural Pragmatics* 5(1): 1–18.
Martin, James H. 2006. A corpus-based analysis of context effects on metaphor comprehension. In: Anatol Stefanowitsch and Stefan Th. Gries (eds.), *Corpus-based Approaches to Metaphor and Metonymy*, 214–236. Berlin/New York: Mouton de Gruyter.
McCarthy, Michael. 1991. *Discourse Analysis for Language Teachers*. Cambridge: Cambridge University Press.
McCarthy, Michael, and Ronald Carter. 1994. *Language as Discourse. Perspectives for Language Teaching*. London: Longman.
Moon, Rosamund. 1998. *Fixed Expressions and Idioms in English: A Corpus Based Approach*. Oxford: Clarendon Press.
Nikiforidou, Kiki. 2010. Viewpoint and construction grammar: The case of "*past+now*". *Language and Literature* 19(3): 265–284.
Nikiforidou, Kiki. 2012. The constructional underpinnings of viewpoint blends: The *past+now* in language and literature. In: Barbara Dancygier and Eve Sweetser (eds.), *Viewpoint in Language: A Multimodal Perspective*, 177–197. Cambridge: Cambridge University Press.
Nikolajeva, Maria, and Carole Scott. 2000. The dynamics of picturebook communication. *Children's Literature in Education* 31(4), 225–239.
Nunberg, Geoffrey, Ivan Sag, and Thomas Wasow. 1994. Idioms. *Language* 70(3): 491–538.
Östman, Jan-Ola. 2005. Construction discourse: A prolegomenon. In: Jan-Ola Östman and Mirjam Fried (eds.), *Construction Grammars. Cognitive Grounding and Theoretical Extensions*, 121–144. Amsterdam/Philadelphia: John Benjamins.
Östman, Jan-Ola, and Graeme Trousdale. 2013. Dialects, discourse, and Construction Grammar. In: Thomas Hoffmann and Graeme Trousdale (eds.), *The Oxford Handbook of Construction Grammar*, 476–490. Oxford: Oxford University Press.
Partington, Alan. 2006. Metaphors, motifs and similes across discourse types: Corpus-assisted discourse studies at work. In: Anatol Stefanowitsch and Stefan Th. Gries (eds.), *Corpus-Based Approaches to Metaphor and Metonymy*, 267–304. Berlin/New York: Mouton de Gruyter.
Penttilä, Esa. 2007. Prototype-based taxonomy of idiomatic expressions. Paper presented at the 10th ICLC, Krakow.
Pinker, Steven, and Ray Jackendoff. 2004. The faculty of language: What's special about it? *Cognition* 95(2): 201–236.
PlentyOfFish Media INC. 2008. PlentyOfFish. Free Online Dating. http://forums.plentyoffish.com/datingposts10180754.aspx
Prince, Ellen F. 1978. A comparison of WH-clefts and *it*-clefts in discourse. *Language* 54(4): 883–906.

Schegloff, Emmanuel, Gail Jefferson, and Harvey Sacks. 1977. The preference for self-correction in the organization of repair in conversation. *Language* 53(2): 289–327.

Schilperoord, Joost, and Alfons Maes. 2009. Visual metaphoric conceptualisation in editorial cartoons. In: Charles J. Forceville and Eduardo Urios-Aparisi (eds.), *Multimodal Metaphor*, 213–240. Berlin/New York: Mouton de Gruyter.

Semino, Elena. 2005. The metaphorical construction of complex domains: The case of speech activity in English. *Metaphor and Symbol* 20(1): 35–70.

Semino, Elena. 2006. A corpus-based study of metaphors for speech activity in British English. In: Anatol Stefanowitsch and Stefan Th. Gries (eds.), *Corpus-Based Approaches to Metaphor and Metonymy*, 36–62. Berlin/New York: Mouton de Gruyter.

Simpson, Paul. 2003. *On the Discourse of Satire*. Amsterdam/Philadelphia: John Benjamins.

Sinclair, John (editor-in-chief). 1987. *Collins COBUILD English Language Dictionary*. London: Harper Collins.

Sinclair, John, and David Brazil. 1982. *Teacher Talk*. Oxford: Oxford University Press.

Sinclair, John, and Malcolm R. Coulthard. 1975. *Towards and Analysis of Discourse*. Oxford: Oxford University Press.

Stefanowitsch, Anatol. 2003. A construction-based approach to indirect speech-acts. In: Klaus-Uwe Panther and Linda Thornburg (eds.), *Metonymy and Pragmatic Inferencing*, 105–126. Amsterdam/Philadelphia: John Benjamins.

Stefanowitsch, Anatol. 2006. Corpus-based approaches to metaphor and metonymy. In: Anatol Stefanowitsch and Stefan Th. Gries (eds.), *Corpus-Based Approaches to Metaphor and Metonymy*, 1–16. Berlin/New York: Mouton de Gruyter.

Stefanowitsch, Anatol, and Stefan Th. Gries. 2003. Collostructions: Investigating the interaction of words and constructions. *International Journal of Corpus Linguistics* 8(2): 209–243.

Swales, John M. 1990. *Genre Analysis. English in Academic and Research Settings*. Cambridge: Cambridge University Press.

Swales, John M. 2009. Worlds of genre – Metaphors of genre. In: Charles Bazerman, Adair Bonini, Débora Figueiredo (eds.), *Genre in a Changing World*, 3–16. Fort Collins, Colorado/ West Lafayette, Indiana: The WAC Clearinghouse & Parlor Press.

The Internet Movie Database. 2011. *Memorable Quotes for* Life of Brian (1979). http://www.imdb.com/title/tt0079470/quotes

Tsakona, Villy. 2009. Language and image interaction in cartoons: Towards a multimodal theory of humor. *Journal of Pragmatics* 41(6), 1171–1188.

Urban Dictionary. 2011. http://www.urbandictionary.com

Van Leeuwen, Theo. 2005. *Introducing Social Semiotics*. London/New York: Routledge.

Washington State University. 2011. *Human Origins: Reconstructing the Story*. http://www.wsu.edu/gened/learn-modules/top_longfor/lfopen-index.html

Watts, Richard. 1984. An analysis of epistemic possibility and probability. *English Studies* 65 (2), 129–140.

Wenger, Etienne. 1998. *Communities of Practice*. Cambridge: Cambridge University Press.

Benjamin Bergen and Kim Binsted
3 Embodied grammar and humor

1 Introduction

Language is so central to humor that it is often taken for granted that the word "humor" refers to humor effected at least in part through language. Types of humor that do not involve language are qualified appropriately – "physical" humor, "musical" humor, and so on. Not only is humor often based on language, but humor is a large part of what language is used for. Humorous utterances constitute a significant portion of normal daily linguistic interactions, and stand as one of language's major and universal functions, along with conveying information and giving orders, among others.

Despite the centrality of language to humor and vice versa, linguists pay very little attention to the use of language for humorous purposes, focusing rather more intently on language in "neutral contexts". Leaving to the side the matter of how it is that a context can be considered "neutral", the important point is that mainstream theories of language use and language structure (e.g. Chomsky 1965, 1995) rarely take into consideration the particular social, cognitive, and structural details of humorous language. Similarly, while most humor researchers take the structure, production, and understanding of humorous utterances as their basic domain of investigation, these studies rarely take into consideration general aspects of linguistic structure and use.

One may have one of several goals in studying the use of language for humor. It could be that one hopes to gain an understanding of the particular linguistic structures that are used in general forms of humor or particular instances of humor. It could alternatively be that one aims to understand the cognitive mechanisms that underlie the use of language for humorous purposes – how exactly does an individual construct an utterance intended to be funny, and how exactly does another individual process the resulting language such that it evokes a humor response? A final reason one might investigate language and humor might be to better understand the nature of linguistic structure and processing more generally, through the study of this particular domain to which it is applied.

Among linguistic theories, those that come closest to providing analytical and theoretical tools for answering questions like these go under the rubric of Cognitive Linguistics (Langacker 1987; Lakoff 1987; Talmy 2000; Fauconnier and Turner 2002), the study of language and the part it plays in the cognitive system. The applicability of Cognitive Linguistics to humor derives from its emphasis on the embodiment of language – how it is used by humans with particular sorts of brains and bodies, with particular physical and social goals in specific physical and social contexts (MacWhinney 1999; Chrisley and Ziemke 2002). This contrasts with mainstream theories of language, which focus more strongly on the formal and abstract nature of linguistic structures.

An emphasis on the embodiment of language benefits an account of its role in humor for two reasons. First, as we argue below, the nature of the language used for humor is strongly influenced by the particular social contexts in which it is used and the social purposes to which it is put. Second, extralinguistic cognitive systems play an important role in processing humorous language. We show below that in order to account for what language users do when producing and understanding humor, an adequate account of how language is used has to have at least the following properties, which reflect these two observations. First, it has to allow for the fact that "sentence patterns have specific pragmatics" associated with them, closely tied to particular usage situations. Second, it has to be able to represent how language serves to cue internal imagination of the content of an utterance.

The next two sections provide the theoretical background for these two claims – that language is structured around specific sentence types that are associated with particular pragmatics, and that language understanding makes use of detailed, embodied imagery. We subsequently demonstrate that both of these observations that hold of language generally apply specifically to humor as well. In the last section, we explore further ways in which embodied theories help explain aspects of humor.

2 Embodied properties of grammar

2.1 Embodied theories of language

Cognitive Linguistic theories of language focus on linguistic knowledge and linguistic processing as they are instantiated in actual language users. Theories of this sort are often referred to as embodied since their focus is on language, not as a formal system, but as a system of declarative and procedural knowledge that humans, endowed with particular types of bodies, make use of in a particular range of physical and social environments. There are a number of approaches to grammar that have such an aim, like Cognitive Grammar (Langacker 1987), and various versions of Construction Grammar (Goldberg 1995, Kay and Fillmore 1999), including Radical Construction Grammar (Croft 2001) and Embodied Construction Grammar (Bergen and Chang 2004). What is centrally shared among these approaches to language is their emphasis on seeking explanations for linguistic form in other cognitive capacities beyond language itself. In particular, these models share two main properties.

First, the basic units of language, rather than being abstract symbols representing just linguistic form, are pairings of form and meaning. These units, called constructions (Goldberg 1995) or symbols (Langacker 1987) range from the very specific (particular words) to the very general (like sentence patterns) but in all cases include aspects of form and meaning. Thus, sentence patterns, as constructions can include meaning components, and among these may be specific pragmatics, based on the particular contexts the constructions are used in and the particular entailments they usually encode. The way language users acquire this constructional knowledge is through use – they learn the details of how to use language and what to use it for on the basis of exposure to language in context, and generalize over it where possible and useful. This means that the human language faculty consists of not only universal and general linguistic knowledge, but also idiosyncratic and specific knowledge.

Second, meaning is seen in these theories as being composed of two parts. Deep understanding of the meanings of constructions and combinations of constructions consists in part of activating detailed and encyclopedic embodied world knowledge. Thus to truly understand a sentence like Groucho hid inside the barrel uses knowledge of what particular Groucho might be referred to, what the barrel might be like (including the size and contents), what the purpose might have been, how tight the fit, and so on. Such a detailed mental model of the described scenario is constructed on the basis of the meanings of the specific linguistic constructions used in the sentence, which meanings themselves are schematic representations of the detailed world knowledge they lead a language understander to access. Based on viewing language as an embodied human cognitive system, the job of the cognitive linguist is to document the full range of linguistic knowledge that people have, which allows them to creatively produce and understand all the language they master. Such an approach may focus on what cognitive processes people actually use when producing or understanding language, on how language is meaningful, or on social aspects of language. In other words, such an approach is interested in how language is actually used, and what it's used for. Since linguistic constructions include a meaning pole, where meaning is defined to include knowledge about language use, the specific pragmatics associated with particular constructions can be represented as part of the constructions themselves. Moreover, idiosyncratic properties of language-specific constructions are learned from language exposure just as more general linguistically universal ones are, and thus constitute an object of linguistic study. Finally, interpreting an utterance as being composed of a set of linguistic constructions yields a mental simulation of the content, which can account for the dependence of language on imagination.

2.2 The pragmatics of constructions

Cognitively oriented theories of language view the building blocks of language as pairings of form and meaning – constructions. In the most straightforward case, simple words like barrel pair a schematic representation of their form (what the word sounds like or how it's spelled) with a schematic representation of their meaning (a schematization over the properties of barrels as experienced by the individual). Not only words but patterns of words also pair form and meaning and thus qualify as constructions. Certain specific sentence patterns, like "What's X doing Y?" (1) have a particular form – in this case a set of words (like what and doing), slots that can be filled in (X and Y), and ordering relations among these (Kay and Fillmore 1999). This sentence pattern actually has a particular meaning associated with it as well – inquiring as to the reason why X is at location Y. Notice that there is another possible interpretation of utterances like these, which ask about the behavior of X at location Y. On this interpretation, the verb doing is interpreted as actually describing some action. Sentences like these arise from a different sentential construction or set of constructions.

(1)   a.   What's that scratch doing in my desk?
       b.   What's that fly doing in my soup?

Most constructions, especially ones larger than a word, are also associated with facts about the way they are used (Lambrecht and Michaelis 1996; Stefanowitsch 2003; Kay To Appear). One way this can occur is through the entrenchment of patterns of inference or other associated cognitive processes with particular constructions. Various lines of research have demonstrated such associations. Consider for example the "X is so y that z" construction (Bergen and Binsted 2004), seen in the examples in (2a) and (2b). Sentences making use of this construction encode a particular relationship between the proposition expressed in the first clause (that Dutch movie-goers are tall, or that Dean was livid) and the one that follows in the second clause (that their heads obstruct one's view or that he almost refused to come out and talk to the crowd). The relationship between the two clauses involves a notion of scale. Specifically, the first clause implies that X (the Dutch or Dean) is extremely Y (tall or livid), and the second clause describes a scenario that results from (and is thus evidence for) this high level of Y-ness. Important here is that for the utterance to be literal and meaningful, the scenario in the second clause must depict X as very Y, not more or less. Thus (2c) is uninterpretable because there is no such relationship between the two clauses; (2d) is pragmatically odd in that one's head usually sticks out over the back of movie seats, and (2e), while perhaps humorous, cannot be interpreted literally. (We will see in detail below how sentences like (2e) are humorous).

(2) a. Dutch movie-goers are so tall that their heads obstruct one's view.
 b. Aides say Dean was so livid that he almost refused to come out to talk to the crowd.
 c. Dutch movie-goers are so tall that their heads are usually covered with blond hair.
 d. Dutch movie-goers are so tall that their heads stick out above the seats.
 e. Aides say Dean was so livid that he punched a hole in the wall with his face.

The point here is that there exists a pragmatic relationship between the first and second clause in sentences that use this "X is so y that z" construction, and utterances that violate this pragmatic relationship are awkward and difficult to process. This implies that part of what language users know about this sentential construction is the particular inferential mechanisms that are conventionally used to interpret it. The same is true of other sentential constructions, such as the "Whats X doing Y" construction, mentioned at the beginning of this section. Sentences like those in (2) are often uttered for a specific purpose, whether it's to enquire as to the origin of the X, to suggest that the X does not belong at the location Y, or even to make accusations about responsibility for the X being located at Y. These pragmatic inferences are conventionally associated with the "Whats X doing Y" construction, and as such, like other pragmatic inferences associated with particular sentential constructions, constitute part of a speaker's knowledge about language.

2.3 Imagery in language understanding

While Cognitive Linguists have long been proponents of a role for mental imagery in linguistic meaning (Casad 1982; Lakoff 1987; Langacker 1987), only recently has this notion accumulated systematic support from behavioral and neural imaging experiments, and started to become fully articulated in a formal and computationally implementable model. The basic idea is that in order to understand an utterance, a language comprehender mentally simulates or imagines its perceptual or motor content. For example, comprehending a sentence like "John kicked the ball over the fence" might entail motor imagery – like what it feels like to kick a ball – as well as visual imagery – such as what it looks like for a ball to be kicked over a fence. On this view, language is meaningful when it effectively evokes mental simulations of this type – when it recreates experiences of "being there" in the mind of a language user. Studies of various types are increasingly demonstrating that language comprehenders automatically and often unconsciously activate both perceptual and motor imagery in order to understand the content of language. Recent work has shown that people make use of particular parts of the visual field (Richardson et al 2003, Bergen To Appear) when a subject is processing simple declarative sentences whose meaning includes objects in those same areas, and that this visual imagination is reflected by actual eye movements (Spivey and Geng 2001). These linguistically evoked visual images include details about the orientation of objects (Stanfield and Zwaan 2001) and their shape (Zwaan et al 2002).

Motor imagery – imagining what it would be like to perform actions described is also activated by language (Glenberg and Kaschak 2002; Bergen et al. 2003). Several recent studies show that parts of motor and pre-motor cortex areas associated with specific body parts become active in response to motor language referring to those body parts. Using behavioral and neurophysiological methods, Pulvermüller et al. (2001) and Hauk et al. (2004) found that verbs associated with different effectors were processed at different rates and in different motor cortex regions. In particular, when subjects perform a lexical decision task with verbs referring to actions involving the mouth (chew), leg (kick), or hand (grab), the motor cortex areas responsible for mouth versus leg versus hand motion received more activation, respectively. Tettamanti et al. (ms.) have also shown through an imaging study that passive listening to sentences describing mouth versus leg versus hand motions activates different parts of pre-motor cortex.

Behavioral methods (Glenberg and Kashak 2002; Bergen et al. 2003) have provided convergent evidence for the role of motor structures in understanding language that encodes actions.The findings from Glenberg and Kaschak's approach show that when subjects are asked to perform a physical action in response to a sentence, such as moving their hand away from or toward their body, it takes them longer to perform the action if it is incompatible with the motor actions described in the sentence. This suggests that while processing language, we perform motor imagery, using neural structures dedicated to motor control. Similarly, Bergen et al's approach has shown that subjects have more trouble deciding that a verb is not a good descriptor for a picture of an action when the action it describes uses the same effector (hand, foot, or mouth) as the action depicted. This finding demonstrates that detailed motor knowledge constitutes part of word meaning.

If, as the various studies described above indicate, understanding language entails performing visual and motor imagery, then this suggests that a complete understanding of how language is used for any given purpose, including its formal configurations, is only possible in a model that takes into account the human cognitive system that linguistic knowledge is embedded in. This system includes motor and perceptual knowledge, based on experiences interacting with the world. An approach to language that can accommodate this constraint along with the finding that grammatical constructions are bound to associated pragmatics, must thus be embodied it must allow the linguistic system to be shaped by the bodily, physical, and social environment in which it is embedded.

3 Funny grammar

Having now seen ways in which an embodied approach to language elucidates aspects of natural language, we turn to ways in which the details of linguistic structure pertain to linguistic humor. It is well known that a limited range of linguistic humor makes direct use of linguistic form – puns like (3a) play on phonological form and double-entendres like (3b) often rely on ambiguities of syntactic form. But beyond these restricted classes of linguistic humor, it may not be obvious how formal properties of sentences and their subparts are particularly relevant to the meaning or function of humorous language. For example, there are no dedicated syntactic structures or configurations that by themselves always trigger humor – there is no humorous equivalent of the ordinary English rule that determiners precede the nouns they modify, such that monkey the is the conventional funny version of the monkey. In other words, there is no such thing as "funny grammar", the content of undergraduate essays notwithstanding. We might then conclude that there is very little room for theories of grammatical knowledge and use in the study of linguistic humor.

(3) a. Q: What's the difference between a sneezing elephant and a spy?
 A: Nothing: they've both got a code in their trunk.
 b. One morning, I shot an elephant in my pyjamas. How he got in my pyjamas I don't know.

However, grammatical knowledge, broadly defined, is quite relevant to humor, in the following way. There exist particular pervasive canonical joke forms, which are specified in syntactic, lexical, and sometimes phonological terms. Knock-knock jokes are a prime example of formally specified jokes. Not only are the first, second, and fourth utterances lexically and syntactically fixed, but in canonical instances of these jokes, the fifth must necessarily begin with a pun on the name proffered in the third turn (4a) or on the response in the fourth turn (4b).

(4) a. A: Knock knock
B: Who's there? A: Nobel.
B: Nobel who?
A: No bell – that's why I knocked!

b. A: Knock knock
B: Who's there?
A: Hawaii
B: Hawaii who?
A: I'm fine. Hawaii you?

Other examples of joke forms that place constraints on form include what's the difference between X and Y (5a), how is X like Y (5b), what do you call X (5c), you know you're an X if Y (5d), how many Xs does it take to screw in a lightbulb (5e), and X was so Y that Z (5f). It's important to note that while these joke forms are all familiar, they vary in their degrees of formal specificity. For example, it's pretty much imperative that jokes like (5e) include the word lightbulb, while utterances like (5f) have very minimal lexical requirements, as shown by the difference between it and (5g).

(5) a. Q: What's the difference between a snow-man and a snow-woman?
A: Snowballs.

b. Q: How is American beer like sex in a canoe
A: Both are fucking close to water.

c. Q: What do you call a Chinese lady with just one leg?
A: Irene.

d. You know you're a redneck if you've got more than one brother named "Darryl".

e. Q: How many flies does it take to screw in a light bulb?
A: Two – the trick is getting them in there!

f. Yo mama's so fat, when I yell "Kool-Aid," she comes crashing through the wall.
g. It was such a cold day in New York City yesterday that the flashers were just describing themselves!

Joke forms like these, however, do not constitute evidence for funny grammar per se. While they are indeed lexically, syntactically, and sometimes phonologically specified, the sentence patterns they use are not used exclusively for humor – the same forms can be put to non-humorous uses. For example, consider the examples in (6). The first of these exemplifies a canonical joke form – you know you're an X if Y, which has saliently been used in recent years in the United States in redneck jokes. The humorous utterance in (6a) contrasts with the non-humorous one in (6b), but the difference in humorousness cannot be attributed to the grammatical forms of the two sentences, which are virtually identical. Rather, humorous utterances like the one in (6a) are specific uses of more general purpose sentence types. Thus, while the grammar itself is not inherently funny, some humor has grammatical constraints, since it often uses particular sentence forms.

(6) a. You know you're a redneck if you think genitalia is an Italian airline.
b. You know you're a prude if you think genitalia should not be discussed.

Moreover, when we look closely at particular joke forms, we find that both the force of the humor and the difference between the humorous and non-humorous versions depend on the particular pragmatics associated with the sentence form used. Recall that many sentence types are associated with a specific inferential structure and knowledge of conditions of use. Both the humorous and the non-humorous uses of the sentence forms rely on a particular inferential structure for their interpretability. For example, the you know you're an X if Y sentence form in (6) above has two clauses, related such that the first identifies a category, and the second describes a salient characteristic of members of that category. We can see in the example above that a significant difference between the humorous and non-humorous examples is that in the first, a particular stereotypical characteristic of rednecks, lack of world knowledge and formal education, is displayed in an exaggerated fashion in the second clause, whereas in the non-humorous example, the second clause provides a fairly reasonable, and thus unfunny, depiction of prudishness. Thus, the inferential structure associated with a sentence form makes non-humorous utterances meaningful, in that it structures the inferential relationship between the two clauses. On the other hand, the breaking of the expectations associated with this inferential structure is at least part of what makes humorous utterances that use this construction funny. Knowledge of the pragmatics associated with particular sentence forms is part of being a competent speaker of a natural language, and being an efficient user of English includes knowing how to understand and perhaps produce jokes in most or all of the various forms discussed above. While their pragmatics are very similar, the humorous and non-humorous utterances differ in the uses to which they are put, a fact of which language users are well aware. Thus, after significant language exposure, speakers know how to participate in responsive joke forms like knock knock jokes, and are not actually surprised when exposed to a you know you're an X if Y joke that the expected inferential relationship between two clauses is violated – rather, they can be surprised by the potentially novel way it is violated. In other words, knowledge about the particular pragmatics of sentence forms does not stop at conventional, non-humorous language; rather, it includes knowledge about the use of particular sentence forms for humorous purposes. It should be noted that sentential pragmatics are used for humor, even when canonical joke forms are not involved, though this is of course harder to document systematically. For example, (7a) uses a sentence form wherein even the subject (a child of five) can be described by the predicate (could understand this), so anyone with greater capacity for doing what's in the predicate (understanding this) should also be able to do so. The implication in this particular case is that anyone unable to perform the task is less intelligent than a child of five. But the speaker of this utterance violates this potential pragmatic interpretation with the second sentence. Similarly, in (7b), the expectation that the second clause will be an example of something less complicated than the content of the first clause is violated by the description of a particularly difficult endeavor.

(7) a. A child of five could understand this. Fetch me a child of five. [Groucho Marx]
   b. Buying the right computer and getting it to work properly is no more complicated than building a nuclear reactor from wristwatch parts in a darkened room using only your teeth. [Dave Barry]

The relevance of grammar to humor, then, is not simply that there exist general rules for constructing humorous utterances. Rather, humorous language plays in part on the particular pragmatics of sentence forms used for humor. Of course, grammatical constructions are not humorous all by themselves – they always require additional mechanisms like imagery to be evoked in order for them to provoke humor responses.

4 Imagery and humor

Humorous utterances use existing linguistic structures, either recruiting their "normal" pragmatics, or, when conventionalized as being used for humor, having a humor-specific pragmatics cued by context. But much of humor depends on subtleties of interpretation relating to imagery.

Imagery is vital not just to understanding basic language about action and movement, as argued above, but also seems essential to linguistic humor as well. One documented example is the case of so-called scalar humor (Bergen and Binsted 2004). Scalar humor plays on a hearer's assumptions about what the possible values of certain scalar properties are, for particular entities. In order for scalar humor like (8) to be interpreted, a hearer must reconcile the claim in the first clause that "your mom is fat" with the alleged result of her fatness depicted in the second clause. A great deal of real-world knowledge contributes to understanding this example, including knowing that when you watch home movies, you often project images onto a large, white surface. But asking someone to wear white when watching home movies doesn't compositionally or conventionally imply that that a person is fat. Rather, only by imagining a very large woman wearing white clothes having a movie projected onto her can the hearer understand the hyperbole.

(8) Yo' mama's so fat, when the family wants to watch home movies they ask her to wear white.

Let us expand briefly on this example, as it demonstrates the roles of both constructional pragmatics and mental imagery in humor comprehension. The linguistic knowledge brought to bear on understanding an utterance like (8) includes, aside from general knowledge of words and grammatical structures, a particular grammatical construction, which we've called X is so y that z (Bergen and Binsted 2004). This construction includes the specifications that first it includes a Noun Phrase, indicating the topic (X), followed by the copula and the word so (or such), then a predicative description of the relevant attribute (Y), then an optional that, and finally a sentence that depicts the resultant state of affairs (Z). All of this is depicted schematically in Figure 1 below, where grammatical form is represented on the top, meaning on the bottom, and constructional characterization of constituents of the construction in the middle.

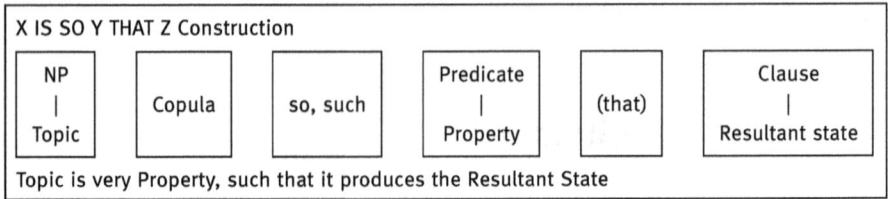

Figure 1: A Schematic representation of the "X is so y that z" construction

A sentence like the one in (8) is easily seen as instantiating this "X is so y that z", at least in terms of its formal and constructional properties. Thus, a language understander will naturally interpret an utterance like (8) as licensed by this construction. This entails that the global meaning of the construction, including the relationships among its constituents (described schematically at the bottom of the construction) is used as a template into which to fit the meanings of each of the constituent parts. But the templatic meaning of the "X is so y that z" construction is not superficially satisfied by its constituents in this particular utterance, since it's not transparently obvious why extreme fatness would result in having to wear white when the family watches home movies. This incompatibility cannot be resolved through basic linguistic or even simple inferential mechanisms alone. Rather, the sentence prompts a search for ways in which being asked to wear white when the family is watching movies indicates fatness. The understander, so encouraged, will consequently engage in the detailed imagery described above, in which a very fat person in white has movies projected onto her.

A second example of imagery playing a central role in making a humorous utterance interpretable is seen in (9). Here, the only relation between the description of the cold weather in the first clause and the description of Dick Cheney rubbing his hands together greedily in the second clause is the similarity of this action with the rubbing together of one's hands in order to stay warm. Thus the motor and visual imagery associated with the scene in the second clause again makes it a comprehensible depiction of a superficially unrelated topic from the first clause.

(9) It was so cold last night I was rubbing my hands faster than Dick Cheney on an Enron payday.

This utterance, too, makes use of the "X is so y that that z" construction, outlined in Figure 1, above. Once again, both constructional pragmatics and imagery are crucial to an understanding of the utterance's intended meaning. The language understander, when trying to interpret this sentence, is once again confronted with the task of satisfying the meaning of the "X is so y that z" construction when the content of the second clause is not transparently a depiction of someone's behavior when it is very cold. The severity of the cold described can only by ascertained by performing two relevant types of imagery – one where Dick Cheney is rubbing his hands together very quickly, due to anticipation of the large sums of money he is to receive from Enron, and a second one, where "I" am rubbing my hands together as just quickly, but due to the cold. A final demonstration of the importance of imagery in understanding humorous utterances can be seen in (10), in which the framing of the scenario described in the question is provided by the punchline. In this case, it's at least partially auditory imagery, rather than the visual or motor imagery seen in the examples above, that fleshes out the scenario described in the punchline, and makes the joke coherent. In addition to general world knowledge, (10) requires more specific encyclopedic knowledge about Amish transportation conventions, and the sound of horse hooves.

(10) Q: What goes clip-clop, clip-clop, clip-clop, clip-clop, bang, bang, clip-clop, clip-clop?
A: An Amish drive-by shooting.

In other cases, as in example (11a), imagery contributes most centrally to the humorousness of an utterance, and less centrally to its interpretability. Thus, while a bear wiping with a rabbit is not a particularly normal scenario, the content may nevertheless be understandable without resorting to imagery that is any more detailed than for understanding a less humorous sentence of the sort in (11b). However, the unexpected perversity of the events described in (11a), which the understander is forced to imagine, contribute to the humorousness of the joke.

(11) a. A bear and a rabbit are shitting in the woods. The bear asks the rabbit: "do you have trouble with shit sticking to your fur?" The rabbit says "no". So the bear wipes his ass with the rabbit.
b. A bear and a rabbit are hanging out in the woods. The rabbit tells the bear it has an itch. So the bear scratches the rabbit against a tree.

We have argued that imagery can be important to linguistic humor in at least two ways. In the first, for the joke to make sense at all, one has to perform detailed imagery, which allows the utterance to be coherent. In other cases, the utterance is interpretable without particularly detailed imagery but it is made funny by properties of evoked imagery.

5 Further embodied properties of humor

We have argued above that a viable account of the use of language for humor must have the following properties. It must be able to account not only for general sentence types, but also for very specific ones, like canonical joke forms. One important aspect of these grammatical patterns that it has to treat is their pragmatics – their conditions of use and the inferential structures they encode. Additionally, the language comprehension faculty must be tightly integrated with the ability to perform mental imagery, which allows for meaningful interpretations of the utterances and inferences that result in a humor effect. Adopting an embodied approach to language affords further predictions about how humor is structured and processed. Two central areas of study within the paradigm of embodied linguistics, conceptual metaphor and frame semantics, have direct applications to the study of humor.

One area of extensive research within the field of Cognitive Linguistics is into how words can have multiple meanings, and how these words are related (e.g. Lakoff 1987; Brugman 1981; Tyler and Evans 2001). In cases of multiple meanings for words, polysemy, certain of the meanings are often more concrete, or literal, than others (Lakoff and Johnson 1980). For example, the word cold can refer to low physical temperature as in (12a), a concrete, literal meaning, or alternatively to emotional detachment, as in (12b), which is more abstract and metaphorical.

(12) a. My water is cold.
  b. Your girlfriend is cold.

Embodied approaches to language have observed that not only are many words conventionally used with these multiple meanings, but in addition words associated with the concrete, literal domain (also known as the source domain) can be used to describe aspects of the abstract, metaphorical domain (the target domain), even if there is no precedent for this use. For example, the word "arctic" has associations with low physical temperature but no conventional usage with respect to emotional accessibility. Nevertheless, it can be used with this novel sense, as in sentences like (13).

(13)   Jane's arctic personality put off her future mother-in-law.

What we can conclude from examples like this is that metaphor isn't simply a matter of particular words having multiple meanings. Rather there are systematic relations between domains of knowledge – in this case temperature and emotional accessibility. Though some words are conventionalized with multiple meanings, these meanings can also be constructed online during language use, because of the relations between the conceptual domains in question. The study of metaphor of this type is known as Conceptual Metaphor (Lakoff and Johnson 1980; Lakoff 1993). Conceptual metaphors pop up in humor use in a variety of places. Puns are often based on them, and can be found in most every form of linguistic humor, for example (14). In the first, there's no conventional meaning of "fall off of" that pertains to a lawyer ceasing to have a professional relationship with someone, and yet this meaning must be accessible for language understanders to make sense of (14). Of course, this alternative, figurative meaning is well motivated by the systematic relationship or conceptual metaphor between abstract difficulties and physical burdens. For example, we talk about having a monkey on one's back, having a heavy burden on one's shoulders, and so on. The online construction of this secondary meaning of the expression "fall off of" can be seen as the result of the application of general, metaphorical knowledge.

(14)   Q: What is the difference between a tick and a lawyer?
         A: A tick falls off you when you die.

The same argument can be made for (15). A chat room isn't a literal room, but rather a metaphorical one. It doesn't have most of the properties rooms do – it has no physical location or structure, it can't act as a literal container for people, etc. This use of the word "chat room" is conventional, despite being non-literal. By contrast, we don't usually use the word fit to describe people's relations to chat rooms. However, in (15), yo mama is described as not being able to fit into a chat room, and this is supposed to be evidence that she is very fat. For this humor to work, the understander must come up with a metaphorical interpretation of fit in a chat room. Since this isn't literally possible – chat rooms have no space, thus no size constraints, there is no way that being physically fat will lead to any plausible lack of such fit. The humor relies on the (fallacious) implication that yo mama is so fat that she can't even fit into a chat room, which has no size at all. The interpretation of this utterance thus relies on the polysemy of room, having a literal (physical) and a metaphorical (non-physical) sense.

(15)   Yo momma's so fat she can't even fit in a chat room.

Frame-based knowledge is also an important component of linguistic knowledge in embodied theories of language (Fillmore 1982). Frames (also known as schemas (Johnson 1987), scripts (Shank and Abelson 1977; Raskin 1985; etc.) are chunks of interrelated knowledge about entities and their relations. A classic example is the Commercial Transaction frame (Fillmore 1982), in which a Buyer possesses some Money and gives it to the Seller in exchange for some Goods. Embodied models of language have argued that much of our linguistic knowledge is grounded in such encyclopedic knowledge. For example, what is a buyer but a role in the Commercial Transaction frame, and what is a hypotenuse, but part of a larger triangle frame? Frames fit into an embodied approach to language since they demonstrate yet another way in which linguistic knowledge is closely bound to the individual human experiences underlying the conceptual structures it is linked to.

Coulson (2000) and Coulson and Kutas (2001) argue that frame-based knowledge constitutes an important part of humor. Since so much of humor plays on world knowledge, one would expect that in understanding language in general and humorous language in particular, understanders regularly activate frames. Humor often requires a modification of the frame the language user is currently maintaining, which is part of what leads to a humor effect. For example, the sentences in (16) each involve a frame shift triggered by the final word. Coulson and Kutas found that when humorous sentences ended with words that did not fit the initial frame, like these examples, event related brain potentials reflected difficulties with semantic integration, significantly more than when they ended with words that did fit the initial frame.

(16)   a.   Statistics indicate that Americans spend 80 million a year on games of chance, mostly weddings.
       b.   She read so much about the bad effects of smoking she decided she'd have to give up reading.

Adopting an embodied perspective on language allows a broad range of cognitive linguistic phenomena studied in this area, like those described above, to be directly applied to humor research.

6 Conclusions

We have demonstrated above that there is a natural fit between the phenomena associated with linguistic humor and the theoretical apparatus of embodied linguistics; in particular, we have argued that humor makes use of constructional pragmatics and mental imagery, as well as metaphor and frames. Embodied grammars elucidate how language is used to produce and understand humor. Humor constitutes a domain of actual language use in which constructional pragmatics and mental imagery are not only obvious, but essential to the function of the language. Without imagery and knowledge of constructional pragmatics, we have argued, the language analyzed above would not only be unfunny, but uninterpretable. Similarly, properties of humorous language help inform the nature of the human linguistic system in general. For example, the central roles of the two embodied characteristics documented above (imagery and constructional pragmatics) highlight the individual, human side of linguistic knowledge. Constructional pragmatics are acquired through exposure to language in particular social and discourse contexts, and as such, knowledge of them is strongly shaped by the individual's particular experiential history. Similarly, the importance of imagery to the meaningfulness and effectiveness of linguistic humor emphasizes the role that components of the human cognitive system other than strictly grammatical capacities play in human linguistic behavior. Together, the importance of constructional pragmatics and mental imagery evident in humorous language testify to the importance of the individual human experience to language use.

Humorous language, such as many of the examples cited in this paper, are instances of creative language use, on the part of the speaker or hearer or both. While creativity has long been an important component of linguistic theory (e.g. Chomsky 1965), this is usually restricted to the study of how words ad morphemes can be combined together in previously unobserved ways, by following general rules or principles (for example, given a new noun wug, how an English speaker knows that the plural is wugs). But the creativity evident in the human ability to produce or understand meaningful humorous utterances clearly far outstrips simple grammatical combination. Rather, it results from play with linguistic practice, including conventional inferences associated with particular constructions, and with the construction of detailed mental imagery. The moral to be drawn from the study of creative humorous language is that creativity cannot be distilled to a single rule-based process, but rather relies on multiple systems, including inference and imagery.

Embodied theories of language focus on language as it is actually used – embedded in a human being with a particular sort of cognitive system and a body of a particular sort, interacting in an environment with certain characteristics. Just as with other types of cognitively and socially integrated language use, such as instruction, argumentation, and requests, humor fundamentally involves a broad range of capacities outside of linguistic form proper, including other sorts of cognitive processes and social interactions. It is not surprising that understanding humorous language requires an understanding of the nature of the human beings that use it.

References

Bergen, Benjamin, and Kim Binsted. 2004. The Cognitive Linguistics of Scalar Humor. In Michel Achard and Suzanne Kemmer (Eds.) *Language, Culture, and Mind*. CSLI.

Bergen, Benjamin, and Nancy Chang. 2004. Embodied construction grammar in simulation-based language understanding. In Jan-Ola Östman and Miriam Fried (eds.), *Construction Grammar(s): Cognitive and Cross-language dimensions*.

Bergen, Benjamin, Shweta Narayan, and Jerome Feldman. 2003. *Embodied verbal semantics: evidence from an image-verb matching task*. Procedings of the 25th Annual Conference of the Cognitive Science Society.

Bergen, Benjamin. 2007. Experimental methods for simulation semantics. M. Gonzalez-Marquez et al. (eds.), *Methods in Cognitive Linguistics*. Amsterdam/Philadelphia: John Benjamins, 277–301.

Brugman, Claudia. 1981. *The story of over*. MA thesis, University of California, Berkeley.

Casad, Eugene. 1982. *Cora locationals and structured imagery*. Ph.D. dissertation, University of California, San Diego.

Chomsky, Noam. 1965. *Aspects of the theory of syntax*. Cambridge: MIT Press.

Chomsky, Noam. 1995. *The minimalist program*. Cambridge: MIT Press.

Chrisley, Ronald, and Tom Ziemke. 2002. Embodiment. *Encyclopedia of cognitive science*, 1102–1108. Macmillan Publishers.

Coulson, Seana. 2000. *Semantic leaps: Frame e-shifting and conceptual blending in meaning construction*. New York and Cambridge: Cambridge University Press.

Coulson, Seana, and Marta Kutas. 2001. Getting it: Human event-related brain response to jokes in good and poor comprehenders. *Neuroscience Letters*, 316: 71–74.

Croft, William. 2001. *Radical construction grammar: syntactic theory in typological perspective*. Oxford: Oxford University Press.

Fauconnier, Giles, and Mark Turner. 2002. *The way we think: Conceptual blending and the mind's hidden complexities*. New York: Basic Books.

Fillmore, Charles J. 1982. Frame semantics. In The Linguistic Society of Korea Linguistics in *Morning Calm*, Seoul: Hanshin Pub. Co., 111–137.

Glenberg, Arthur M., and Michael P. Kaschak. 2002. Grounding language in action. *Psychonomic Bulletin and Review*, 9: 558–565.

Goldberg, Adele. 1995. *Constructions. A construction grammar approach to argument structure*. Chicago: University of Chicago Press.

Johnson, Mark. 1987. *The body in the mind*. Chicago: University of Chicago Press.

Kay, Paul, and Charles J. Fillmore. 1999. Grammatical constructions and linguistic generalizations: The What's X doing Y? construction. *Language*, 75(1): 1–33.

Kay, Paul. to appear. Pragmatic aspects of grammatical constructions. In Laurence Horn and Gregory Ward (eds.), *Handbook of Pragmatics*, Blackwell.

Lakoff, George. 1987. *Women, fire, and dangerous things*. Chicago: University of Chicago Press.

Lakoff, George. 1996. The contemporary theory of metaphor. In Knud Lambrecht and Laura A. Michaelis, Toward a construction-based theory of language function: The case of nominal extraposition, *Language*, 72(2): 215–247.

Lakoff, George, and Mark Johnson. 1980. *Metaphors we live by*. Chicago: University of Chicago Press.

Langacker, Ronald. 1987. Foundations of cognitive grammar: *Theoretical Prerequisites*. Stanford, CA: Stanford University Press.

MacWhinney, B. 1999. The emergence of language from embodiment. In B. MachWhinney (ed.), *Emergence of Language*. Hillsdale, NJ: Lawrence Earlbaum Associates.

Pulvermüller, F., M. Haerle, and F. Hummel. 2001. Walking or talking?: Behavioral and neurophysiological correlates of action verb processing. *Brain and Language*, 78: 143–168.

Pulvermüller, F., O. Hauk, and I. Johnsrude. 2004. Somatotopic representation of action words in human motor and premotor cortex. *Neuron*, 41(2): 301–7.

Raskin, Victor. 1985. *Semantic mechanisms of humor*. Dordrecht, Holland: D. Reidel.

Richardson, D.C., M.J. Spivey, K. McRae and L.W. Barsalou. 2003. Spatial representations activated during real-time comprehension of verbs. *Cognitive Science*.

Shank, R.C., and R. Abelson. 1977. *Scripts, plans, goals and understanding*. Hillsdale, NJ: Erlbaum Association.

Spivey, M., and J. Geng. 2001. Oculomotor mechanisms activated by imagery and memory: movements to absent objects. *Psychological Research*, 65: 235–241.

Stanfield, R.A., and R.A. Zwaan. 2001. The effect of implied orientation derived from verbal context on picture recognition. *Psychological Science*, 12: 153–156.

Stefanowitsch, Anatol. 2003. A construction-based approach to indirect speech acts. In Klaus-Uwe Panther and Linda L. Thornburg (eds.), *Metonymy and Pragmatic Inferencing*.

Talmy John Benjamins, Leonard. 2000. *Toward a cognitive semantics*. Cambridge: MIT Press.

Tettamanti, M., G. Buccino, M.C. Saccuman, V. Gallese, M. Danna, D. Perrani, S.F. Cappa, F. Fazio and G. Rizzolatti. Unpublished Ms. Sentences describing actions activate visuomotor excecution and observation systems.

Tyler, Andrea, and Vyvyan Evans. 2001. Reconsidering prepositional polysemy networks: The case of over. *Language*, 77(4): 724–765.

Zwaan, R.A., R.A. Stanfield and R.H. Yaxley. 2002. Do language comprehenders routinely represent the shapes of objects? *Psychological Science*, 13: 168–171.

Tony Veale
4 The humour of exceptional cases: Jokes as compressed thought experiments

1 Introduction

As much as one might seek certainty and simplicity in life, the category boundaries that shape our perception and guide our behaviour are neither fixed nor certain. Rather, these boundaries are frequently the subject of examination, renegotiation and sometimes, even outright rejection, by creative individuals ranging from philosophers to artists, and jokers to scientists. In this paper we consider two of the cognitive activities that can influence these boundaries. Both are, we argue, remarkably similar in terms of the conceptual manipulations and strategies that they employ, yet both are used in very different domains, one primarily for scientific discourse, the other for social intercourse.

The first of these cognitive activities is a powerful conceptual tool for probing the underbelly of received scientific wisdom. The thought experiment, or *Gedanken* experiment (the latter term is often attributed to Ernst Mach; Mach 1960, 1976; Kuhn 1964), is armchair science at its most cerebral, presenting a purely conceptual means of probing the limits of a theory not with any physical apparatus, but wholly in the mental laboratory of the imagination. This cerebral quality notwithstanding, physical intuition about the world still plays a key role in most thought experiments. As Mach notes, the goal of a good thought experiment is to construct a conceptual scenario that dredges up, from the realm of the intuitive and the instinctive, previously unarticulated knowledge that can be manipulated at the level of concepts and categories. A thought experiment is a form of embodied reasoning that brings not just concepts, but instincts, intuitions and emotions to bear on a problem, motivating a sceptic to want to accept the conclusions of the experiment's logical argument.

The second of these activities is humour. Thought experiments and jokes both take aim at the limitations of received wisdom, often employing the same high-level strategies to provoke an audience – perhaps even a hostile audience – into accepting an alternative conceptual perspective. In each case the inconsistencies of habitual thinking are exposed, frequently with a hint of derision, satire or superiority. And in each case, the role of imagination is vital, for jokes ask us to imagine scenarios that are so out of the ordinary that conventional modes or rules of behaviour appear to break down, in much the same way that thought experiments ask us to imagine scenarios for which conventional scientific theories fail to offer a consistent explanation. We shall argue then that many jokes are, in fact, humorous thought experiments, in which the theories under revision are social norms, genre conventions and taboos. Even off-hand witticisms and one-liners can possess the argumentative force of a good thought experiment, and we shall consider here examples that demonstrate a remarkable density of implicit argumentation. Conversely, we shall see that many thought experiments are philosophical jokes, in which the subversive logic of humour is used to induce a contradiction in an opponent's theory.

1.1 Category-juxtaposition and category-subversion

It is perhaps not surprising that thought experiments and jokes should appear so similar when viewed from the appropriate level of abstraction. Both employ a tightly structured narrative to guide an audience to a particular, and often shocking, conclusion. More generally, science and humour each thrive on insight and innovation, which in turn require a high degree of creativity. With this in mind, Koestler (1964) describes a psychological mechanism he calls 'Bisociation' to explain both, going as far as to suggest that bisociation is implicated in all varieties of creativity, from science to humour to art. Koestler's influential theory can be considered the fore-runner of Attardo and Raskin's (1991) General Theory of Verbal Humour (henceforth GTVH), Fauconnier and Turner's (1998) Conceptual Integration Theory (or blending theory), and Coulson's (2000) frame-shifting theory of humour. De Mey (2002) in turn presents an account of thought experiments in terms of conceptual blending theory.

Bisociation, blending, frame-shifting and the script-switching of the GTVH are all multi-space juxtaposition theories. Each describes a mechanism whereby multiple input categories (whether the matrices of bisociation, the mental spaces of blending and frame-shifting, or the scripts of the GTVH) can be integrated, and through which the oppositions between these inputs can be identified and resolved. Since juxtaposition can only meaningfully apply to a plurality of inputs, humour and thought experimentation are consequently viewed as combination operations: given the appropriate input categories to combine, the desired output category can be generated. Juxtapositional theories are capable of describing a good many instances of humour, and as De Mey illustrates, a variety of celebrated thought experiments also. At a trivial level, of course, humour appreciation is inherently juxtapositional, since some form of comparison will always be required to detect deviation from that which is normative or expected to that which is innovative (Giora 2002). The key issue concerns the nature of the structures that are actually juxtaposed: do they comprise different input structures that are to be cross-mapped or blended, or are they variations (normative and creative) of a single input structure? We reserve the label "juxtapositional theory" for theories that non-trivially presuppose the former view. However, many creative jokes, specifically of the kind to be discussed in sections 3 and 4, appear to presuppose the latter view, as do many creative thought experiments. In these cases, it seems that what is juxtaposed is not a pair of different but overlapping categories, but a single source category and a creative subversion of this category. For all intents and purposes, comprehension of these constructs does not involve the juxtaposition of multiple inputs, but the manipulation of a single input, to probe its boundary conditions and identify interesting counter-examples.

1.2 Structure of this paper

It is our goal here to explore the role of subversive counter-examples in thought experimentation and humour. We begin by considering the structure of thought experiments in section two, where we elaborate on Gendler's (1998, 2000) notion of an *exceptional case* and consider how one might be constructed for a given theory. Gendler sees such cases as both appropriate examples of a theory and surprising counter-examples of that theory, insofar as these cases plainly belong to the theory's domain of application yet produce conclusions that are incongruous relative the claims of the theory. As such, these appropriate counter-examples exhibit what Oring (2003) terms the "appropriate incongruity" that he claims is the very motor of humour. In section three we explore the mechanics of subversion via appropriate counter-examples in verbal humour, and demonstrate how exceptional cases can be constructed from the raw lexico-conceptual components of conventional linguistic constructions. We also briefly describe a particular genre of humour called 'trumping' whose form more clearly echoes the adversarial dialogue that lies at the heart of thought experiments. In section four we look to inter-personal considerations in both jokes and thought experiments to better understand why humour arises from some exceptional cases and not others. In section five we offer a case study of a particular linguistic form, the stereotypical simile, to see how (and how often) commonplace stereotypical associations are subverted by exceptional cases. Finally, we conclude in section six with a consideration of the implications of this synthesis of thought experiments and humour.

2 Thought experimentation

Thought experiments derive their distinctive argumentative force from a grounding in physical reality. Most describe activities that are physically realizable, if given enough time or resources, and thus engage the corresponding physical intuitions and instincts. Scenarios that do not require us to delve into the level of physical intuition and exploit what Mach (1976) calls "our store of instinctive knowledge" are not truly thought 'experiments'. It is not enough then to merely ask "what if", for the thought process must engage in some simulacrum of an experimental activity. Consider Euclid's demonstration of the infinitude of prime numbers. This proof by contradiction neatly demolishes the notion of a largest prime number by first asking us to conceive of such a number, before then demonstrating how an even larger prime can be constructed. Yet this can hardly be called an experiment, since there is little here to actually visualize, and the key mental operation has no experimental analogue in the physical world. In contrast, the argument provided by Lucretius for the infinitude of space *is* an experiment, of sorts. Imagine yourself lobbing a spear at the boundary of known space, he says. If the spear bounces back, then the boundary is real, but there must be something on the other side for the boundary to block access to; but if the spear passes through, then the boundary is not real to begin with. In either case, we can conclude that space is not bounded at this particular point, and since we can repeat the experiment everywhere, it is not bounded anywhere.

For thought experiments to preserve a definite philosophical function of their own (in the sense of Kuhn 1964), and be seen as more than a conventional logical argument in fancy-dress (as has been argued by critics such as Norton 1996), they must bring more than pure logic to the table. The sense of physical embodiment that comes from imagining a real world action, whether the throwing of a spear at an imagined boundary or the dropping of stones from the top of a tower, is intrinsic to how we interpret the experiment and its outcomes. For one, this embodiment serves a psychological purpose to be sure (as Norton concedes). But more importantly, the appropriate physical descriptions can engage the image schemas that best support the sceptic's arguments (Johnson 1987). For instance, the image schema of boundary is a symmetric one, for we are asked to imagine a wall-like barrier separating two regions of space[1]. By successfully invoking this schema in the mind of the reader, Lucretius establishes

---

[1] More specifically, because Lucretius depicts the boundary as acting as a potential obstacle to the flight of his imaginary spear, the Blockage schema becomes activated (Johnson, 1987: 45). Inherent in this schema is the idea that one can "get past the blockage" and hence the idea that there is something beyond the blockage.

not just an experiential basis for his argument, but a strong conceptual basis also, for his very language presupposes the existence of space on the other side of the boundary.

A strong emotive basis is also important in nurturing the desired response to a thought experiment, much as it is in humour, which often seeks a visceral reaction to a joke. As such, the mocking tone of some thought experiments is intended not just to persuade, but to deride and lampoon, as though to make an opponent embarrassed to espouse the theory under attack. It seems clear, for instance, that Galileo is having fun at the expense of his opponents in his Dialogue Concerning The Two Chief World Systems when he puts Aristotle's opposing theory into the mouth of a character he derisorily calls "Simplicius" (Gendler 1998). Likewise, Searle (1980) creates a *mise en scene* for his Chinese Room argument against Artificial Intelligence (as typified by the work of Schank and Abelson 1977) that is so vaudevillian that it elevates this particular thought experiment to the level of parody. Searle asks us to imagine a man much like himself who is locked in a room and who receives a series of incomprehensible Chinese markings through a slot. By following a set of complex mapping rules in a huge rulebook, the man assembles a response that is returned through another slot. Though the response may seem germane and intelligent to the outside observer, who may well believe the room to be occupied by a native Chinese speaker, those who are privy to the experiment know that the man inside remains ignorant of Chinese and the meaning of the symbols that he processes. Were the man to be replaced by a computer, and the rule book by a program, Searle concludes that the computer would likewise be ignorant and would thus not exhibit true intelligence. In a display of verbal mastery, Searle formulates the perfect exceptional case of an abstract computer (a man using a rule book) to subvert the idea of an intelligent computer.

2.1 Exceptional cases

Gendler (1998, 2000) claims that all thought experiments describe the construction of exceptional cases, since it is exceptional cases that best expose the limits of the conventional uses of categories. In this view, the history of thought experiments is the history of exceptional cases that beg the right questions at the right time in the development of science. For instance, the "ship of Theseus" experiment asks us to imagine a ship in which every single piece of wood has been replaced over time, raising an important question about the nature of identity. The Chinese room experiment of Searle (1980) asks us to imagine a book of rules with which a person ignorant of Chinese can meaningfully process any

Chinese query. But Gendler's view begs an important question of its own, namely, what is an adequate definition of an exceptional case?

Gendler begins by assuming that not all of the features of a category are of equal importance, but that some will be of primary or central importance in defining membership, while others will be secondary and peripheral. Therefore, the primary features are either necessary for category membership (in a classical view of category structure) or for defining prototypes (in a non-classical view), while those features that one tends to habitually associate with primary features, are considered secondary. This dichotomy of features is consistent with both Lakoff's (1987) notion of a *radial category* (which has a prototype member at its centre, and less representative members on its periphery) and Sowa's (2000) *egg-yolk theory* of meaning (where primary features occupy the yolk, and secondary features occupy the egg-white).

Consider Aristotle's theory of falling objects, which claims that all objects fall at a speed proportional to their weight. Paradoxically, Aristotle provides no consistent explanation of how entities are to be individuated into discrete objects, yet offers a theory of falling speed that crucially depends on the nature of this individuation. Galileo's classic thought experiment (perhaps the most celebrated example of the genre), exposes this theory as contradictory by imagining an exceptional case where the issue of individuation is foregrounded, by asking us to imagine a composite object comprising two stones, one large and one small, flexibly connected by a rope. This exceptional object is simultaneously a single entity (a system of connected stones) and two individual entities falling in concert. This simultaneity reveals a fundamental confusion in the Aristotelian world view, since the composite object should fall both faster than the heavier stone alone (because the composite is heavier still), *and* slower (because the lighter stone would act as a drag on the heavy stone). Implicit in Aristotle's theory is the expectation that the objects of interest are either atomic (non-composite) or rigid. However, Galileo recognizes that atomicity and rigidity are not primary but secondary features of the category that can safely be contradicted to form an exceptional case.

Galileo demonstrates that to create an exceptional case, one must first have an appreciation of what constitutes the *un*exceptional or stereotypical examples of a category, so one can perceive where the category is most vulnerable to criticism. One can then choose a highly conventional example of the category to subvert (e.g., a physical *and* non-composite object), separating those components that are primary and central to membership in the category (e.g., physical) from those that are secondary and merely habitual or accidental (e.g., non-composite). One can then reassemble these components to arrive at an example that is, technically at least, a member of the category while contradicting certain of the habitual expectations that have been stripped away (e.g., an object that is physical *but* composite).

2.2 Exceptionality and consistency

As this example demonstrates, an exceptional case will successfully subvert a category only when it forms a valid yet uncomfortable fit with this category. This is, it must possess enough primary characteristics to be recognized as an appropriate category member, if only technically so, yet once admitted, it must prove itself to be an incongruent member of this category (and thereby exhibit Oring's notion of appropriate incongruity). But consistency is often relative in thought experiments, especially those that rely on instinctive knowledge. In a purely logical argument, contradiction is defined in absolute terms via negation, whereas an embodied argument must pit one qualified belief against another. An inconsistency will arise then whenever a theoretical belief is shown to imply a conclusion that contradicts a more deeply entrenched belief or physical instinct. A subverted theory thus faces a serious dilemma when presented with a suitably exceptional case: either the case should be excluded from the theory, in an admission that the theory is necessarily incomplete, or admitted into the theory, where its presence forces the theorist to reject an even more fundamental and treasured belief. For example, Galileo forces Aristotle (via Simplicius) to either reject the idea that weight determines falling speed, or to accept the bizarre outcome that two different speeds can be simultaneously ascribed to the same falling entity. Ultimately then, consistency is judged against a set of baseline beliefs that one is more loathe to reject than the theory itself.

These baseline beliefs can be a matter of simple common sense (e.g., that an object has a single speed at any given moment), or a scientific belief that one takes as a near-absolute. For instance, Mach (1960) recounts a thought experiment in which a chain is draped over a frictionless triangular wedge, and demonstrates that the chain must be in a state of rest by asking us to further imagine joining the loose ends of the chain so that they form a loop that hangs around the wedge. If the chain is not to reach a state of equilibrium, its circular shape ensures that it must slip endlessly around the wedge, and in doing so, form a perpetual motion machine. Mach suggests that we instinctively find such an outcome impossible, though it is perhaps truer to claim that the conservation of energy is a principle that physicists are instinctively driven to defend and are loathe to dismiss.

3 Verbal humour

The categories of most interest in verbal humour, in particular the narrative humour of "story" jokes, are those that pertain to event structure, social convention and genre expectations. This realization has lead computationally minded theorists of humour to view the *script* (a notion given computational form by Schank and Abelson 1977) as the most appropriate level of categorization for resolving the meaning of narrative jokes (Raskin 1985). Indeed, one cannot discuss theories of humour without granting centre-stage to the script-based General Theory of Verbal Humour (or GTVH) of Attardo and Raskin (Attardo and Raskin 1991; Attardo et al. 2002). The GTVH is a juxtapositional theory of humour that is a modular reworking of Raskin's (1985) Semantic Script Theory of Humour (or SSTH). Like the SSTH, the GTVH views a joke as a narrative that is compatible with multiple scripts, one of which will at first appear primary until the punch-line contrives an *incongruity* that must be resolved (Suls 1972; Ritchie 1999; Veale 2004). Resolution is achieved, either partially or fully, by a special logical mechanism that analyses the nature of the mismatch between the primary script and the text, before switching the thrust of interpretation from this script to another.

GTVH scripts can be activated by a text in one of three ways: lexically (by association with a single word, called the *lexical handle* of the script); sententially (by a pattern of words and lexical scripts); and inferentially, as a by-product of common-sense reasoning (e.g., as when one intuits that a joke is racist and activates a Racism script). Furthermore, since certain elements in a script will be more salient and foregrounded than others, these elements are marked to distinguish them from less salient background elements. More recently, Attardo et al. (2002) augment this view with a graph-theoretic account of script representation that views scripts as arbitrarily complex symbolic structures, to which juxtapositional processes like sub-graph isomorphism can be applied. This representational shift allows the GTVH to encompass even punning as a script-level operation, provided the notion of script is sufficiently generalized to accommodate phonetic as well as semantic information. With this generalization, the GTVH moves further from Schank and Abelson's vision of a script, toward a generalized data structure that perhaps buys its increased descriptive flexibility at the cost of explanatory power.

The GTVH views the process of incongruity-resolution as the work of a particular logical mechanism (henceforth LM) that operates across script representations. Understandably, LMs have proved to be the most enigmatic elements of the GTVH, prompting Attardo et al. (2002) to enumerate a taxonomy of 27 different LMs. For instance, it is suggested that an LM called *false-analogy* is central to jokes whose humour derives from ill-judged comparisons, as in the old joke where a mad scientist builds a rocket to the sun but plans to embark at night to avoid being cremated. Here a false analogy is created between the sun and a light-bulb, suggesting that when the sun is not visible it is not "turned on", and hence, not hot. Different LMs may be employed in different jokes, bringing a distinctive logical flavour to each. Indeed, insofar as jokes that employ the same LM may possess the same identifiable character, LMs resemble the *Ur-jokes* of Hofstadter and Gabora (1989). These are joke skeletons that can be re-instantiated in different settings with different protagonists while preserving a distinctive character that runs through each of their manifestations (in this respect, Ur-jokes are productive humour schemas that in turn resemble the metaphor schemas of Lakoff and Johnson 1980 and Johnson 1987). The individuation of different LMs make the GTVH a highly modular theory of humour in which research can proceed on many different fronts simultaneously. Nonetheless, such extreme modularity, when combined with the GTVH's juxtapositional view of humour, tends to reduce jokes to the level of particular dishes as defined by standard recipes. In this view, the GTVH begins to resemble a kitchen appliance, in which logical mechanisms are little more than the optional whisks and cutting blades that can be attached in different contexts to meet different production needs.

3.1 Subversion of verbal meaning

As noted in the context of thought experiments, one constructs an appropriate counter-example by stripping away the layers of conventionality and habitual thinking that have accreted around a category. Fauconnier and Turner's (1998, 2002) theory of blended concepts explains why integrative ideas can have so many accreted meanings that do not directly derive from their individual parts. In this view, the integrated concept occupies its own mental space, a special blend space, in which recruitment of additional concepts and a process of gradual elaboration can occur. To undo the after-effects of blending, one must dismantle the chosen concept into its fundamental parts, so that it may be reconstructed devoid of these layers of recruited and elaborated meaning. Consider the following witticism from serial divorcee Zsa Zsa Gabor, which shows that in verbal humour, these parts are often directly accessible as individual words and morphemes.

(1) "Darlink, actually I am an excellent housekeeper. Whenever I leave a man, I keep the house!"

While the GTVH entreats us to view jokes like this as a juxtaposition of scripts, this merely begs the question of where these scripts originate. For while can expect to find a conventional housekeeping script in the lexicon, indexed by its lexical handle "housekeeper", it is unlikely that any *a priori* structure expressing the meaning "a taker and keeper of houses" can be found so readily. As conventionally defined, scripts "are not subject to much change, nor do they provide the apparatus for handling totally novel situations" (Schank and Abelson 1977). It follows that this new meaning must arise not from a script, but as a creative product in itself, via an exceptional reading of the phrase "housekeeper" that describes an exceptional member of the category of housekeepers. The subsequent inclusion of this exceptional reading in the housekeeper category, whose prototypical members are thrifty and hard-working rather than spendthrift and pampered, is a creative act of category subversion that in turn undermines the tacit value system to which Gabor is responding, In doing so, she pointedly (via "actually") undermines the suggestion that conventional housekeeping skills are the valid measure of a woman.

Derived categories are those that depend on a logically prior category for their conventional meaning. For instance, the category Hypotenuse depends on the category of triangles, for without right-angled triangles there would be no hypotenuses, or, in the language of Cognitive Grammar (Langacker 1991), Hypotenuse is a profiled element of the base concept Right-Angle-Triangle. However, this dependency can be subverted by witticisms such as "Hypotenuse seeks two straight lines to form love triangle". Likewise, the category Meat is conventionally conceived as logically dependent on the category Animal, since instances of Meat are derived from instances of Animal. Conventional wisdom thus holds that without animals there can be no meat, and without meat there could be no vegetarians. However, this is a form of habitual thinking that can be wittily subverted, as in the following one-liner:

(2) "If God wanted us to be vegetarians he wouldn't have made animals out of meat."

Which categories are subverted here, Vegetarian, Animal or Meat? The answer appears to be all three, for we seem to be presented with three quite exceptional objects that simultaneously subvert three different categories. First we are directed to imagine an exceptional member of the Animal category, the animal as meat machine, from which all non-utilitarian aspects are divorced; if such an animal were not sentient, there could be no moral basis for vegetarianism. Secondly, we are asked to imagine an exceptional kind of meat, one that possesses all the biological properties of conventional meat yet one that may not derive from an animal source. Thirdly, we are directed to imagine an exceptional kind of Vegetarian, one that would eat meat if it did not derive from an animal source. All three subversions together lead to a subversion of the category Vegetarianism, for what moral force would this lifestyle preserve if a vegetarian could freely eat meat yet remain a vegetarian? The above joke is, in fact, a highly compressed thought experiment that attempts to undermine the conventional theory that vegetarianism is a morally superior way of life, while justifying a moral laissez faire on the part of the meat-eaters.

Some of the most effective uses of subversion aim for a more visceral effect:

(3) "Eating is over-rated. Remember, food is just excrement waiting to happen."

This witticism succeeds in constructing a quite exceptional member of the category Food, that of excrement-in-waiting, for prototypical members of the category Food are expected to be edible and tasty, while excrement is neither. We can thus view this joke as another compressed thought experiment, one that uses a time-shifted view of food to subvert the conventional wisdom that to eat well is to live well. It achieves this appropriate incongruity through a visceral form of metonymic *tightening* (Fauconnier and Turner 1998; Veale and O'Donoghue 2000), a compression of relations that strengthens the connection between Food and Excrement to uncomfortably suggest that when one is eating the former, one is also eating the latter (Fauconnier and Turner 2002).

3.2 Subversion of conceptual mappings

One might well argue that while thought experiments involve a deep form of conceptual subversion, wherein a conceptual construct like a scientific theory in undermined, jokes merely subvert the semantic (or script-based) expectations of an audience. But this kind of expectation-subversion often goes hand-in-hand with a subtle subversion of conceptual viewpoints, as illustrated by the following exchange between two vagabonds:

(4) Tramp #1: 'ave you seen yesterday's newspaper?

Tramp #2: Can't says that I 'ave. What's in it, anyhow?

Tramp #1: My lunch, that's what!

Listener expectations are here based on a number of common metonymies: "to see" a newspaper is usually taken to mean "to read" a newspaper, while the "contents" of a newspaper usually refers to news stories rather than physical objects. But these metonymies do not, in themselves, provide the humour of the exchange; non-sequitors and nonsense behaviour will also thwart listener expectations, but to produce bafflement rather than humour. The subversion we find here is also conceptual, and works at several levels simultaneously. First we see the subversion of the concept Newspaper, which is demoted from its usual standing as a container of knowledge (an organ of the truth) to a lowly container of food: "today's news is just tomorrow's wrapping for fish and chips". Secondly, we see the subversion of the speaker himself, who is transformed from a consumer of "high" knowledge to a consumer of "lowly" food. And thirdly, we see a subversion of the concept News, or Knowledge in general, where "food for thought" is seen as less important to human existence than food itself.

3.4 Trumping: Subversions of figures of speech

The subversion of verbal meaning allows a witty speaker to overtly agree with a critic while simultaneously subverting the critic's argument. Veale et al. (2006) describe this particular combination of category subversion and overt agreement as conversational 'trumping', and note that trumping is not a form of deliberate *mis*-understanding, but is actually a form of *hyper*-understanding, in which the respondent exhibits a greater understanding of verbal meaning than does the critic. Trumping heightens the social dimension of category subversion by requiring that the parties to the dialogue do not overtly disagree, but this in turn heightens the creative demand placed on the respondent. The result is not only an ideational subversion of the initiator's pragmatic goals (via a given category), but a highly effective (and thus humour inducing) interpersonal subversion of the initiator as a social agent.

Trumping is a form of subversive humour that thrives on idioms and conventional figures of speech, since close analysis often reveals these figures to be built upon on a foundation of active conceptual metaphors. From this perspective, even the most frozen of idioms can be appreciated as a manifestation of metaphoric reasoning (Gibbs 1993). So where one finds metaphors, one also finds theory-like assumptions that can be subverted for humorous ends. The joke below nicely demonstrates that figures of speech, like theories, make claims that can be subverted using a potent exceptional case:

(5) CEO: (indignantly) I do the work of two people for this company!
 Chairman: Yes, Laurel and Hardy.

The idiomatic expression "to do the work of two people" makes the theory-like claim that two typical workers can achieve more than one alone (or, proverbially, that "many hands make light work"). They key assumption here is typicality: two unexceptional workers might do more work than one alone, but one unexceptionally competent worker is surely preferable to two exceptionally incompetent ones. The goal of trumping is not simply to invalid the initiator's use of a particular category, but to validate this usage while simultaneously undermining the tacit assumptions that determine the effects of the usage. Since the pairing of "Laurel and Hardy" serves as a recognizable prototype of the bumbling duo, it also serves as the ideal exceptional case for the assumption of typicality that governs the use of this idiom, to the detriment of the initiator.

4 Interpersonal dimensions of conceptual subversion

It is not the act of subversion in itself that gives rise to a humorous effect, but the pragmatic, largely social, uses to which the subversion is put. Conventional scientific thought experiments can employ exceptional cases to achieve appropriate incongruity without being overtly humorous, but may become humorous to the extent that they are grounded and understood in social terms (for example, as attacks on the originating theorist). That is, to the extent that a given subversion has a strong social and interpersonal dimension, we should expect the effect to be perceived as more humorous, *ceteris paribus*[2], whether the context is an explicit joke or a scientific thought experiment. Consider the following exchange between the boxer Muhammad Ali (at the height of his sporting and verbal prowess) and a flight attendant:

(6) Flight attendant: Buckle your seat belt, Mr. Ali, we're about to take off.
     Muhammed Ali: Superman don't need no seat belt!
     Flight attendant: Superman don't need no airplane neither.

Though an off-the-cuff remark rather than a considered scientific claim, Ali's description of himself as "Superman" constitutes a world-view that one can either defend or attack., much as one might react to a novel scientific claim. But what makes Ali's claim particularly ripe for humorous subversion is that

---

[2] Other factors, like aptness, topicality, conciseness and intellectual depth, are also extremely important.

the claim concerns *himself*: few scientists advance scientific claims about themselves, so most thought experiments only tangentially represent an assault on the proponent of the claims themselves. In undermining Ali's use of the concept Superman, the attendant simultaneously undermines Ali himself in a way that demonstrates her authority over a disruptive passenger and her verbal mastery over a smart-mouthed aggressor. Ali's particular world-view of himself as a "Superman" is thereby shown to be inconsistent, much as Aristotle's world-view was posthumously shown to be untenable by Galileo.

The distinction between funny and unfunny thought experiments is not at all a binary one. As we have seen, scientific thought experiments are not the abstract expression of a socially disinterested thought process, but the forceful expression of a criticism that can be rich in satire and humorous intent. Galileo, for instance, was less interested in attacking Aristotle than he was his contemporaries, who he labels simpletons through his none-too-subtle naming of the interlocutor "Simplicius". Likewise, Searle's Chinese room argument has many humorous qualities, not least the extreme caricature he paints of A.I. research. He lampoons the rules of conventional A.I. programs by stating that his imaginary Chinese rulebook contains rules of the form "*squiggle squiggle* means *squoggle squoggle*" (Searle 1980). His goal is to show that A.I. is not just inconsistent with our conception of human intelligence, but quite ridiculous in its own right. The baroque elements of Searle's argument place his experiment into the realm of a joke but his exposition never strays so far that the butt of the joke, symbolic A.I., becomes inaccessible or obscured. As such, Searle strives to construct an argument that is *optimally innovative* in the sense of Giora (2002).

In these thought experiments we see an attempt to subvert not just a theory but the proponents of the theory themselves. For instance, Searle (1980) claims that only those "in the grip of an ideology" would attempt to critique his Chinese room argument via the "system's reply" (which states that it is the combination of *man + rulebook*, rather than the man alone, that truly understands Chinese). This suggests that thought experiments, like jokes and metaphors, can have both an ideational and an interpersonal function (Halliday 1985). Thought experiments with a pronounced interpersonal dimension are more likely to engage the social instincts of a listener and achieve both an emotive and an intellectual effect. So to the extent that our social instincts lead us to enjoy the humbling of the mighty (e.g., Aristotle), the pompous (e.g., the religious supporters of Aristotle), the arrogant (e.g., Roger Schank, as perceived by John Searle) or the stupid (e.g., perhaps all of the above), we may tend to find humour in such thought experiments (1938). The precise degree of humour will depend, of course, on other factors, such as the quality of execution (e.g., cleverness, conciseness) and the social connection of the listener to the category and its proponents.

5 Subverting cultural stereotypes: A case study

Language is the primary means through which cultural knowledge is preserved and transmitted from one generation to the next, yet it does so in a manner that is not always maximally informative. Indeed, idioms and other stock phrases represent this cultural knowledge in a fossilized form that can often appear inscrutable to modern speakers. For instance, Charles Dickens opens "A Christmas Carol" by stating that "Old Marley was as dead as a door-nail" before going on to wonder what it is about door-nails that makes them so suited to the evocation of death. Suggesting that "coffin nails" might make a more suitable metonymy (noting "I might have been inclined, myself, to regard a coffin-nail as the deadest piece of ironmongery in the trade"), Dickens admits defeat by concluding "the wisdom of our ancestors is in the simile, and my unhallowed hands shall not disturb it, or the Country's done for" (Dickens [1843] 1984: 1). In raising the inscrutability of commonplace similes, Dickens is, in fact, having fun at the expense of received wisdom as it is encoded in language. By subverting listener expectations in the way such stock phrases are used creatively, a witty speaker can also subvert the received wisdom that underpins these phrases, to point out the limitations of this wisdom.

We take our cue from Dickens in this section, and demonstrate how commonplace similes can be subverted via counter-examples to achieve a humorously appropriate incongruity. We first describe how a large corpus of such similes is automatically harvested from the texts of the World Wide Web (in section 5.1.) before showing how the simile pattern can be used to ironically subvert listener expectations in section 5.2, and less frequently, to subvert the concepts underlying these similes, in section 5.3.

5.1 Acquiring a corpus of commonplace similes

For our current purposes we consider stock similes of the form *"as ADJECTIVE as a/an NOUN"*, and we attempt to collect all commonly-used values of ADJECTIVE for a given value of NOUN. To do this, we first extract a list of antonymous adjectives, such as "hot" or "cold", from the lexical database WordNet (Fellbaum 1998); the intuition here is that explicit similes will tend to exploit properties that occupy an exemplary point on a scale. For every adjective ADJECTIVE on this list, we then send the query "*as ADJECTIVE as **" to the Google search-engine and scan the first 200 snippets returned for different noun values for the wildcard *. From each set of snippets we can ascertain the relative frequencies of different noun values for ADJECTIVE. The complete set of nouns extracted in this way is then used to drive a second phase of the simile-harvesting process. In this phase, the query "*as * as a NOUN*" is used to collect similes that may have lain beyond the 200-snippet horizon of the original search, as well as similes that hinge on adjectives not in the original list. Together, both phases harvest a wide-ranging series of core samples (of 200 hits each) from across the web, yielding an initial set of 74,704 potential simile instances (of 42,618 unique types) relating 3769 different adjectives to 9286 different nouns.

However, many of these instances are not sufficiently well-formed for our purposes. In some cases, the instance does not convey a stereotypical association, but a highly contingent one that only holds in a specific, ephemeral context. In other cases, the noun value forms part of a larger noun phrase: it may be the modifier of a compound noun (as in "bread lover"), or the head of complex noun phrase (such as "gang of thieves"). A human judge is thus used to annotate those instances that correspond to bona-fide similes, by which we mean, similes that associate an adjectival property with a noun concept for which that property stereotypically holds (such as "hot" for "oven", "humid" for "sauna", or "busy" for "beaver"). Overall, 30,991 of these simile instances are accepted as bona-fide expressions of a stereotypical association, yielding 12,259 unique adjective-to-noun associations, from 2635 adjectives to 4061 different nouns. As such, we believe that this collection represents the largest resource of its kind for the study of similes.

5.2 Subverting listener expectations

When one uses the syntactic pattern "as ADJECTIVE as a ..." there is a clear listener-expectation that what follows is a noun description that is highly evocative of the property ADJECTIVE. But among those instances of the simile pattern that our judge rejects, we find 4685 instances (or 2798 unique associations of an adjective to a noun) that can be classified as *ironic*. An ironic simile is here taken to be any comparison of the form "as ADJECTIVE as a NOUN" for which NOUN is not merely un-stereotypical for ADJECTIVE, but for which NOUN actively evokes the opposite property *not*-ADJECTIVE. Examples include "as subtle as a freight-train", "as bullet-proof as a sponge-cake" and "as private as a shopping-mall". Surprisingly then, the number of ironic similes constitutes a larger proportion of well-formed similes than one might have previously imagined, with bona-fide similes (those that express a stereotypical association) out-numbering ironic similes by just 3 to 1. Of course, the bona-fide simile remains the norm, as one would expect, but these findings point to a large-scale subversion of the simile frame to achieve humorous effects in web texts.

Similes like "as hairy as a bowling-ball" do an effective and humorous job of subverting listener expectations by promising one thing (e.g., a stereotype of hairiness) and delivering another (e.g., a stereotype of baldness). In doing so, they doubly accentuate the lack of an expected property and re-create in the mind of the listener the surprise initially experienced by the speaker. In other words, speakers use such similes when they themselves expect to find the property ADJECTIVE but are surprised to instead perceive *not*-ADJECTIVE. As such, these similes are clearly amenable to analysis by the GTVH, wherein the syntagmatic pattern "as ADJECTIVE as ..." triggers a script that expects a stereotype of ADJECTIVE, but a stereotype of *not*-ADJECTIVE is discovered instead. The conflict between ADJECTIVE and the implicit evocation of *not*-ADJECTIVE yields the semantic incongruity demanded by the GTVH, while this incongruity is resolved (or seen to be appropriate) by recognizing that "as ADJECTIVE as ..." can have two meanings: ADJECTIVE can denote an extreme point on the scale of ADJECTIVE-ness (e.g., "hairy" may denote a state of extreme hairiness) or the scale of ADJECTIVE-ness itself (e.g., "hairy" may denote the extent to which something is more or less hairy).

5.3 Subverting arguments based on stereotypes

Simple ironic similes such as these are amenable to the GTVH because they merely succeed in subverting listener expectations, and such expectations are eminently conducive to formalization as scripts (indeed, this is the goal of a script in Schank and Abelson's original formulation). But because these similes do not exhibit any traction at the conceptual level, they cannot succeed in changing our views of the concepts concerned. For instance, the ironic simile "as ruthless as a bunny-rabbit" does not make us think of rabbits as any more callous, nor does it make our stereotypes of ruthlessness, such as sharks and wolves, seem any less cold-blooded. In short, while such similes can be novel, they are not optimally innovative in the sense of Giora (2002), since they fail to identify a specific stereotype to which any innovation can apply.

To be optimally innovative, an ironic simile should both evoke a stereotype and simultaneously subvert it. For instance, while someone who is "as fast as a cheetah" is very fast indeed (since speed and agility are properties of the stereotypical cheetah), someone who is "as fast as a *three-legged* cheetah" is, conversely, remarkably slow. Examples like the latter do not simply subvert listener expectations, but subvert the very logic of stereotype-based reasoning itself. Just as ironic similes are less frequent than their bona-fide counterparts, we expect optimally-innovative ironic similes to be less frequent than ironies that simply challenge listener expectations.

We test this hypothesis by harvesting similes from the web that have the syntactic form "as ADJECTIVE1 as an ADJECTIVE2 NOUN", since – as illustrated by the cheetah example above – this form can both evoke a salient stereotypical association ("as ADJECTIVE1 as a NOUN") and innovatively subvert this association (insofar as "ADJECTIVE2 NOUN" denotes a sub-kind of entities that strongly suggest the opposite property, not-ADJECTIVE1). Taking the 12,259 stereotypical adjective-to-noun associations harvested in section 5.1, we use these to construct queries of the form "as ADJECTIVE as a|an * NOUN" that retrieve elaborations of these basic similes from the web. We find 5729 elaborations in total, such as "as invulnerable as an *armoured* tank", "as ugly as a *shaved* mule" and "as delicious as a *fresh* peach".

Unsurprisingly, most elaborations serve to augment and reinforce the stereotypical association on which they are based. Thus, we find "as bright as an *exploding* star", "as supple as a *young* willow" and "as blue as a *cloudless* sky", where, in each case, the elaboration prompts the listener to construct a more detailed mental picture of the stereotype underlying the comparison. In some cases these reinforcing elaborations add humour to an otherwise unfunny association, such as "as white as a *frightened* ghost", "as green as a *pickled* toad" and "as dry as a *Syrian* martini". Interestingly, these examples do not subvert listener expectations (a pickled toad is still green) but do subvert the stereotypes underlying these expectations (a frightened ghost is not a stereotypical ghost, a pickled toad is a quite exceptional toad, and a Syrian martini is an unlikely concoction at best). However, we have as yet no formal basis for deciding whether a non-ironic elaboration presents an exceptional case or not, as this depends crucially on the perceived absurdity of the mental image that is constructed (is a "shaved mule" more or less exceptional than a "pickled toad" or an "exploding star"?). In each case, these reinforcing elaborations have the following argumentative form:

(7) Speaker 1: If you think a NOUN is ADJECTIVE1, an ADJECTIVE2 NOUN is even more ADJECTIVE1

Speaker 1: X is not just as ADJECTIVE1 as a NOUN, but as ADJECTIVE1 as an ADJECTIVE2 NOUN!

When humorous, these examples just stop short of subverting the associated stereotype, but do show how the stereotypical category can be elaborated to include increasingly bizarre category members. The more incongruous (yet appropriate) these members, the funnier the elaboration is likely to seem. One can consider this a mild form of subversion, of a kind that does not undermine the stereotype but which incongruously stretches the stereotype to achieve ridiculous ends. As such, these examples can be seen as a weak form of thought experiment, one that does not strive for contradiction or inconsistency, but one that cleverly explores the limits of what is possible and what is meaningful.

We also find a number of ironic elaborations that more obviously correspond to the stronger formulation of a thought experiment discussed earlier: these subvert both the listener's expectations (by offering a comparison for which *not*-ADJECTIVE1 is more salient than ADJECTIVE1) and the explicitly provided stereotype: we find, for instance, "as white as a *bloody* sheet", "as edgy as a *dulled* razor", "as explosive as a *wet* firecracker" and "as accurate as a *drunken* archer". Each is a compressed dialectical argument, or trumping:

(8) Speaker 1:   X is as ADJECTIVE1 as a NOUN
     Speaker 2:   Yes, an ADJECTIVE2 NOUN!

Speaker 1's claim can here be seen as a culturally received theory about NOUN (as well as a personal theory about X), to which Speaker 2's trumping elaboration can be seen as an exceptional case for which this theory *should* hold, but does not.

Our study reveals that just 2% of the elaborations we harvest from the web (or 109 cases among 5079) have this doubly subversive form. While we make the strong prediction that these forms, which subvert both listener expectations and stereotype-level expectations, should be perceived as funnier than corresponding forms that subvert neither, *or* that subvert just one (expectations or stereotypes), this prediction still remains to be empirically validated.

6 Conclusions

By examining the similarities between thought experiments and jokes, we see that both forms of discourse are similar by virtue of their subversive role in the undermining of habitually-held world-views. As such, we argue that rather than view humour as a juxtapositional mechanism that combines different scripts, frames or mental spaces, it is often more fruitful to view humour as a rather pointed use of a more fundamental cognitive mechanism: the ability to probe the boundaries of existing categories, to illuminate the unspoken limitations of these categories, and to offer appropriate counter-examples that expose these limitations to ridicule. In this view, jokes and thought-experiments can be seen as language games that posit exceptional cases to subvert or undermine patterns of conventional thinking and the people that exploit them (Veale 2002). The construction of exceptional cases, as advocated by Gendler (1998, 2000), relies on an ability to dismantle concepts into their component parts, to reveal what is truly central to the workings of a category. In this way, jokes and thought experiments provoke a sceptic to undertake a radical re-analysis of a category, one that reveals how a category can be used and, perhaps more importantly, misused.

Jokes and thought experiments can both be used to prompt a reappraisal of a particular mindset or mode or behaviour, but it is important to note that jokes are granted a special licence in this regard, one that is off-limits to the scientific thought experiment. Crucially, jokes are free to exploit hyperbolae, irony, sarcasm and metaphor, while the effectiveness of a thought experiment is predicated upon the perceived fairness, factuality and descriptive plainness of the arguments used. Jokes are not expected to be either fair or factual, and their effectiveness is measured in terms of their ability to provoke laughter. People rarely, if ever, laugh at semantics: humour is a social phenomenon, and semantics can provoke laughter only when it is given a pragmatic social dimension, explicitly or otherwise. We laugh not just because categories are subverted and their boundaries shown to be fuzzier than previously believed, but because there are social consequences of this subversion that we find psychologically satisfying (Freud 1938).

Crucially then, we do not claim that all jokes can be interpreted as thought experiments in the strongest sense, for shoehorning all of verbal humour into a single philosophical paradigm would inflict a serious injustice on both phenomena. For instance, there exists a substantial body of jokes – such as those that nurture stereotypes of women and ethnic minorities – that attempt to promulgate conventional thinking and buttress existing belief structures. While such jokes can be subversive to the point of being socially corrosive, they do not fit comfortably into the *Gedanken* mould. However, they do have a corresponding form in scientific discourse, since most scientific experiments are designed to buttress rather than undermine a particular theory. Jokes then, like experiments, can be used to bolster or to undermine, *and* just as thought experiments cause us to question the unspoken assumptions that surround a theory, jokes can prompt us to question the habitual associations that surround a word or category.

This *Gedanken*-based subversion view of humour is not antagonistic to, but complementary to, the juxtaposition view of humour as embodied in mechanisms like bisociation, script switching and frame shifting. Subversion explains how, and why, new categories are created from old: to demonstrate the limitations of conventional wisdom as captured in conventional categories. We thus believe that the subversion view, as illuminated by a comparison to the workings of scientific thought experiments, goes further to explain (rather than simply describe) the creativity inherent in both joke production and joke understanding.

References

Attardo, Salvatore, and Victor Raskin. 1991. Script theory revis(it)ed: Joke similarity and joke representational model. *Humor: International Journal of Humor Research* 4(3): 293–347.

Attardo, Salvatore, Christian F. Hempelmann, and Sara Di Maio. 2002. Script oppositions and logical mechanisms: Modeling incongruities and their resolutions. *Humor: International Journal of Humor Research* 15(1): 3–46.

Brône, Geert, Kurt Feyaerts, and Tony Veale (eds.). 2006. Special issue on 'cognitive linguistic approaches to humor'. *Humor: The International Journal of Humor Research* 19(3).

Coulson, Seana. 2000. *Semantic Leaps: Frame-shifting and Conceptual Blending in Meaning Construction*. New York/Cambridge: Cambridge University Press.

De Mey, Tim. Thought experiments, conceivability arguments and conceptual blending. In: Anders Hougaard and Stephen Nordahl (eds.) *Odense Working Papers in Language and Communication* 24, 143–156.

Dickens, Charles. 1984. Reprint. *A Christmas Carol*. Middlesex, UK: Puffin Books. Original edition, 1843.

Fauconnier, Gilles, and Mark Turner. 1998. Conceptual integration networks. *Cognitive Science*. 22(2): 133–187.

Fauconnier, Gilles, and Mark Turner. 2002. *The Way We Think. Conceptual Blending and the Mind's HiddenComplexities*. New York: Basic Books.

Fellbaum, Christiane (ed.). 1998. *WordNet: An Electronic Lexical Database*. MA: MIT Press, Cambridge.

Freud, Sigmund. 1938. Wit and its relation to the unconscious. In: Abraham Arden Brill (ed.) *The Basic Writings of Sigmund Freud*, New York: Modern Library.

Gendler, Tamar Szabó. Galileo and the indispensability of scientific thought experiment. *The British Journal for the Philosophy of Science* 49(3): 397–424.

Gendler, Tamar Szabó. 2000. *Thought Experiment: On the Powers and Limits of Imaginary Cases*. London UK: Garland Publishing.

Gibbs, Raymond W. Jr. 1993. Why idioms are not dead metaphors. In: Cristina Cacciari and Patrizia Tabossi (eds.) *Idioms: Processing Structure and Interpretation*. Hillsdale, NJ: Erlbaum, 57–78.

Giora, Rachel. 2000. Optimal innovation and pleasure. In: O. Stock et al. (eds.) *The April Fools' Day Workshop on Computational Humour:* Proceedings of the Twentieth Twente Workshop on Language Technology (Series TWTL20). Enschede: UT Service Centrum.

Halliday, Michael A. K. 1985. *An Introduction to Functional Grammar*. London: Edward Arnold.

Hofstadter, D. and Gabora, L. 1989. Synopsis of the workshop on humor and cognition. *Humor: International Journal of Humor Research* 2(4): 417–440.

Johnson, Mark. 1987. *The Body in the Mind*. Chicago, IL: Chicago University Press.
Koestler, Arthur. 1964. *The Act of Creation*. New York: Macmillan.
Kuhn, Thomas. 1964. A Function for Thought Experiments. In: Thomas Kuhn (ed.) *The Essential Tension*. Chicago: University of Chicago Press, 240–265.
Lakoff, George, and Johnson, Mark. 1980. *Metaphors We Live By*. Chicago: Chicago University Press.
Langacker, Ronald W. 1991. *Concept, Image and Symbol: The Cognitive Basis of Grammar.* Cognitive Linguistics Research. Berlin/New York: Mouton de Gruyter.
Mach, Ernst. 1960. *The Science of Mechanics*. trans. Thomas J. McCormak. LaSalle, Illinois: Open Court Press.
Mach, Ernst. 1976. *On Thought Experiments. Knowledge and Error*. Dordrecht: Reidel.
Norton, John D. 1996. Are thought experiments just what you always thought? *Canadian Journal of Philosophy*.
Oring, Elliott. 2003. *Engaging Humor*. University of Illinois Press.
Ortony, Andrew (ed.). 1979. *Metaphor and Thought*. Cambridge: Cambridge University Press.
Ritchie, Graeme. 1999. Developing the incongruity-resolution theory. In: Kim Binsted and Graeme Ritchie (eds.) *Proceedings of the AISB Symposium on Creative Language: Stories and Humour* 75–85. Edinburgh, Society for the Study of Artificial Intelligence and the Stimulation of Behaviour.
Raskin, Victor. 1985. Semantic Mechanisms of Humor. Dordrecht: D. Reidel.
Schank, Roger C., and Abelson Robert P. 1977. Scripts, Plans, Goals and Understanding. New York: Wiley.
Searle, John. 1980. Minds, brains and programs. *Behavioural and Brain Sciences* 3(3): 417–457.
Suls, J. M. 1972. A two-staged model for the appreciation of jokes and cartoons: An information processing analysis. In: Jeffrey H. Goldstein and Paul E. McGhee (eds.) The Psychology of Humor, 81–100. New York: Academic Press.
Veale, Tony, and Diarmuid O'Donoghue. 2000. Computation and blending. *Cognitive Linguistics* 11(3–4), 253–288.
Veale, Tony. 2002. Compromise in multi-agent blends. In: Anders Hougaard and Stephen Nordahl (eds.) Odense Working Papers in Language and Communication 23.
Veale, Tony. 2004. Incongruity in humor: root-cause or epiphenomenon? *The International Journal of Humor Research* 17(4): 410–428.
Veale, Tony, Kurt Feyaerts, and Geert Brône. 2006. The cognitive mechanisms of adversial humor. *Humor:. International Journal of Humor Research* 19(3): 305–339.

Salvatore Attardo
5 Humorous Metaphors[1]

It is a well-known fact, indeed an obvious one, that some humor comes from taking literally a metaphorical expression or vice-versa. This is not the topic of this paper. This paper is concerned with metaphors that are humorous. The central issue of any account of humorous metaphors is to answer the question of why some metaphors are humorous and some are not.[2] Most accounts of humorous metaphors rely on variants of the "distance theory" (Fónagy 1982, Morrissey 1989, Pollio 1996), which essentially consists in postulating a threshold of "semantic distance" beyond which the linkage between the two domains in the metaphorical construal becomes "stretched" (i.e., too distant) and is therefore perceived as humorous. The most obvious problem for the distance theory is that no precise (or even approximate) quantification of the threshold exists. But a subtler and more damaging argument can be brought up against it. Consider the example:

(1) Life is a journey.

In what sense are *life* and *journey* not "too distant"? After all, life is not a journey and a journey is not life. Why is

(2) Life is an apple.

more distant than "life is a journey"? And if so, what about

(3) Life is a box of chocolates.

---

[1] I am grateful to Margerita Dore, Phillip Hamrick, Elliott Oring, Elena Semino, and Tony Veale for examples and suggestions, and generally being supportive. The paper was submitted in its present form to the editors in 2008. It has not been updated or altered, in any way, except for correcting typos. The materials were presented originally at the 2007 Cognitive Linguistics conference in Krakow, Poland.

[2] The same question, *mutatis mutandis* applies to blends, metonymies, incongruities, or any other cognitive phenomenon involved in humor. This is not the place for an account of humor theory (for which see Attardo 1994, updated in Attardo ([1996] 2005), and Attardo (2008), nor is it for an account of the applications of cognitive linguistics to humor, for which see the references in Attardo (2008).

the example made famous by the Forrest Gump movie? Are chocolates and apples equidistant from life?[3]

For example, Emily Dickinson's poem 280 *I felt a funeral in my brain* includes the wonderful line

(4) And then a Plank in Reason, broke. (Dickinson 1976)

from which we infer the metaphor "reason is a wooden construction (with a floor)" which surely has to qualify as the mapping of two distant domains, no matter what metric of distance is used. Yet, the line is not interpreted as humorous.[4]

In this paper I will present an alternative (but not necessarily antagonistic) approach grounded in the most recent developments of humor research within the incongruity/resolution framework. No familiarity with humor research is assumed or necessary as the term "incongruity" can be assumed to have its non-technical meaning, and "resolution" will be defined in the text.

The first step of the analysis is to problematize the very concept of humorous metaphor. Analysis of a small corpus of "humorous metaphors" collected from web pages and press reports[5] shows that "humorous metaphors" is an umbrella term covering at least three completely different phenomena:
1. metaphors that are funny in and of themselves
2. metaphors that describe a referent that is inherently funny
3. failed metaphors (metaphors that are involuntarily funny, or that are produced pretending to be involuntarily funny)

It does not seem possible or even desirable, at this point in the research, to reduce the idea of "humorous metaphor" to a unique category. It is not even that the concept is organized prototypically: I think it is safe to say that this is

---

[3] This is not to say that semantic distance is impossible to calculate, in principle. See for example Budanitsky and Hirst (2001), Maki, McKinely, and Thompson (2004) and references therein. However, the methods are neither mature enough to be applicable to the lexicon at large, nor sophisticated enough to tackle the examples examined below. It is quite possible that in a few years the distance theory may be completely vindicated and integrated with what I present in this paper.

[4] Obviously, the issue may be keying, not the metaphor itself. This is not the place to address these issues. See Attardo (Forth.) for a treatment of the problem.

[5] The paper is based on a small corpus of humorous metaphors collected primarily on the Internet, online lists of humorous metaphors, and in publications, such as the *New Yorker*.

All the examples in the corpus were explicitly labeled as humorous metaphors (except the samples from the *New Yorker*, where the label is implicit).

an umbrella concept, that collects a number of heterogeneous phenomena, some semantic, some pragmatic, and some not even linguistic (but still obviously conceptual). This is a price we have to pay for dealing with a folk-concept, which does not necessarily have clearly definable theoretical counterpart.[6] Perhaps further research will uncover a unifying category underlying all linguistic expressions that are considered humorous metaphors by speakers, but given the results I will present, this seems unlikely. At best, humorous metaphors may share a family resemblance. However, I am skeptical even of that possibility. As I said, I think the term is an umbrella term, covering heterogeneous phenomena.

It seems useful to start the analysis by restating the cognitive approach to metaphors, which sees them as mappings between two different conceptual domains (Lakoff and Johnson 1980). The conceptual domains mapping approach has been developed in the "blending theory of metaphor" (Grady, Oakley and Coulson 1999), which is programmatically complementary to Lakoff's approach.

Blending theory has its origins in the work of Gilles Fauconnier (1997) and Mark Turner (1996). Blending theory is based on mental spaces. Mental spaces (Fauconnier 1985) are similar to possible worlds, although they do not share their ontological commitments. Essentially, a mental space is some intellectual construct imagined, wished for, etc., which consists of mental entities organized in some relation. The relationship between mental spaces and domains is one of instantiation, particularization, and specification: "a mental space is a short-term construct informed by the more general and more stable knowledge structures associated with a particular domain" (Grady, Oakley and Coulson 1999).

Blends involve four mental spaces: two input spaces, a generic space, which represents the information shared by both input spaces, and finally the blended space, where the two input domains interact. A significant aspect of blending theory is that it accounts for "emergent" properties: thus in "this surgeon is a butcher" the "incompetent" feature is not present in either domain/mental space "butcher" or "surgeon", it emerges from the interplay of the mental spaces. The nature of the "emergence" is inferential: "The incongruity of the butcher's means with the surgeon's ends leads to the central *inference* [emphasis mine, S.A.] that the butcher is incompetent" (Grady, Oakley and Coulson 1999). This is related to the other distinctive feature of blending theory: whereas conceptual domains theory of metaphor is mostly concerned with codified metaphors, blending theory is more concerned with the online processing of novel metaphors, even explicitly mentioning "cartoons, jokes, newly coined terms, terms we apply in unusual ways" (Grady, Oakley and Coulson 1999).

---

6 It should be noted that this does not mean that a folk concept cannot have a clearly definable theoretical counterpart.

The differences between the conceptual domains theory of metaphor and blending theory can be summarized in the table 1:

Table 1: Differences between the conceptual domain and blending theories of metaphor

	Conceptual Domain Mapping	Blended Mental Spaces
Domains	Directly mapped	Inform mental spaces
Mental Spaces	NA	Directly mapped
Mappings	One-to-one	Two-to-one
Emergent	NA	Inferential
Type of metaphor	Codified	Novel

Blends are governed by a set of five principles (Fauconnier and Turner 1998). Of particular interest in this context is the fifth: Metonymic Tightening, thus defined, "Relationships between elements from the same input should become as close as possible within the blend. For instance, Western images of personified Death often depict the figure as a skeleton, thus closely associating the event of death with an object that, in our more literal understandings, is indirectly but saliently associated with it" (Grady, Oakley and Coulson 1999). This principle may be the source of the "distance theory" of humorous metaphors, mentioned above.

Another observation, which is similarly interesting is the distinction, introduced by Tsur (1992; 2003), between metaphors that have a 'split focus' and metaphors that have an 'integrated focus'. The former "emphasize the incongruous, discordant elements of source and target concepts and, according to Tsur, tend to be perceived as witty, ironic, paradoxical, and in some cases, emotionally disorientating". (Semino 2008) The purpose of split focus metaphors is "to achieve mainly witty effects" (Tsur 2003: 124). Integrated focus metaphors, conversely, "background the incongruity between source and target concepts, and emphasize the similarity or congruence between them". (Semino Forth.) Their purpose is to achieve "emotional effects." (Tsur 2003: 124). Relatedly, Pollio (1996: 248) claims that a metaphor is humorous if there is an emphasis on "the boundary or line separating them" whereas it is not "if the boundary between the joined items (or the act joining them) is obliterated and the two items fuse to form a single entity." Both Tsur and Pollio, recognize the problem we started from at the beginning of the paper: some metaphors are funny and some are not. The problem remains: why is this so? I believe an answer may come from a proposal by Elliott Oring, to be presented next.

As we saw, traditional accounts of humorous metaphors rely on the vague and unspecified idea of "distance" between conceptual domains or restate the problem by noting that some metaphors focus on or emphasize the incongruity, while other do not. However, Oring (2003) has proposed a different approach to humorous metaphors, which relies on ideas commonly used in humor theory: incongruity and resolution.[7] According to Oring, metaphors seek to find an appropriateness in an incongruous connection between two frames, but they are not humorous because the appropriateness they find is "genuine" (i.e., legitimate), whereas riddles and jokes find "spurious" appropriateness (2003: 5) in the connection of two frames. Humor always involves non-fully resolved incongruities. Metaphors, conversely, fully resolve the incongruity of the mapping between domains.

The proposed explanation for humorous metaphors (*stricto sensu*) is that they are metaphors in which the incongruity of the mapping of different domains is not fully resolved by the interpretation (finding appropriateness/resolution) of the metaphor (Oring 2003). This explanation combines semantic and pragmatic factors: the incongruity of the mapping is a semantic fact, the research for appropriateness a pragmatic one. It is obvious that it can be recast in blending terms without any loss of analytical power. It differs, as noted above, from the distance approach in that the distance between domains is not a factor relevant to the humorous effect, whereas the processing of the blend/metaphor is assumed to be the crucial factor. It should be noted, as I mentioned in passing above, that this account is not necessarily antagonistic to the distance theory, which could possibly be integrated in the present account.

A further difference between Oring's approach and the "distance" theories should be clear: Oring's is a dynamic theory, based on the inferential process of finding appropriateness in (i.e., resolving the incongruity of) the comparison of two different domains. The distance theories are based on a-priori metrics, or on vague "emphasis" or "focus" on the incongruity/congruity of the comparison. It is tempting to read both Tsur and Pollio's proposal as less precise formulations of Oring's theory, but as I noted these proposals merely restate the problem. Moreover, Oring's approach has the further advantage of being fully integrated, even terminologically, with humor theory.

It is worth noting, in passing, that even those critical of the Lakoff Johnson theory of metaphors assume that conceptual mapping are in use with novel or unusual metaphorical expressions (Keysar et al. 2000). So, while this discussion of humorous metaphors is couched in conceptual mapping/blending terms, it is

---

[7] This is not the place to discuss the incongruity and resolution theory of humor. A thorough discussion of the psychological aspects, broadly construed to include also applications outside of psychology, can be found in Martin (2007); a discussion focusing on linguistics in Attardo (1997).

probably independent of the particular theoretical apparatus.[8] Let us note also in passing that the incongruous aspect of metaphors is acknowledged by blending theorists. It is called "anomaly" and is defined as follows:

> part of what defines metaphors is that they involve (temporary) suppression of critical knowledge of a given conceptual domain, and therefore are *not compatible with our understanding of reality*. We refer to this particular phenomenon, in which structure from one fused element is blocked, as 'accommodation': the target material yields to the source material, which is explicitly represented in the blend. (Grady, Oakley and Coulson 1999; my italics, SA)

It is fairly obvious that "incompatibility with our understanding of reality" is equivalent to "incongruity."

1 Funny Metaphors

Let us consider some examples of humorous metaphors.

(5) *His thoughts tumbled in his head, making and breaking alliances like underpants in a dryer without Cling Free.*

This example can be clearly explained as a blend between the domain of ideas and of underwear: the partially emergent aspect of the blend is that ideas form connections among themselves by coming in contact with other ideas (note the mapping between static cling and connections between ideas). The blend is further complicated by a minor (intrusive?) third source domain of diplomacy (connections are alliances). According to Oring's theory (2003), the appropriateness of the connections between the domain of ideas and underwear is insufficient to justify the mapping and hence the resolution is only partial, making the metaphor humorous. This is probably due to the differential in status between ideas and underwear. Needless to say, the disparagement theory of humor assumes that a significant part of humor (or all of it, depending on the formulation) comes from status differentials.

Consider the following (fabricated) example, provided by Oring (p.c.):

(6) *His thoughts tumbled in his head, making and breaking alliances like an Italian Renaissance prince.*

---

[8] To put it differently, this approach can be stated in a number of other approaches to metaphor, for example a metaphor-as-trope, or a metaphors-as-implicature.

In this example, the alliances are more motivated, but the loss of incongruity is almost complete. Presumably this is due to the high status of Italian Renaissance princes.

(7) *A review of Frederic Raphael's Novel A Double Life is quoted as saying: "[B]eautifully written. There is suspense, irony, breathtaking raccourcis [pithy descriptions] and humorous metaphors – for instance, picturing Pia, a good professional making love 'like a typist'."* Marie-Alice de Beaumarchais, *The Spectator*

Technically, "making love like a typist" is a simile, but we can ignore the differences since the example can be readily rephrased as "Pia was a typist as far as making love went". The blend/mapping in the metaphor is fairly clear on the one hand we have *sex* and on the other *typing*. Why should this be perceived as humorous is somewhat more complex: for starters, the distance theory stumbles right off the gate[9]: both sex and typing involve fine motor activities done (in part) with the fingers. Sex can be performed in a sitting position (Kakar and Doniger 2003), which is the prototypical position for typing. In fact, the humorous effect of the metaphor is to be found in the stereotypes associated with typists, in the frame semantic information activated by the lexical item "typist". While the dictionary definition of "typist" is simply "someone who operates a typewriter" encyclopedic information tells us that typists were overwhelmingly female and that a steady production of pornographic material focused on the interplay between the (male) bosses and the female typists. However, in this case the sexual innuendo is not the focus of the humor, but rather the prototypical characteristics of females employed in low-paying jobs, i.e., daintiness, lack of imagination/initiative, etc.[10]

According to Oring's theory (2003), the metaphor is humorous because, despite the partial resolution I have sketched, the incongruity of mapping sex to typing is not completely resolved by the interpretation "Pia made love in a dainty, unimaginative way". There is no need, *stricto sensu*, to evoke the typist domain, to express the interpretation "Pia made love in a dainty, unimaginative way".[11] This is similar to what I have called the "residual violation" of irony: after the hearer has processed the irony and reached the two meanings of the

---

9 Theories are race horses...
10 As is well known, often humor is based on entirely mythical stereotypes.
11 Incidentally, I am *not* saying that the metaphor expresses the proposition "Pia made love in a dainty, unimaginative way." On the contrary, the sentence "Pia made love in a dainty, unimaginative way" serves only to evoke a vast, unspecified, and possibly unbounded set of weak implicatures (to use the Relevance Theoretic term) triggered by the metaphor.

ironical expression, he/she reaches a reasonably good interpretation of what the intentions of the speaker must have been in uttering the ironical sentence. However, it remains that the speaker could have spoken literally. I wish to suggest that Oring's incomplete resolution is, in this instance, the fact that the speaker could have avoided the metaphorical expression.

From the above discussion it follows then that the present approach makes a strong empirical prediction: no *stricto sensu* humorous metaphor should occur within a metaphorical schema. Examples such as "rug rat" or "couch potato" should no longer be perceived as humorous, or at least much less so than novel humorous metaphors.

2 Metaphors that describe inherently funny referents

(8) "As independent as a hog on ice" (Funk 1985; Morrissey 1989).

It can be argued that here it is the referent of the metaphorical expression that is funny, not the metaphor itself. It should be noted that the expression is of course a contradiction, since the hog is not independent, and that creates part of the humor, however, I agree with Morrissey's interpretation that most of the humor comes from the image evoked by the hog slipping on the ice, as evidenced by the fact that most people use the expression without the comparison, i.e., just as "hog on ice", consider, for a rough estimate, that the expression without the "as independent" phrase occurs in 216,000 pages according to Google, and in a mere 750, in the full expression.

If the analysis of the referent-as-source-of-the-humor is correct, then this category is of little interest for the analysis of humorous metaphors, since one could describe a hog slipping on the ice and get (most of) the same effect, without the metaphor. Having said this, I will complicate matters a bit. Consider that the expression's implied comparison may be the logical mechanism (i.e., resolution), as in the following example, collected from the internet:

(9) *[hog on ice] was probably said of me, big football player and wrestler when I went out for basketball. I remember that we had this real delicate guy come out for football, he looked like he was going to be just like a hog on ice – but, it turned out he was the best kicker we had ever had.*
(Awarulz 2007).

To paraphrase: the "delicate guy" was going to be clumsy and out of his element *like* a hog on ice, but then he was not. If this analysis is correct, then characterizing these referential humorous metaphors as such is correct.

3 Failed metaphors

The following sections examine the various kinds of failed metaphors that emerged from my corpus. Relatively more attention is paid to novel categories. It should be noted that it is irrelevant whether these failed metaphors were produced deliberately or as a result of inappropriate performance. In either case, the hearer/reader has to interpret them as humorous. The only difference might be that if they were produced inadvertently, one can make a case that the target of the humor becomes the speaker of the utterance.

3.1 Un-metaphors

In the case of "un-metaphors" the explanation is fairly straightforward: since the definition of metaphor is a conceptual mapping between two different domains, if one maps one domain upon itself, one does not get a successful metaphor (while preserving the construction which signals the metaphor) and conversely, if one attempts to map two domains that have no connection, no well-formed metaphor emerges. Intuitively the incongruity between the expected metaphor and its failure is enough to explain the humor.

Here are some examples of un-metaphors.[12]

(10)   *The red brick wall was the color of a brick red Crayola crayon.*

This is a straightforward example of self-mapping (mapping a domain upon itself).

(11)   *The thunder rumbled ominously, making a sound much like the sound of a thin sheet of metal being shaken backstage during the storm scene of a play.*

---

[12] One could object that these are not metaphors. However, native speakers label them as humorous metaphors. This presents a conundrum for a usage-based analysis: either retreat in the abstraction of theoretical models or accept the inherent messiness of data.

This example is slightly more complex: the mapping/blend between the domain of *storm* and *sound effect* is incongruous, insofar the sound effect is supposed to imitate (or at least evoke fictionally) the source domain and hence obviously should resemble it. It is a case of mapping between a domain and its representation, and hence ultimately a case of self-mapping.

(12) *The little boat gently drifted across the pond exactly the way a bowling ball wouldn't.*

Example (12) is interesting because it explicitly denies the mapping (which in itself would cause the metaphor to fail) but it also lends itself to manipulation. First of all, the explicit denial of similarity can be removed, without loss of humorous effect, yielding (13).

(13) *The little boat gently drifted across the pond exactly like a bowling ball.* [constructed]

Since bowling balls are notoriously heavy and non-buoyant, it is obvious that they would not float on a pond's surface (evoked by "drifting across the pond"). This formulation can be generalized into a formula for producing humorous/ironical un-metaphors. Consider (14)

(14) *As silent as a garbage truck.* [constructed]

or

(15) *As easy to grasp as a lecture on string theory.* [constructed]

This suggests strongly that, for one class of humorous metaphors and similes, it is enough to predicate a feature of one domain onto another, Whereas the feature is conspicuously absent from the either domain.[13] Finally, let us consider a sophisticated case:

(16) *Her vocabulary was as bad as, like, whatever.*

---

13 On the subject of ironical similes, promising research is being done by Veale and Yao (2007, 2008). They find that a remarkably large number (20%) of similes of the "as X as NP" structure, retrieved through Google searches, are ironical (2007: 684).

In (16) we find no mapping, as in the previous examples, but the lack of mapping is motivated thus providing the appropriate incongruity (Oring 2003). Comparison of this failed metaphor to the following light bulb joke is enlightening:

(17)   *How many Surrealists does it take to change a light bulb? Fish!*

In Attardo (2001: 77), I analyzed this joke as a meta-joke in the light bulb joke cycle. Essentially, it is a joke that fails to deliver the light bulb joke evoked by the canonical first line of the text (the construction "How many X does it take to change a light bulb?"), but does so by making reference, as light bulb jokes do, to the stereotypical characteristics of a given group: in this case, surrealists. Since surrealists enjoyed connecting things that had nothing in common, the answer "Fish!," which has no connection to the question, is thus appropriate. In (16), we see the same mechanism: the expression "whatever" literally means that the speaker is not interested in any of the specifics of the discourse at hand, hence *a fortiori* of vocabulary choices. Hence, the speaker of (16) is guilty of the very same fault he/she is accusing the referent of "her". This self-defeating nature of the utterance is a common feature of humor.

3.2 Mixed metaphors

A metaphor is "mixed" when more than one metaphor occurs in the same expression. Lakoff and Johnson (1980: 92, 95) noted that mixed metaphors may (but need not) result in "a conflict of concepts": "At this point our argument doesn't have much content. In what we've done so far, we have provided the core of our argument. If we keep going the way we're going, we'll fit all the facts in." (1980: 92)

The reason some metaphors can be mixed is that they have shared "entailments" (Lakoff and Johnson 1980: 92), i.e., they reach the same conclusion: in the examples above the metaphors are "an argument is a journey" and "an argument is a container"; the shared entailment is "as we make an argument, more of a surface is created" (1980: 94). A metaphor such as "the direction of his argument has no substance" (1980: 95) is not acceptable, because it mixes the two metaphors without a shared entailment.

Lakoff and Johnson's position is fairly clear. However, we find that some of the examples that are in our corpus seem to operate differently:

(18) "I'm tired of being Charlie Brown and putting in more hoops for teachers to jump though and then pulling the football of higher salaries away at every turn." (From the *Des Moines Register*. Qt., New Yorker March 6, 2006, 78)

(19) "A restraining order at this point would throw a monkey wrench in the whole procedural apple cart that has already left the station' said lawyer Marc Cohen, arguing on behalf of the state." (From the *Macon (Ga.) Telegraph*, qt. New Yorker August 21, 2006, 78)

(20) "This is the margin of patience. It takes a special player or coach with a strong back for scrutiny to transition from a wide-eyed country mouse to a position in a rat race of expectations without losing his marbles." (From the *Times*, qt. New Yorker April 2, 2007, 83)

In example (18)–(20), we do not see so much metaphors that lack shared entailments, but rather partially or completely unrelated metaphors that are piled up by the speaker, even sequentially: consider (20), we see "having a strong back" for "resilient"; "wide-eyed" for "innocent" (metonymy?); "country mouse" for "simpleton" or perhaps "unsophisticated"; "rat race" for "stressful situation"; and finally, "losing one's marbles" for "going insane."

The operating principle here seems to be more along the lines of a "restraint" rule (do not use too many metaphors either at the same time or in close sequence). It should be kept in mind that any reasonably long text will inevitably include several, perhaps tens or even hundreds of different metaphors. The issue is that they occur at a sufficiently large distance (measured in words, for example, and not to be confused with the semantic distance we discussed at the beginning of the article). The prohibition for using several metaphors at the same time follows from the shared entailments rule. However, the avoidance of too many metaphors in sequence does not follow from the shared entailment rule and is thus unpredictable from within that framework. It is explained on pragmatic grounds in the discussion section.

Note how examples (18)–(20) can be paraphrased in completely non humorous and non-metaphorical[14] counterparts: e.g., (19) can be turned into (21).

(21) *A restraining order at this point would impede the whole procedure, which is already in an advanced stage of implementation.*

---

14 Ignoring conventional metaphors, of course.

Finally consider the following example

(22) *So now what we are dealing with is the rubber meeting the road, and instead of biting the bullet on these issues, we just want to punt.*
(From the *Chicago Tribune*, qt. New Yorker, August 13, 2007, 79)

which can also be paraphrased completely seriously, as

(23) *So now what we are dealing with is the most significant part of the problem, and instead of doing what we have to do on these issues, we just want to get rid of them.*

It is unclear to me why since the "rubber meeting the road" metaphor is complete and gets referred to no further, its entailments should still conflict with the "biting the bullet" metaphor.

It should be noted in passing that blending theory explicitly allows for more than two input spaces. This makes it harder to explain why mixed metaphors are "anomalous" unless we allow for the "restraint" rule proposed above.

An interesting explanation, suggested to me by Elena Semino (p.c.) is that in all of these cases, we have a combination of two things:
1) relatively infrequent and therefore salient expressions[15] (e.g., monkey wrench)
2) which evoke metaphorical concepts that are odd when combined into a single metaphorical scenario.

This explanation has the advantage that it reduces straightforwardly to the script opposition/incongruity scenario (a monkey wrench in an apple cart, etc.). Furthermore, it also has the advantage that it does not require the intervention of a pragmatic rule. The two explanations are not incompatible, so it is conceivable that both are at play. For example, we may note that the *New Yorker* examples involve three metaphors in close sequence. So, perhaps there exists a threshold (more than two metaphors?) that triggers the perception of clash.

3.3 Overdone metaphors

These are metaphors that violate primary metaphors relations (Grady 2005), such as

(24) "I am building a theory of metaphor from the ground up" (unfunny)

and

---

[15] Semino notes that mixed metaphors are very common, but mostly go unnoticed, as for example in the expression "a key step in the argument" where both "key" and "step" are metaphors, but no "clash" emerges.

(25) "I am building a theory of metaphor with many windows" (funny or at least odd).

This takes care also of

(26) "He was faster than a speeding .25 caliber bullet, fired by a Beretta Jetfire pistol" [fabricated example]

since presumably there is no primary metaphor involving Beretta guns. Note in passing the exaggeration of the speed.

Or consider (27), supposedly produced by a student,

(27) He was as lame as a duck. Not the metaphorical lame duck, either, but a real duck that was actually lame. Maybe from stepping on a land mine or something.

Let us ignore in this context the literalization of the conventional metaphor "lame duck." The incongruous detail whereby the duck would have been rendered lame by the explosion of a land mine is both clearly outside of the primary metaphors and completely unnecessary (why would it matter how the duck was injured?).[16] Moreover, it is also a clear exaggeration (a duck would be pulverized by a land mine).

Another example of exaggeration is (28), also supposedly produced by a student.

(28) *It hurt the way your tongue hurts after you accidentally staple it to the wall.*

Many of the overdone metaphors violate primary metaphor relations because they provide excessive detail (such as the type of handgun that fired the speeding bullet, the event that crippled the duck) or are overt exaggerations. It is unclear whether this is a necessary condition for overdone metaphors (as the label I have used seems to imply) or whether one can have a metaphor that violates primary metaphor relations and is funny without being exaggerated.

3.4 Erroneously categorized metaphors

In passing let us mention that some of the examples are "fake metaphors": there are in fact cases of antanaclasis, i.e., the use of a word in two different senses, such as in the following examples, the antanaclastic word bolded:

---

16 Unless you are the duck, it goes without saying.

(29) *"Oh, Jason, take me!" she panted, her breasts **heaving** like a college freshman on $1-a-beer night.*

(30) *He **fell** for her like his heart was a mob informant and she was the east river.*

(31) *The plan was simple, like my brother-in-law Phil. But unlike Phil, this plan just might **work**.*

Here, as was the case in the metaphors that describe inherently funny referents, we face a possible complication: the connection between the two unrelated senses of the word may create a (failed) metaphor connecting two unrelated domains. If that is the case, then these cases of antanaclasis become failed metaphors by default and then there exists a *prima facie* plausibility in labeling them as metaphors (however "failed ones").

3.5 Discussion of failed metaphors

The explanation for failed metaphors is both pragmatic and semantic. On the pragmatic side, it relies on an extension of the principle of cooperation (CP), which has been justified on independent grounds elsewhere (Attardo 1999; Eisterhold, Boxer and Attardo 2006). Essentially, this entails the postulation of a "principle of non-cooperation" (NCP), which governs the violation of the principle of cooperation. Applied to metaphors, the NCP prescribes avoidance of excessive or unnecessary detail (overdone metaphors), avoidance of multiple metaphors (mixed metaphors), avoidance of exaggeration, etc. Most (all?) of these rules follow directly from the tenets of the NCP, or perhaps from a straightforward extension of the CP to metaphorical discourse (e.g., do not exaggerate). Conversely, it should be stressed that failed metaphors are not completely pragmatic in nature: un-metaphors and overdone metaphors are clearly also semantic (no mapping, unwarranted mappings).

4 General discussion

Given that we have dealt with heterogeneous materials, it will be useful to examine a summary chart of the types of humorous metaphors we find in the folk-definitions of the phenomenon, with their explanation in linguistic terms (see table 2).

Table 2: Types of humorous metaphors

	Type	Explanation	Example
A	Funny metaphors	Partially resolved incongruity of cross domain comparison	Thoughts are underpants
B	Metaphors with funny referent	Referential humor and possibly implied comparison	Hog on ice
C	Un-metaphors	Mapping a domain upon itself or no mapping	Red brick wall the color of a brick-red crayon
D	Mixed metaphors	Multiple metaphors that do not share entailments and possibly too many metaphors	Throw a monkey wrench in the procedural apple cart that has already left the station
E	Overdone metaphors	Metaphors that violate primary metaphorical relations	A lame duck, lame from stepping on a land mine.
F	Erroneously categorized	Antanaclasis	Unlike Phil, this plan may work.

As I anticipated, I do not think that a unified theory of why some metaphors are humorous and some are not is possible. This is because the reasons why they are funny are different. Metaphors are funny because of different semantic reasons (compare types A and B, in the chart above, to the remaining types). Other metaphors are humorous because of semantic and pragmatic reasons (D, E). Others, because they describe humorous referents, and would be funny even without the metaphorical medium (B). Others yet are not metaphors at all (F) and are rather puns.

For a theoretical point of view then, depending on the type of humorous metaphor, a given theory may be ideally suited to explain the mechanisms of the text. For example, Grady's primary metaphorical relations explain very nicely overdone metaphors. Oring's humor theoretic account of metaphor as fully resolved incongruities, with the converse theorem that partially resolved incongruous metaphors are humorous, is the best explanation for the class of humorous metaphors. The lack of, or improper, mappings across domains explain the un-metaphors. Finally, a pragmatic account can explain aspects of overdone and mixed metaphors. Once more, however, we must come to the conclusion that no single approach/theory can explain all the phenomena that folk-definitions label "humorous metaphors". In a sense, we could get a family resemblance definition of humorous metaphors if we were willing so sacrifice categories C and F, which are technically not metaphors at all. The price to pay is to retreat from the usage/corpus-based stance into the abstraction of theory (as well as the nice explanation of the failure of category C to generate metaphors as an extension of the same metaphorical processes of the other categories (except F).

5 Metaphors and humor theory

Finally, we need to address briefly the issue of the connection between humor theory and the discussion of humorous metaphors. As I mentioned, the examples above are perfectly amenable to a standard analysis in terms of various humor theories. Take example (19) here repeated for convenience:

(19)   "*'A restraining order at this point would throw a monkey wrench in the whole procedural apple cart that has already left the station' said lawyer Marc Cohen, arguing on behalf of the state.*" (From the *Macon (Ga.) Telegraph*, qt. New Yorker August 21, 2006, 78)

A standard analysis in terms of humor theory[17] would identify a series of incongruities, deriving from script/frame oppositions: monkey wrench vs. apple cart; apple cart vs. train (as in "the train has left the station"), etc. Further abstraction would show that in each case the opposition involves the "literal" and the "metaphorical" sense of the expression. Furthermore it would identify a butt of the humor (in this case "lawyer Marc Cohen" the speaker of the sentence (and thus would label this form of humor as "involuntary humor"). The specific linguistic features of the text are also obviously involved and specifically the lexical choices of the collocations/idiomatic expressions "throw a monkey wrench", "apple cart", and "has (...) left the station". The text is too short to have a specific narrative form or to refer to a specific situation intelligible out of context, expect that it is a case of legal discourse.

One may be tempted to ask then whether the fact that the presence of three metaphors in the text was a mere coincidence. This would be in error. The metaphors are the aspect of the text that brings about the incongruity, which makes

---

17 The analysis is kept deliberately neutral in theoretical terms. Formulation in terms of the GTVH is easy enough: Script Opposition: monkey wrench/apple cart, etc.; literal/metaphorical; actual/non-actual. Logical Mechanism: Metaphors. Situation: Legal discourse. Narrative Strategy: irrelevant (reported discourse). Language: the specific metaphorical idiomatic expressions: throw a monkey wrench; apple cart; the train has left the station.

possible and playfully justifies ("partially resolves") the script opposition. To put it in different terms, the metaphoricity of the text is its Logical Mechanism.

I propose this as a general hypothesis to be investigated (Hamrick 2007): metaphors, blends, metonymies, and similar cognitive phenomena may be a class of Logical Mechanisms. This would account nicely as to why some metaphors are humorous and some are not: just like reasoning from false premises or stating the obvious[18] may or may not be humorous depending on whether they occur as logical mechanisms of an incongruity/script opposition, similarly metaphors, blends, metonymies, etc. may or may not be humorous depending if they enable or bring about an incongruity and/or partially resolve it. Further research will be necessary to address this question.

Other issues also remain open: for example, is the high/low status of the elements in the mapping significant? Consider examples (1–3) in which "life" is mapped on "food". Food is a "low status" item (presumably because of its "bodily" associations. Is it possible that (2) and (3) are seen as humorous, whereas (1) is not is (at least in part) due to the fact that the mapping involves food? After all, consider the known logical mechanism of juxtaposition, exemplified, among other cases, by coordination, as in Achille Campanile's novel titled: *Asparagus and the immortality of the soul* in which the incongruity is provoked by the wide disparity of the two coordinates (the NPs "asparagus" and "the immortality of the soul") and the (feeble) resolution by the coordination "and".

Finally, we can note that there seem to be degrees of incongruity across the humorous metaphors. Can they be measured? Is there a threshold? Does this avenue bring us back to the distance theory? Once more we can only call for further research.

References

Attardo, Salvatore. 1994. *Linguistic Theories of Humor.* Berling: Mouton de Gruyter.
Attardo, Salvatore. 1997. The semantic foundations of cognitive theories of humor. *Humor: International Journal of Humor Research* 10(4): 395–420.
Attardo, Salvatore. 1999. The place of cooperation in cognition. European Conference of Cognitive Science (ECCS '99) Siena, Italy. October 27–30. 459–464.
Attardo, Salvatore. 2001. *Humorous Texts*. Berlin: Mouton de Gruyter.
Attardo, Salvatore. 2005. Humor. In: J. Verschueren, J-O Ostman, J. Blommert and C. Bulcaen (eds.) *Handbook of Pragmatics*. Amsterdam/Philadelphia, PA: Benjamins. 2nd ed., 1–18. Original edition 1996.

---

[18] Reasoning from false premises and stating the obvious are logical mechanisms that have been identified in humor theory.

Attardo, Salvatore. 2008. A primer for the linguistics of humor. In: Victor Raskin (ed.) *A Primer for Humor Research*. Berlin: Mouton de Gruyter.
Attardo, Salvatore. Forth. Salience of incongruities in humorous texts and ther resolution. In: Grzegorz Szpila and Elzbieta Chrzanowska-Kluczewska (eds.) *Proceedings of the IALS Conference*. Oxford UP.
Awarulz. 2007. *Askville by Amazon*. http://askville.amazon.com/expression-hog-Ice/Answer-Viewer.do?requestId=3972023.
Budanitsky, Alexander, and Graeme Hirst. 2001. Semantic distance in WordNet: An experimental application-oriented evaluation of five measures. In: *Proceedings of WordNet and Other Lexical Resources Worksho,p* 29–34. Pittsburgh, PA.
Dickinson, Emily. 1976. *The Complete Poems of Emily Dickinson*. New York, NY: Back Bay Books.
Eisterhold, Jodi, Diana Boxer, and Salvatore Attardo. 2006. Reactions to irony in discourse: Evidence for The Least Disruption Principle. *Journal of Pragmatics* 38(8): 1239–1256.
Fauconnier, Gilles. 1985. *Mental Spaces*. Cambridge, MA: MIT Press.
Fauconnier, Gilles. 1997. *Mappings in Thought and Language*. Cambridge: Cambridge University Press.
Fauconnier, Gilles, and Mark Turner. Conceptual integration networks. *Cognitive Science* 22(2): 133–187.
Fónagy, Ivan. 1982. He is only joking: Joke, metaphor and language development. In: Ferenc Keifer (ed.) *Hungarian Linguistics*, 31–108. Amsterdam: Benjamins.
Funk, Charles Earle. 1985. *A Hog on Ice & Other Curious Expressions*. New York: Harper Colophon Books.
Grady, Joseph E. 2005. Primary metaphors as inputs to conceptual integration. *Journal of Pragmatics* 37(10): 1595–1614.
Grady, Joseph E., Todd Oakley, and Seana Coulson. 1998. Blending and metaphor. In: G. Steen and R. Gibbs (eds.) *Metaphor in Cognitive Linguistics*. Philadelphia: John Benjamins.
Hamrick, Philip. 2007. Notes on some cognitive mechanisms of humor. In: Diana Popa and Salvatore Attordo (eds.) *New Approaches to the Linguistics of Humor*. Galati: Dunarera de Jos University Press, Rumenia.
Kakar, Sudhir, and Wendy Doniger. 2003. *Kamasutra* (Oxford World's Classics). Oxford: Oxford University Press.
Keysar, Boaz, Yeshayahu Shen, Sam Glucksberg, and William S. Horton. 2000. Conventional language: How metaphorical is it? *Journal of Memory and Language* 43: 576–593.
Lakoff, George, and Mark Johnson. 1980. *Metaphors We Live By*. Chicago, IL. University of Chicago Press.
Maki, Williams S., Lauren N. McKinley, and Amber G. Thompson. 2004. Semantic distance norms computed from an electronic dictionary (WordNet). *Behavior Research Methods, Instruments, & Computers* 36(3): 421–431.
Martin, Rod A. 2007. *The Psychology of Humor: An Integrative Approach*. Burlington. MA/London: Elsevier.
Morrissey, Maureen M. 1989. Script Theory for the analysis of humorous metaphors. In: Shaun F. D. Hughes and Victor Raskin (eds.) *WHIMSY VII. Proceedings of the 1988 WHIM conference Held April 1–4, 1988 at Purdue University* 124–125. West Lafayette. IN/Tempe (AZ): International Society for Humor Studies.
Oring, Elliott. 2003. *Engaging Humor*. Urbana and Chicago. IL: University of Illinois Press.
Pollio, Howard R. 1996. Boundaries in humor and metaphor. In: Jeffrey Scott Mio and Albert N. Katz (eds.) *Metaphor: Implications and Applications* 231–253. Mahwah (NJ): Lawrence Erlbaum.

Semino, Elena. 2008. *Metaphor in Discourse*. Cambridge: Cambridge University Press.
Tsur, Reuven. 1992. *What Makes Sound Patterns Expressive: The Poetic Mode of Speech-Perception*. Durham N. C.: Duke UP.
Tsur, Reuven. 2003. *On the Shore of Nothingness: Space, Rhythm, and Semantic Structure in Religious Poetry and its Mystic-Secular Counterpart – A Study in Cognitive Poetics*. Exeter: Imprint Academic.
Turner, Mark. *The Literary Mind*. Oxford: Oxford University Press.
Veale, Tony and Y. Hao. 2007. Learning to understand figurative language: From similes to metaphors to irony. In: *Proceedings of CogSci, The 29th Annual Meeting of the Cognitive Science Society*, 683–688. Mashville, USA.
Veale, Tony and Y. Hao. 2007. A context-sensitive framework for lexical ontologies. *The Knowledge Engineering Review* 23(1): 101–115.

Ralph Müller
6 A metaphorical perspective on humour

1 A metaphorical perspective on humour

In Western philosophy and poetics we can find a longstanding belief that there is a conceptual similarity underlying both humour and metaphor. However, another obvious connection between metaphor and humour which has been neglected is the metaphorical description of humorous experiences, the reason being that metaphor analysts have mostly focused on negative emotions, such as anger or grief. Not only are theoretical terms such as "superiority theory" or "degradation" and "incongruity" of metaphorical origin. Even basic experiences such as 'comic relief' or various kinds of laughter are often understood in terms of metaphorical mappings.

The following study will first sketch the intellectual history of the conceptual metaphor-humour-connection. The second part of the study will then investigate metaphorical mappings that describe humour in German. The question of whether metaphors have a particular affinity to humour or vice versa will also be addressed throughout this study in order to contribute to the investigation of cognitive mechanisms of creativity from a stylistic perspective that underlie humour and many instances of metaphors (Brône, Feyaerts and Veale 2006: 214).

2 A short history of dualism in humour and metaphor

The most prominent tenant of a conceptual or cognitive similarity between humour and metaphor is the notion of conceptual duality. Jean Paul,[1] a German writer and critic, captured this belief in the phrase that "Wit in its narrowest sense" is the disguised priest who marries every couple (Jean Paul 1963: 173). This metaphor has become one of the most frequently cited definitions of humour in German, and even Sigmund Freud did not miss out on the opportunity to start his famous book on *The Joke and Its Relation to the Unconscious* with this witty metaphor (Freud, 1960: 8f.).

---

[1] Alias Johann Paul Friedrich Richter (1763–1825).

Jean Paul's witticism combines a dual-structure of metaphor with a dual contrastive structure of humour. On the one hand, his phrase is a witty formulation of the *incongruity theory* of humour, as wit seems to be able to couple concepts which are incongruent by their semantic background. On the other hand, this is a witty metaphor: it draws an analogy between a misalliance of a couple and the relation between incongruent ideas or words.

The idea that both metaphor and humour derive from duality can be traced back far beyond Jean Paul to Aristotle's *Rhetoric* (Aristotle 1970: III, 1412a). Aristotle demanded that metaphors should be drawn from "objects closely related", but not obvious to "everyone at first sight". The aptitude of finding metaphors is compared to philosophy where "to observe the resemblances in widely distant things is characteristic of a sagacious penetrating intellect". Aristotle also finds that jokes and riddles are similar to metaphor as they all lead to pleasure derived from the unexpected surprise. By emphasising the dual structure of metaphor and connecting it explicitly to the expectation-delusion-structure of riddles and jokes Aristotle has formulated the most important tenants of the metaphor-humour connection. And this view has been influential up to the present day. On the one hand, it has promoted the idea that metaphors consist of two (distant) ideas which indirectly inspired I. A. Richards' differentiation of metaphorical meaning in vehicle and tenor (Richards [1936] 1976: 96f.). On the other hand, it has offered the foundation of the incongruity theory through a long and complicated history of reception, as traditional incongruity theories have described humour in terms of contrasts between perceptions or ideas (Beattie 1809: 152f.; Breitenbürger 1975; Hecken 2005; Müller 2007). Even the underlying spatial view of metaphor can be found in contemporary definitions of metaphor and humour, as, for instance, in Mio and Graesser, who basically claim that the humour of jokes increases with the "distance between the circles of ideas", (Mio and Graesser 1991).[2]

3 Duality in contemporary theories of humour and metaphor

A dualistic view on metaphor is not inevitable, and not all theories of metaphor assume dual structures (Mooij 1976: 31). In fact, there are even some methodological problems with dualistic views of metaphor. The traditional dualistic view assumes that metaphors consists of fusing two ideas, one of which is

---

[2] For the problematic consequences of this metaphorical view cf. also Attardo (in this volume).

called "vehicle" and conveys the "literal meaning of the words used metaphorically", whereas the other one – the "tenor" respectively the "topic" – conveys the idea of the vehicle (Kittay 1987: 16). One of these ideas is often implicit and has to be reconstructed in order to complete the dual structure. On the one hand, the topic of a metaphorical expression may be implicit. On the other hand, utterances such as *Our marriage is on the rocks* imply in dualistic terms that a marriage is understood to be a travelling ship, even if there is no underlying vehicle explicitly stated (e.g., *The ship of our marriage is on the rocks*); thus metaphors may require a "vehicle reconstruction" (Reinhart 1976). As a consequence, Beardsley has rejected the dualistic view, because it would invite us to make unfounded inferences (Beardsley 1962: 294f.). However, vehicle reconstructions make dualistic theories more powerful in explaining novel and unconventional metaphors by making assumptions about their cognitive processes.

Most cognitive theories of metaphor have adopted a dualistic stance. This stance is evident for early cognitive theories, such as Richards' differentiation of "tenor" and "vehicle". Similarly, Karl Bühler, a trained gestalt-psychologist, understood metaphors as a mixture of two spheres (Bühler [1934] 1999: 348). However, contemporary approaches to metaphor in Cognitive Linguistics do not easily fit the traditional understanding of duality. The Theory of Conceptual Metaphor applies duality on a higher level of abstraction, where single concepts (or ideas) and their related expressions are subsumed under two larger conceptual domains, the so-called source domain and the target domain. The Theory of Conceptual Blending describes particular metaphorical meanings with two input spaces, but it also adds additional spaces in order to explain new emerging features in the metaphorical blend (Coulson and Oakley 2000).

In humour studies, the dualistic stance is very important for incongruity theories, which explain humour as emerging from apprehending two related but contrasting, inconsistent or incongruent ideas. The traditional understanding of incongruity has been significantly formalised in terms of the overlap and oppositeness of scripts, a notion that is central to the Script-Semantic Theory of Humour and its extended version, the so-called the General Theory of Verbal Humour (henceforth GTVH) (Attardo and Raskin, 1991; Raskin, 1985). Coulson has proposed a description of humour in terms of an elaborated version of the Theory of Conceptual Blending which assumes more dynamic meaning structures than the General Theory of Verbal Humour (cf. Coulson, Urbach and Kutas 2006; Ritchie 2005). She describes humour as "frame shifting" which is essentially also a dualistic approach.[3]

---

[3] In the period between the writing and publication of this paper, additional studies by Dynel (2009) and Veale (2013), but also chapters in the monographs by Kövecses (2015) and Goatly (2012) have appeared.

In summary, duality has played a continuous role in cognitive studies of both metaphor and humour. However, the terminology used to describe the entities that may participate in dual structures is often defined on different levels of abstraction or formalisation, which makes, for instance, the Theory of Conceptual Metaphor and the General Theory of Verbal Humour incomparable. Nevertheless, there are various descriptions of a shared duality by metaphor and humour which will be examined now.

4 The conceptual metaphor-humour connection

It was Arthur Koestler who most prominently (albeit not very scientifically) suggested that metaphor and humour shared the same conceptual mechanisms. He referred to it as "bisociation", and believed it to be a common base of metaphor, humour and scientific invention (Koestler 1964). On a more abstract level, Hofstadter and Gabora have explored analogies as underlying patterns of humour (Hofstadter and Gabora 1989), and in the GTVH the incongruity resolution, more specifically the Logical Mechanisms, has also been described as a "general mapping function which introduces a spurious similarity between elements in the scripts involved" (Attardo 2001: 25). Such observations emphasize that both metaphor and humour are based on incongruent concepts which are, nevertheless, connected by some cognitive mechanisms similar to metaphorical analogy. Still, there is – to my knowledge – no study that would claim humour and metaphor to be the same. In fact, identity of metaphor and humour is rather unlikely, since not every metaphor strikes us as funny, nor can we base humour identification on metaphor analysis (Fónagy 1982: 64f.; Oring 2006: 51). Moreover, there are various statements in favour of cognitive differences between humour and metaphor. Fónagy emphasizes that jokes carry "clean-cut semantic limits", whereas a metaphor is often vague and open (Fónagy 1982: 64). Giora assumes that joke comprehension, on the basis of the graded salience hypothesis and in contrast to metaphor comprehension, suppresses salient meaning (Giora 2003: 175). Mio and Graesser admit that both humour and metaphor contain paradoxes, but they suppose that the paradoxes are of different sorts: Comprehension of jokes and metaphors would be different, since a joke that has to be explained is no longer funny, but explaining a metaphor may contribute to our understanding (Mio and Graesser 1991: 94). This assumption that metaphor increases insight, and humour merely triggers laughter is widely held. Fónagy goes further in believing that metaphors, in contrast to jokes, have the power to bring about new ideas (Fónagy 1982: 82). This view has also led to the judgement that metaphors are nobler by being more insightful. For instance, Pollio says that metaphor would seem the "more subversive of the two phenomena.

Not only do the category-crossings of figurative language serve to alter (or destroy) the boundary between the categories crossed, they also provide a novel vision or at least a changed perspective" (Pollio 1996: 251).

In summary, studies on the metaphor-humour-connection seem to agree that humour and metaphor process duality differently: On the one hand, humour seems to have a tendency to retain an opposition between two concepts, whereas understanding of metaphor seems to conflate two different concepts. However, any differentiation in humour and metaphor begs the question of whether we can explain how humorous metaphors function in contrast to non-humorous metaphors. In particular, we should be able to explain why we rarely laugh at the inherent incongruity of metaphors. Why is it usually not funny to call somebody a "flower"?[4]

Pollio explains the difference between metaphors that elicit humour and metaphors that are not humorous by a split reference (Pollio 1996: 248): metaphors usually fuse the split reference; only when they are humorous, do they retain the two references in such a way that the tension has to be dissipated through laughter (Pollio 1996: 251). One would expect many answers from approaches in the context of the Theory of Conceptual Blending, as this theory has, so far, provided descriptions of both metaphor and humour. However, the position of this theory towards a possible metaphor-humour connection is still unclear, since few studies have dealt with humour and metaphor as related phenomena. For instance, although Coulson investigates both metaphor and jokes, and although she describes humorous metaphors (Coulson 2001: 193), she does not discuss such connections. Fortunately, Kyratzis gives a detailed account of the conceptual form of humorous metaphors in terms of the Theory of Conceptual Blending, and he offers some explanations, starting with Pollio's observation that humour draws attention to the boundaries, and metaphor "fuses" the two input spaces: Kyratzis claims that "metaphor becomes a joke and causes mirth in discourse when attention is drawn to the boundaries between the two concepts it brings together; speakers, either intentionally or unintentionally, disjoin the domains that are relevant to the metaphor and emphasise their dissimilarities" (Kyratzis 2003: 15). Kyratzis understands this process as a "de-blending" or 'breaking up of the blend', which leads to a "de-automatisation" of a conventional metaphor. However, Kyratzis observes in his corpus also one instance of an innovative metaphor in which the fusion of boundaries led to humour. He supposes that these kinds of novel blends keep their duality and tension by virtue of their unconventionality (Kyratzis 2003: 17).

---

4 This question reverses the usual question of humour analysts, which is also the reason why this question is not a central issue of humour studies.

Kyratzis' analyses are convincing, as there is an intuitive difference, for instance, between an ambiguous pun on a conventional metaphorical meaning and a humorous unconventional metaphor; however, his explanation that humour may emerge from blending or from de-blending applies two contradictory explanations to humorous metaphors in such a way that one of the two explanations will always be applicable. A more promising approach lies in locating the humorous effect not only in the blended space itself, but in the relationships between the blended space and its input spaces. First of all, this would be more in tune with the hypothesis that metaphorical meaning is not limited to the blended space, but emerges also from its relationships to other spaces (Coulson 2001: 196f.). In fact, the existence of humorous metaphors is a strong argument in favour of a dual view of metaphor which retains the input spaces as a part of the meaning of the whole blend. In this respect, it is not necessary to assume a de-blending effect, instead we assume that humorous metaphors differ from non-humorous metaphors by an additional emphasis on the input spaces. Consequently, humorous metaphors are particular examples of metaphors where the inherent incongruity of the input spaces is made apparent (Dynel 2009). At the same time, the so-called blended space may serve as a part of the incongruity resolution, which re-motivates the incongruity in terms of the Logical Mechanisms (Attardo 2001: 22–28) or Oring's "appropriate incongruity" (Oring 2006).

The idea that humour is a particular quality that characterises a metaphorical conceptual structure in certain circumstances casts another light on the questions of co-occurrence of metaphor and humour in discourse. If novel or poetic metaphors and humour are different ways of creatively exploiting similar conceptual phenomena, then they could also co-occur more frequently in similar discursive contexts. In fact, there are some studies that observed a tendency of humour and metaphor to co-occur in discourse. Pollio (1996: 232) reports observations that puns and metaphors appear frequently in the same linguistic environments. Kyratzis analysed a range of de-automatised funny metaphors in conversation (Kyratzis 2003: 15). Veale et al. have discovered that metaphor and metonymy are important techniques in humorous trumping (Veale, Feyaerts and Brône 2006: 318). At the same time, we can find observations by metaphorists that innovative metaphors are often used to elicit humour (Deignan 2005: 29; Goatly 1997: 162). Can we thus infer that metaphoricity is a typical feature of humour in discourse? An answer to this question should differentiate between a strong and a weak hypothesis. The strong hypothesis assumes that metaphors appear systematically to enhance humour or as inherent parts of humorous utterances. This hypothesis can be discarded. A comparison of metaphorical and humorous elements in Oscar Wilde's *Lord Arthur Savile's Crime* did not show a particular conceptual relationship of metaphor and humour: Oscar Wilde, an author of exquisitely elaborated humorous style, applied only a few humorous metaphors (Müller 2007). Nevertheless, the data suggested that humour is often accompanied by metaphorical expressions. Even if it seems that humorous metaphors in discourse are rather exceptional among both metaphorical and humorous expressions, it is still possible that creative metaphors and humour tend to 'bloom' under similar conditions. They presuppose a "ludic spirit" or a playful attitude (Brône et al. 2006: 222) which is ready or eager to deviate from current usage in order to "de-automatise" conventional conceptual combinations. Such conditions are favourable for both creative metaphors and humour. In this respect, metaphor and some forms of humour have common roots in conceptual creativity, if we understand "creativity" as novel combinations or expansion of concepts with an emerging structure that cannot be fully explained by its components (Ward, Smith and Vaid 1997: 1).

This observation raises the question: to what extent does humorous incongruity function as a "foregrounding" device for creative metaphors? In the practice of stylistic analysis, foregrounded elements are often identified by a rule of thumb: Anything that "sticks out" against the background of linguistic routine can be regarded as foregrounded (Leech [1969] 1991: 57); hence in foregrounding, the expression draws the attention of the reader toward the form of the utterance (Mukařovský 1964: 19), and leads to further effects such as surprise and slower processing (Peer 2007: 102). In applying this definition to the study of metaphor (and following the Czech structuralist Jan Mukařovský) we may understand "creative metaphors" to be all metaphors which draw the attention to their metaphoricity by virtue of deviating from automatised schemes. Mukařovský, as a structuralist, emphasised the role of linguistic deviation in foregrounding; however, on the background of the Theory of Conceptual Blending we could complement this deviational approach with a conceptual view: Metaphors may be foregrounded by an emphasised duality of the input spaces. Of course, the degree of conventionality seems to play an important role for emphasised duality, as de-automatisation seems to work differently with metaphorical puns (which exploit a conventional use of the same metaphorical expression) and creative metaphors (Kyratzis 2003). Creative Metaphors that express uncommon conceptual combinations tend to be foregrounded, because these combinations retain a tension between the input spaces by virtue of not yet being automatised, whereas metaphorical puns confront automatised conventional meanings of an expression. The question remains, under what circumstances can an emphasised duality be exploited for humorous incongruities. The following chapter will provide a more detailed description of this issue by analysing conventional and creative metaphor about humour and probing their humorous background.

5 Creative and conventional metaphors about humour

Creative metaphors should not only be regarded in terms of selection of metaphorical expressions. It is also necessary to take into account additional aspects such as the context of use, the particular reference of the metaphor, and the arrangement of the expressions. In addition, creativity depends to a large degree on the amount of deviation from conventional ways of talking (and thinking) about things. As a consequence, identifying creative metaphors also presupposes a reconstruction of a backdrop of conventional metaphors about humour against which an analyst's judgement on the degree of creativity may be established. Unfortunately, the research on metaphorical conceptualisations of humour is scarce. Metaphor analysts have mostly focused on negative emotions such as fear, anger or grief. As a result there is no comprehensive account of metaphors conceptualising humour, let alone conceptual metaphors about humour in German. At this early stage, the following overview can only give an outline of conventional ways of talking metaphorically about humour based on the analysis of a corpus of German novels. Several texts by Jean Paul, one of the most renowned masters of metaphor in German, are included in the corpus used for this study.[5] In addition, several novels from the literary period of German realism,[6] which were used for comparisons, have been added. All texts are available on the internet allowing citations to be verified with the help of common

---

[5] The corpus contains the following of Jean Paul's work, counting 1.4 Million words: *Flegeljahre* (FJ, 1804), *Des Feldpredigers Schmelzle Reise nach Flätz* (FSRF, 1809), *Hesperus oder 45 Hundposttage* (HH, 1795), *Katzenbergers Badereise* (KB, 1809), *Des Luftschiffers Gianozzo Seebuch* (LGS, 1801), *Das Leben des Quintus Fixlein* (QF, 1796), *Siebenkäs* (S, 1796/97), *Titan* (T, 1800), *Die unsichtbare Loge* (UL, 1793), *Vorschule der Ästhetik* (VA, 1804). All texts are novels with the exception of *Vorschule der Ästhetik*, which is a poetological treatise.

[6] The Realism corpus contains 2,3 Million words; it includes T. Fontane: *Effi Briest* (F-EB, 1895), *Grete Minde* (F-GM, 1880), *Irrungen und Wirrungen* (F-IW, 1888), *Vor dem Sturm* (F-V, 1878); G. Freytag: *Soll und Haben* (Fr-SH, 1 855); K. Gutzkow: *Ritter vom Geiste* (G-RG, 1850/51); G. Keller: *Das Fähnlein der sieben Aufrechten* (K-FA, 1878), *Der Grüne Heinrich*, 2nd edition (K-GH, 1879), *Kleider machen Leute* (K-KL, 1856), *Romeo und Julia auf dem Dorfe* (K-RJ, 1876), *Der Landvogt von Greifensee* (K-LV, 1878), *Martin Salander* (K-MS, 1886), *Das Sinngedicht* (K-SG, 1881); C.F. Meyer: *Das Amulett* (M-A, 1873), *Jürg Jenatsch* (M-JJ, 1876), *Der Schuss von der Kanzel* (M-SK, 1877), *Gustav Adolfs Page* (M-GAP, 1882), *Plautus im Nonnenkloster* (M-PN, 1882), *Die Hochzeit des Mönchs* (M-HM, 1884), *Angela Borgia* (M- AB, 1891); W. Raabe: *Die Chronik der Sperlingsgasse* (R-CS, 1856), *Der Hungerpastor* (R-H, 1864), *Hoexter und Corvey* (R-HC, 1875), *Pfisters Mühle* (R-PM, 1884), *Die Akten des Vogelsangs* (R-AV, 1896); A. Stifter: *Der Nachsommer* (S-N, 1854); T. Storm: *Immensee* (Sm-I, 1849), *Staatshof* (Sm-S, 1859), *Pole Poppenspäler* (Sm-PP, 1875), *Acquis submersus* (Sm-AS, 1877), *Der Schimmelreiter* (Sm-SR, 1888).

search engines. The corpus has been analysed according to several keywords related to humour, including 'laughter' and 'joke', and all concordances have been searched for metaphors following a formalised procedure of metaphor identification (Pragglejaz Group 2007).

6 Lachen – to laugh

A straight forward way to describe the challenges of an analysis of metaphors in relation to the vocabulary of humour may be provided by a preliminary discussion of different ways of using 'to laugh' in German (1024 concordances in the corpus).[7] First of all, many concordances had to be discarded from the analysis. For instance, in almost one half of all concordances the act of laughing was merely recorded as the fact that somebody laughed, stopped laughing or did not laugh at all – without further description of the way of laughing or clear indication of the actual cause of laughter. In 13% of all concordances 'to laugh' was used to introduce direct speech *(Susanne lachte: "Wie [...]")*. Moreover, 'to laugh' was used several times in paradoxical statements with other verbs similar to 'to cry' or 'to swear' which indicated complex and contradictory emotional states that have not been treated as descriptions of humour. Similarly, the diverse and interesting metaphorical uses of 'to laugh', e.g., when 'to laugh' is attributed to non-human actors such as the sky or trees, have been discarded from the analysis. As a result, from a metaphorical point of view, a majority of concordances were not relevant to the analysis of metaphorical conceptualisations of humour.

In the remaining concordances, most metaphorical expressions in the co-text of 'to laugh' turned out to be conventional. Depending on whether one is ready to consider prepositions as metaphorical (even if their metaphoricity is hardly noticed by native speakers), the biggest group of metaphorical use is *lachen über* ('to laugh about', 156 occurrences), which would suggest that the superiority theory (*über* = 'above, over') is entrenched in the German language. The same preposition *über* can also be found in many other humour related expressions such as 'making fun of something or somebody' *(sich lustig machen über, spotten über)*.

A second important group consists of evaluation of laughter via sensory perceptions such as *bitter lachen* ('laugh bitterly'), *hell lachen* ('laugh brightly'),

---

7 Separable verbs such as *aus-lachen* ('to laugh at somebody') or *auf-lachen* ('to burst out laughing') and other verbs with affixes such as *ver-lachen* or *belachen* ('laugh at somebody') were not included in this count.

hart lachen ('laugh callously'). These kinds of metaphors have recently attracted the interest of psychologists who try to differentiate different types of laughter (Huber 2006).

'Laughing' also provided examples which are similar to the famous ANGER IS A HOT LIQUID IN A CONTAINER conceptual metaphor, by locating laughter in the body:

(1) *Alles lachte ja in ihm.* (G-RG)
    'Everything in him laughed'

(2) *..., sondern ich lachte innerlich ganz frohmütig darüber [...]* (K-GH)
    'instead I laughed [*inwardly] quite happily about it'

However, this way of conceptualising laughter could also be seen in a broader framework of laughter as an object that is located in or on particular parts of the body. For instance, laughter is often located in parts of the face, since somebody may have a merry laugh on her lips (*mit einem fröhlichen Lachen auf den Lippen*, Fr-SH), the eyes may laugh (*Des Paters dunkle Augen lachten, [...]*, M-AB) or the 'heart laughs' (*daß einem deutschen Mann das Herz im Leibe lachen mußte.* M-GAP). Many instances of such localisations of laughter are based on metonymical motivation where a prominent part of the body (e.g., lips) may stand for the laughing person.

The ways of locating laughter figuratively become even more complex, when the analysis is extended to local adverbs such as *hinein* ('into') which can be treated as prefixes in German:

(3) *Und solch Kellner, der immer so still vor sich hinlacht oder wenigstens in sich hinein[lacht], [...]* (F-IW)
    'And such a waiter who quietly laughs to himself or at least laughs into himself, [...]'

In German, it is not uncommon to say that one can laugh in some direction. Interestingly, this particular kind of laughter which is directed inwards (but alos laughter that is located in body parts), tends to be connotated positively. In contrast, conceptualisations of laughter and humour as moving behind or toward somebody else, has often aggressive or denigrating connotations, as, for instance, 'to laugh *after someone' (*Die Kinder lachten hinter der Schwester her*, G-RG) or the expression 'to laugh in someone's face' (*Ich mußte ihm in's Gesicht lachen*, G-RG).

7 Conceptualisations of humour and humorous events

The previous discussion of metaphors accompanying the verb 'to laugh' gives an impression of both a range of conceptual metaphors and the challenges that are related to such an analysis, e.g., the vague meaning of humour-related words or the question of dead metaphors. In a second step, the scope of analysis was broadened to include not only the noun *Lachen* ('Laughter'), or separable verbs *(anlachen, auflachen, verlachen)*, but also by taking into account additional humour related vocabulary such as *Humor, Witz* ('joke/wit'), *Lächerlichkeit* ('Ridicule') and their various derivates (Santana López 2006: 54).

The broadened focus provided additional theoretical challenges as it provided examples where both a metaphorical and a metonymical interpretation were possible at the same time. Expressions such as 'timid banter' or 'grim joke' *(schüchternen Scherz,* K-GH; *grimmigen Witz,* R-PM) may be regarded as metaphorical personifications which present humour in analogy to a person, but one could also argue that these examples metonymically reflect properties of the person producing the joke. The figurativeness of both cases is based on the observation that a joke itself does not typically carry human features such as timidity; however, the explanation of how these expressions are figurative differs very much depending on a metonymical or a metaphorical perspective. Considering observations that metaphor and metonymy are not necessarily mutually exclusive (Deignan 2005: 70) it seems justifiable to consider these cases as metaphorical mappings.

Many findings in the preliminary analysis of 'to laugh' could be differentiated by a broader focus. First of all, expanding the focus of humour-related vocabulary yielded more conventional metaphors that conceptualised laughter as a force or an object that can move. For instance, laughter as the most directly perceivable symptom of humour is often conceptualised in terms of an irresistible force of *unbändiges Lachen* ('irrepressible laughter'). Sometimes it is even described as a kind of explosion, in such a way that somebody may 'burst out into loud laughter' *(Jeannette brach über diese Worte in lautes Lachen aus,* G-RG*)* or 'burst forth with long repressed laughter' *(Ernst und platzte mit längstverhaltenem Lachen so hervor,* G-RG*)*.

The analysis also provided more examples of the metaphorical use of sensory features. Several of these examples had already been found in the preliminary analysis of 'to laugh': 'Bitter' and 'hard' tend to characterise a mixture of negative feelings and humour. 'Dry', as in *ein trockener Scherz* (Fr-SH), an unpretentious form of presenting humour. Mellow colours, 'sweet', 'bright or lightweight tend to characterise positive humour (*ich lachte hell und fröhlich [...]*, Sm-AS; *leichtem Scherz*, Fr-SH) in contrast to intensive colour impressions, e.g., 'glaring farces' (*grelle Possen*, M-AB). There were also some examples of creative metaphors from Jean Paul's oeuvre that could be attributed to the conventional mapping of sensory perception onto humour, and the following citation may give a first glimpse of particularities of creative use of metaphors (metaphorical expressions are underlined).

(4) *Indes ist wahr, daß der Humor <u>im Widerschein</u> der Erzählung <u>weichere Farben annimmt</u> als in der <u>grellen</u> Wirklichkeit.* (S)
'However, it is true that humour receives mellower colours in the reverberation of narration than in the glaring reality'.

An interpretation of this metaphor requires the reconstruction of underlying conceptual structure, as only 'humour', the topic, is stated explicitly; hence, we need a vehicle reconstruction to know more about the metaphorical object that is set in analogy to humour. In its literal sense *Widerschein* ('reverberation') is used to describe the reflection of a light source – e.g., the sun – onto a body – e.g., the moon (*Der Mond gab jetzo durch den Widerschein der Sonne [...] der Freude hellere Farben*, HH). The German adjectives *weich* ('mellow, soft') and *grell* ('glaring') are themselves already synaesthetical expressions which evaluate visual impressions in terms of tactile or acoustic experiences. As a consequence, they have – in contrast to *heiter* ('bright, hilarious') – in their metaphorical usage no particular association to humour. Nevertheless, in the context of this analogy they add to the overall analogy of humour as an object that is perceived differently in the moon-like light of narration than in the (glaring daylight) of reality. Several elements of this analogy are implicit and have to be recovered by vehicle reconstruction. This need for vehicle reconstruction suggests that reading this metaphorical utterance requires additional attention and may, therefore, have a particular poetic effect; however, the lack of an explicit object to complete the analogy may also attenuate the inherent contrast of this creative metaphor and, therefore, reduce the humorous incongruity.

The conventional mapping of weather or atmospheric phenomena onto feelings is closely related to the sensory metaphors mentioned above. This is apparent when humour is described in terms of good weather such as *heiteres Lachen* (Fr-SH, 'bright laughter') or *sonnenhelle Lustigkeit* (K-RJ, 'sun-bright merriness'). In terms of conventionality this is a very important group if we consider the very frequent noun *Heiterkeit* (exhilaration). However, the group also included examples where it became increasingly difficult to discern a difference between humour and vague positive emotions of wellbeing or happiness. Of course, humour comes in different degrees and therefore has vague borders. Similarly vague borders of humorous effects have also been observed in the analysis of humour (Attardo 2001: 103f.), and the opposition of momentarily striking punch-lines and diffuse humour is also put forward in another quotation from Jean Paul's *Vorschule der Ästhetik*:

(5) *Den Witz und den komischen Einfall <u>erschöpft</u> und <u>entladet</u>, wie <u>den zickzackigen Blitz</u>, der erste <u>Schlag</u>; aber der Humor ist ein <u>still spielendes unschuldiges Wetterleuchten</u>, nicht über unserm <u>Haupte</u>, sondern <u>am fernen Horizonte, das schöne Tage verkündigt</u>.* (VA)
'Wit and comical idea are exhausted and discharged at the first hit like the zigzag lightning; humour, however, is a quietly playing sheet lightning which is not above our head, but on a distant horizon which announces beautiful days.'

In each case, the syntactical arrangement of the analogies makes both elements of the dual structure explicit. In the first simile, wit and ideas are set in an explicit analogy to the lightning. In the second part of the quotation, the effect of humour is metaphorically identified with pleasant sheet lightning. This citation also seems to be a good example of what Lakoff and Turner called "composing", the formation of composite metaphors by "putting complex metaphorical concepts together" (Lakoff and Turner 1989: 70f.), as weather condition metaphors ('sheet lightning' and 'beautiful days') are used in the same context of a lightning metaphor. 'Lightning', which is used at several occasions in Jean Paul's work, should be seen in a broader framework of other metaphors on light and heat such as 'fireworks' *(Raketen des Witzes*, UL; *buntesten Feuerwerke des Witzes*, HH*)* or 'sparks' *(Witz-Funke*, VA*)*. In fact, Jean Paul also liked to draw complex analogies to physical experiments with light or electricity which were quite in fashion at that time:

(6) *[...] und so wie der Blitzfunke ohne Zünden durch Schießpulver, aber am Eisenleiter, fährt, so läuft am komischen Leiter jene Flamme nur als Witz ohne Schaden durch die brennbare Sinnlichkeit hindurch.* (VA*)*
'As the spark of lightning can move without detonation through gunpowder on an iron conductor, so this flame runs only as joke on a comical conductor through the inflammable sensuality.'

As a consequence, all metaphors of flashing heat or light have been considered as another kind of mapping, different from weather phenomena.

The concordances also showed that some mappings yielded fewer examples than expected. For instance, animal metaphors in humour were not often found. Formulations such as *grelles, thierisches Auflachen* (G-RG, 'a gaudy, beastly outburst of laughter') or *zum wiehernden Lachen bringen* (G-RG, 'to incite neighing laughter') suggest that conventional mappings exist, but seem to be appropriate only in particular situations. Metaphors which illustrate the quality of laughter by drawing on analogies of childishness (*kindlicher Heiterkeit*, F-EB) or sickness (e.g., *totlachen, krank lachen* 'laugh oneself to death/sickness') were more frequent, but with the exception of *Fleckfieber des Witzes* ('typhus of wit', UL) they were rarely creative. There were also only few metaphors that were based on analogies between weaponry and humour (e.g., *satirische Pfeile*, 'satirical arrows', K-SG; *satirische Dornen*, 'satirical thorns', HH). The rather small number seems to be due to the fact that, in line with a more general mapping of potential harmfulness of humour, these uses are associated with a particular type of humour such as 'injuring satire' *(verwundende Satire,* K-LV*)* or 'cutting derision' *(schneidendem Spott*, G-RG). Even *Stich* ('sting'), or its derivates *sticheln, Stichelei* ('teasing'), were rather rare; *Stachel* ('barb') – although it belonged to the traditional terms of satirical humour and punch-lines (Müller 2003) – was mostly used not in the context of humour, but that of emotional distress.[8]

So far, the analysis could establish a range of conceptual metaphors that are frequently used to conceptualise humour and humorous events. First of all, the conventional preposition *über* indicates that the superiority theory is conceptually important. At the same time, the analysis also yields many metaphors that conceptualise humour and laughter as a force that is located in the body, may move in the body or may burst forth. These conventional metaphors are to some degree compatible with "comic-relief metaphors" or Sigmund Freud's explanation of humour as a release of retained psychic energy (Freud 1960: 148). Whereas some prominent mappings were less frequent than expected (e.g., animal-like laughter, harmful humour) there was a surprising range of sensory metaphors of humour. Metaphors which conceptualised humour in terms of light, energy or heat seemed to be to some extent compatible with sensory metaphors. However, these metaphors also included several elaborate examples which made it difficult to assign them to a particular conventional mapping.

Many sensory metaphors presupposed a concretisation of humour as an object which can be perceived, touched or tasted. Thus, these metaphors seemed

---

[8] In fact, uses in the sense of satirical humour were basically confined to the works of Jean Paul: [...] *Xenophon, die attische honigvolle und stachellose Biene!* (VA), *Schon die Sprache setzt Hohn, Spott, Stachelschrift, Hohnlachen scharf dem Scherzen, Lachen, Lustigmachen entgegen.* (VA). One exception was found in an early novel of realism: *Führe ihn sanft und liebevoll, wenn es muß mit erlaubtem stachellosem Scherze, auf die Erkenntniß Dessen, was ihm mangelt!* (G-RG)

to presuppose a reification of humour. Since this reification was only apparent in some cases, the question arises of whether one should assume a very broad mapping that conceptualises humour as an object. The following example, where humour is recommended as a 'handle' on difficult issues, may illustrate this kind of metaphors.

(7)   *An einer Menge <u>schwerer Materien</u>, <u>wovon euch alle Handhaben abbrechen</u>, <u>hält</u> bloß die des Scherzes <u>fest</u>, und ihr könnt sie damit regieren;* ... (UL)
'A lot of difficult/heavy matters, from which all handles break off, only the [handles of] jests stay on and you can control them by them;'

Materien is ambiguous as it may refer to 'matter' as well as to 'topics of conversations', thus, this example is a metaphorical pun which sets up an analogy between difficult topics of conversation which may be mastered by humour and bulky items which can only be handled by good handholds.

At first sight, reification seems to provide a very interesting and, in terms of creativity, very copious mapping. However, reification of abstract things is quite common in metaphorical use, and such a broad mapping would also include very heterogeneous metaphors, e.g., metaphors where humour and laughter are conceptualised as objects we can hide behind, e.g., 'hide behind banter' (*die eigne Rührung nur hinter Scherz verbergend*, G-RG). Considering the difference of such metaphors to other reification metaphors, it seems appropriate to take such differences into account by assuming, if possible, more particular mappings, e.g., humour as a potential device to hide behind. Here a mildly funny example of the elaboration of such a metaphor from Jean Paul's *Titan*:

(8)   *Sie verbarg öfters, wie andere hinter den schwarzen Trauerfächern der Trauer und Empfindung, so hinter dem heitern Putzfächer des Lachens, der den Zuschauern die bemalte Seite zukehrte, ihren Kopf mit seinen Entwürfen; [...] (Titan).*
'Frequently, she hid her mind with its ideas, as others hide behind black fans of grief and sentiment, behind the bright finery fan of laughter, which showed the spectators the painted side'

Interestingly enough, in this example it is not clear whether 'black fans of grief and sentiment' is literal or not. It is, however, apparent that the 'finery fan of laughter' is a metaphorically elaborated way to talk about the potential of humour as a means to hide one's emotions and/or intentions, in the same way a fan might hide facial expressions.

8 Conclusion

Searching for metaphors in the co-text of humour related expression demonstrates that evaluation of humour and reasoning about its functions is strongly influenced by metaphors. At the same time, it has demonstrated that looking for humour related vocabulary does not yield a lot of examples of humour. In fact, most metaphors – including creative metaphors – about humour were not funny. Nevertheless, there were also some witty metaphors about humour which could be analysed in depth and in contrast to other non-humorous elaborated metaphors.

It seems that vehicle reconstruction – which was, for instance, necessary in example 4 – tended to be less funny. This would lead to the hypothesis that metaphors which leave the analogy partly implicit by only hinting at the metaphorical vehicle need further explanation and are less disposed to trigger humour.

The case is different with metaphorical punning where vehicle and topic are expressed simultaneously. These examples build up a clear incongruity between literal and figurative sense and show, therefore, a stronger disposition to trigger humour. Moreover, funny creative metaphors, such as Jean Paul's wit as priest in disguise elaborated the vehicle in terms of a rich scenario. This elaboration seems to be important. For instance, one can talk quite seriously about an artist as performer of religious functions, and in this context it is also possible to use "priest" in a rather serious way, e.g., *Die Musen weihten dich zum Priester* (Hölderlin). However, in Jean Paul's witticism 'priest' refers not to another person, but to something abstract (wit) which is disguised as a priest, and this metaphor is elaborated as a caricature of prototypical activities of a priest. This could point towards a particular technique of humorous creative metaphors which consists of pushing analogies even further, thereby accentuating the inherent incongruity of cross-domain analogies. For instance, Friedrich Theodor Vischer (1807–1888) elaborated Jean Paul's metaphor even further by adding that the priest marries couples with preference against the consent of their relatives.[9] We could call this technique "exploration of analogies". Exploring a metaphor means to treat a target domain entirely according to the logic of the source domain, in such a way that one commits deliberately categorical mistakes to the verge of absurdity. "Exploring analogies" might produce new incongruent metaphors: "How do words divorce? How many patchwork families have been left in Jean Paul's work?" etc. This is very different from explaining

---

9 (Vischer, 1922/1846: 457): *Geistreich nennt J. Paul (ebenda) den Witz den verkleideten Priester, der jedes Paar kopuliert. Er ist aber der Schmied zu Gretna-Green, der lauter Paare traut, deren Trauung die Verwandten (der methodisch wahre Zusammenhang) nicht dulden wollen.*

analogies, which would probably increase understanding without making us laugh. This proves again that the study of humour and metaphor is a deadly serious subject.

References

Aristotle. 1970. *The Rhetoric of Aristotle*. With a Commentary by Edward Meredith Cope. Edited by J. E. Sandys. Hildesheim, New York: Georg Olms.
Attardo, Salvatore. 2001. *Humorous Texts. A Semantic and Pragmatic Analysis*. Berlin, New York: Mouton de Gruyter.
Attardo, Salvatore, and Victor Raskin. 1991. Script theory revis(it)ed: Joke similarity and joke representation model. *Humor: International Journal of Humor Research* 4(3): 293–347.
Beardsley, Monroe C. 1962. The metaphorical twist. *Philosophy and Phenomenological Research. A Quarterly Journal* 22(3): 293–307.
Beattie, James. 1809. An essay on laughter and ludicrous composition. In: B. Fabian (ed.) *Essays* Vol. 1: 127–301. Hildesheim: Olms.
Breitenbürger, Gerd. 1975. *Metaphora. Die Rezeption des aristotelischen Begriffs in den Poetiken des Cinquecento*. Kronberg/Ts.: Scriptor.
Brône, Geert, Kurt Feyaerts, and Tony Veale. 2006. Introduction: Cognitive linguistic approaches to humor. *Humor: International Journal of Humor Research* 19(3): 203–228.
Bühler, Karl. 1999. Reprint. *Sprachtheorie. Die Darstellungsfunktion der Sprache. Mit einem Geleitwort von Friedrich Kainz*. Stuttgart: Lucius and Lucius. Original edition, 1934.
Coulson, Seana. 2001. *Semantic Leaps: Frame-Shifting and Conceptual Blending in Meaning Construction*. Cambridge: Cambridge Univ. Press.
Coulson, Seana, and Todd Oakley. 2000. Blending basics. *Cognitive Linguistics* 11(3/4): 175–196.
Coulson, Seana, Thomas P. Urbach, and Marta Kutas. 2006. Looking back: Joke comprehension and the space structuring model. *Humor: International Journal of Humor Research* 19(3): 229–250.
Deignan, Alice. 2005. *Metaphor and Corpus Linguistics*. Amsterdam: Benjamins.
Dynel, Marta. 2009. Creative metaphor is a birthday cake: Metaphor as the source of humour. In: metaphorik.de 17, 27–48.
Fónagy, Ivan. 1982. He is only joking: Joke, metaphor and language development. In: Ferenc Kiefer (ed.) *Hungarian Linguistics*, 31–108. Amsterdam: Benjamins.
Freud, Sigmund. 1960. Jokes and their relation to the unconscious (1905). In: James Strachey, Anna Freud, Alix Strachey and Alan Tyson (eds.), *The Standard Edition of the Complete Psychological Works of Sigmund Freud*. Vol. 8. London: Hogarth Press.
Giora, Rachel. 2003. *On Our Mind. Salience, Context and Figurative Language*. Oxford: University Press.
Goatly, Andrew. 1997. *The Language of Metaphors*. London: Routledge.
Goatly, Andrew. 2012. *Meaning and Humour*. Cambridge: Cambridge Univ. Press.
Hecken, Thomas. 2005. *Witz als Metapher. Der Witz-Begriff in der Poetik und Literaturkritik des 18. Jahrhunderts*. Tübingen: Francke.
Hofstadter, Douglas R., and Liane Gabora. 1989. Synopsis of the workshop on humor and cognition. *Humor: International Journal of Humor Research* 2(4): 417–440.
Huber, Tanja. 2006. Differenzierung verschiedener Arten des Lachens: ein historischer Überblick. Presentation at the Congress „Humor gewinnt", Bad Zurzach (Switzerland), 22–24

September 2006. Retrieved 23.5.2008, from www.psychologie.uzh.ch/perspsy/texte/zurzach/huberzurzach_06.pdf.
Kittay, Eva Feder. 1987. *Metaphor. Its Cognitive Force and Linguistic Structure*. Oxford: Clarendon.
Koestler, Arthur. 1964. *The Act of Creation*. London: Hutchinson.
Kövecses, Zoltán. 2015. *Where Metaphors Come from. Reconsidering Context in Metaphor*. Oxford: Oxford Univ. Press.
Kyratzis, Sakis. 2003. *Laughing Metaphorically. Metaphor and Humor in Discourse*. Paper presented at the Cognitive Linguistics, Functionalism, Discourse Studies: Common Ground and New Directions. Panel: Cognitive Linguistic Approaches to Humour (July 20–25, 2003), La Rioja. Retrieved 30.6.2006 from http://wwwling.arts.kuleuven.ac.be/iclc/Papers/Kyratzis.pdf.
Lakoff, George, and Mark Turner. 1989. *More than Cool Reason. A Field Guide to Poetic Metaphor*. Chicago: Univ. of Chicago Press.
Leech, Geoffrey N. 1991. Reprint. *A Linguistic Guide to English Poetry*. London: Longman. Original edition, 1969.
Mio, Jeffrey Scott, and Arthur C. Graesser. 1991. Humor, Language and Metaphor. *Metaphor and Symbolic Activity* 6(2): 87–102.
Mooij, Jan Johan Albin. 1976. *A Study of Metaphor. On the Nature of Metaphorical Expressions, with Special Reference to Their Reference*. Amsterdam: North-Holland Publishing Comp.
Mukařovský, Jan. 1964. Standard language and poetic language. In: Paul L. Garvin (ed.) *A Prague School Reader on Esthetics, Literary Structure and Style*, 17–30. Washington: Georgetown Univ. Press.
Müller, Ralph. 2003. The pointe in german research. *Humor: International Journal of Humor Research* 16(2): 225–242.
Müller, Ralph. 2007. The interplay of metaphor and humor in Oscar Wilde's "Lord Arthur Savile's crime". In: Diana Popa and Salvatore Attardo (eds.), *New Approaches to the Linguistics of Humour*, 44–54. Galati: Editura Academia.
Oring, Elliott. 2006. *Engaging Humour*. Urbana/Chicago: University of Illinois Press
Peer, Willie van. 2007. Introduction to foregrounding: A state of the art. *Language and Literature* 16(2): 99–104.
Pragglejaz Group. 2007. MIP: A method for identifying metaphorically used words in discourse. *Metaphor and Symbol*, 22(1): 1–39.
Raskin, Victor. 1985. *Semantic Mechanisms of Humor*. Dordrecht: D. Reidel.
Reinhart, Tanya. 1976. On understanding poetic metaphor. *Poetics* 5: 383–402.
Richards, Ivor Armstrong. 1976. *The Philosophy of Rhetoric*. London, Oxford, New York: Oxford Univ. Press. Original edition, 1936.
Ritchie, David. 2005. Frame-shifting in humor and irony. *Metaphor and Symbol*, 20(4): 275–294.
Santana López, Belén. 2006. *Wie wird das Komische übersetzt. Das Komische als Kulturspezifikum bei der Übersetzung spanischer Gegenwartsliteratur*. Berlin: Frank and Timme.
Veale, Tony. 2013. Humorous similes. *Humor: International Journal of Humor Research* 26(1): 3–22.
Veale, Tony, Kurt Feyaerts, and Geert Brône. 2006. The cognitive mechanisms of adversial humor. *Humor:. International Journal of Humor Research* 19(3): 305–339.
Vischer, Friedrich Theodor. 1922. *Aestehtik oder Wissenschaft des Schönen*. Erster Teil: Die Metaphysik des Schönen (2nd ed.). München: Meyer and Jessen. Original edition, 1846.
Ward, Thomas B., Steven M. Smith, and Jyotsna Vaid (eds.). 1997. *Creative Thought. An Investigation of Conceptual Structures and Processes*. Washington: American Psychological Association.

Rachel Giora, Ofer Fein, Nurit Kotler and Noa Shuval
7 Know hope: Metaphor, optimal innovation and pleasure

1 Introduction: Processing models

What are the processes involved in language comprehension? Do literal and nonliteral instances of language use require different interpretation mechanisms or do they follow the same processing routes? To illustrate the question, consider the following example:

(1) On Wednesday, February 20th, 2002, Yinnon Hiller, aged 20 and Amir Malenky, aged 18, will appear before the Israeli High Court of Justice... Both ask to be released from military service on the grounds of their pacifist beliefs... Both conscientious objectors ask to perform alternative civilian service instead of military service, but the Israeli army so far refused to allow them this option.

New Profile – Movement for the Civil-ization of Israeli Society supports Yinnon Hiller and Amir Malenky in their struggle. We believe that the State of Israel should recognize that an individual can participate in society in ways other than bearing arms. http://www.gush-shalom.org/archives/forum_eng.html (19.2.02)

How do we make sense of these utterances? What makes us interpret the last word (*arms*) or collocation (*bearing arms*) *nonliterally* (as 'weapons') rather than literally (as 'hands')? Is it contextual information biased toward the military sense of *arms* that makes us select this appropriate sense? Is it the salience or dominance of the military sense of the word that makes that meaning available swiftly? What about the meaning of *struggle*, then? Given the contextual bias toward the military interpretation, would its literal ('battle') meaning be primed during its processing on account of its contextual relatedness?

Whether it is context or the lexicon that affects our understanding primarily has been an enduring debate in linguistics and psycholinguistics for over three decades or so (Gibbs 1994; Glucksberg 2001; Giora 1997, 2002, 2003). Indeed, various models of figurative language have come up with different proposals as to how we make sense of literal and nonliteral utterances.

The Standard Pragmatic Model (Grice 1975; Searle 1979) assumes the temporal priority of the literal interpretation of utterances. In this view, literal meanings are obligatory – they are automatic and immune to contextual information. Nonliteral meanings, on the other hand, are derivative and optional. They are induced only when a literal interpretation fails to resonate with contextual information. In this view, then, it is the literal meaning ('hand') of *arms* that should be accessed first and adjusted to contextual information only as an aftermath; similarly, it is the literal ('battle') meaning of *struggle* that should be induced first and revisited later. The Standard Pragmatic Model thus assumes different processing routes for literal and nonliteral language uses, regardless of strength and bias of context. While both literal and nonliteral utterances are being processed literally initially, only nonliteral language is expected to involve an additional phase of adjustment to contextual information. According to the Standard Pragmatic Model, then, comprehending the *figurative utterances* in (1) should incur some integration difficulty compared to their interpretation in a literally biasing context.

Unlike the Standard Pragmatic Model, the Direct Access View (or its more recent version entitled the Constraint Satisfaction Model) does not assume that lexical processes are immune to contextual information. Rather, context interacts with lexical processes very early on and if it is sufficiently constraining, it should result in selecting the contextually appropriate interpretation exclusively or at least initially. Such a view disputes the temporal priority of literal meanings (Glucksberg 1998, 1995, 2001; Glucksberg, Gildea and Bookin 1982; Keysar 1989, 1994). Instead, in realistic, social contexts, comprehenders should be able to understand the figurative interpretations of metaphors, irony/sarcasm, idioms, proverbs and indirect speech acts directly without having to first analyze and reject their literal interpretations (Ferretti, Schwint and Katz 2007; Gibbs, 1994, 2001; 2002; Katz and Ferretti 2001, 2003). The Direct Access View thus assumes no processing differences for literal and nonliteral language, provided prior context is supportive and specific enough. Rather, both types of language should be comprehended directly, without involving an inappropriate interpretation first. According to this view, then, in the strongly biasing context of (1), the utterance including *struggle* and *arms* should be interpreted metaphorically; no integration difficulties are anticipated compared to their interpretation in a literally biasing context (Ortony et al. 1978).

Following Fodor's modular assumptions (1983), the Graded Salience Hypothesis (Giora 1997, 1999, 2003; Giora and Fein, 1999a, b; Giora, Fein and Schwartz 1998; Peleg, Giora and Fein 2001, 2004; Peleg and Eviatar 2008) assumes that comprehension involves two distinct mechanisms that run in parallel, without interacting initially. One is bottom-up, sensitive only to domain specific (here) linguistic stimuli; another is top-down involving inferential and integrative processes, susceptible to both linguistic and nonlinguistic information. Diverging from the classical modular view (Swinney 1979), however, the Graded Salience Hypothesis further assumes that bottom-up processes are ordered: Salient responses/meanings are accessed faster than less-salient ones (Duffy, Morris and Rayner 1988; Rayner et al. 1994).

To be salient, a meaning has to be coded in the mental lexicon and be foremost on our mind due to e.g., conventionality, frequency, familiarity, or prototypicality. Coded meanings, low on these parameters, are less-salient and slower to reach sufficient levels of activation than salient meanings. According to this view, then, coded meanings would be accessed automatically upon encounter, regardless of contextual information or authorial intent. Meanings not coded in the mental lexicon, although nonsalient, may be made available via the contextual, predictive mechanism.

Indeed, when specific enough, contextual information may affect comprehension immediately. A highly predictive context would yield meanings on its own accord very early on. However, it would not interact with lexical access and would therefore not block coded but inappropriate responses upon encounter of the lexical stimulus (Giora 2003; Peleg et al. 2001; Peleg and Eviatar 2008).

Given that both the literal and nonliteral meanings of *arms* and *struggle* are salient, the Graded Salience Hypothesis predicts that the metaphorical utterances in (1) should incur no integration difficulties compared to their interpretation in a literally biasing context. Since both meanings should be accessed automatically in both types of context, the contextually appropriate meaning is made available swiftly and effects seamless integration processes.[1]

In sum, whereas the Standard Pragmatic Model assumes that nonliteral language should cohere less smoothly with prior context than literal language, the Graded Salience Hypothesis and Direct Access View have different predictions. Both theories assume equivalent processes for figurative and nonfigurative language, though apparently for different reasons. The Direct Access View attributes to a constraining context the role of neutralizing the differences found between literal and nonliteral language embedded in poorly informative contexts so that when context is sufficiently strong and supportive, literal and nonliteral interpretations cohere as smoothly (Ortony et al. 1978; but see Janus and Bever 1985; Peleg et al. 2004 and Giora et al. 2007 for a critique). Particularly, nonliteral language would be tapped directly without having to involve an analysis of the literal interpretation first (Gibbs 2002). The Graded Salience Hypothesis discards the literal-nonliteral distinction altogether and replaces it with the salient-nonsalient continuum (Giora 1997, 2002, 2003). Diverging from the Direct

---

[1] In Giora (2003) and Giora and Fein (1999a) we further argue that the contextually inappropriate literal meanings should not be suppressed.

access View, it thus anticipates processing difficulties for language uses whose less or nonsalient meanings or interpretations are invited. Given that salient meanings get accessed automatically upon encounter of the relevant stimulus, when contextually incompatible, they would result in extra adjustment processes resulting in less-salient or innovative meanings and interpretations. When such interpretations are invited, processing would be more effort consuming, at least, locally, compared to when salient meanings are invited, regardless of literality or figurativeness.

Given the Graded Salience Hypothesis, then, the idiom *He is singing a different tune* in (2c, taken from Gibbs, 1980), or the fixed expression *black on white* in (3c), or the idiom *you don't know your right from left* in (4c) should cohere more smoothly with prior context (e.g., take shorter to read) following (2a, 3a, 4a) than following (2b, 3b, 4b). Whereas the contexts in (2a, 3a, 4a) invite the salient (figurative) meaning of the idioms and the salient (literal) meaning of the fixed expression, the contexts in (2b, 3b, 4b) invite their low-salience (literal and figurative) interpretations. According to the Graded Salience Hypothesis, reading (2c, 3c, 4c) following (2b, 3b, 4b), then, should involve accessing (and reinterpreting) the salient meaning of the expressions in spite of their contextual incompatibility. Such predictions, however, are not invited by either of the alternative views. Both theories predict equal reading times for (2c, 3c, 4c) in all types of context (either 2a, 3a, 4a or 2b, 3b, 4b). According to the Standard Pragmatic Model, both interpretations of (4c) involve a figurative comprehension phase; hence no processing differences are anticipated. Since, however, there are literality differences involved in idioms, processing difficulties would be predicted only for the figurative reinterpretation. According to the Direct Access View, both interpretations of (2c, 3c, 4c) are invited by similarly strong and supportive contexts; hence no processing differences are anticipated. Findings, however, support the Graded Salience Hypothesis. They show that low-salience interpretations took longer to read than salient alternatives, regardless of figurativeness (Brisard et al. 2001; Frisson and Pickering 2007; Gibbs 1980; Giora and Fein 1999a, b; Giora et al. (2009); Giora et al. 2007; but see Ortony et al. 1978):

(2) a. On TV there was a program discussing Carter's first year in office. One reporter talked about the military budget. "In the campaign Carter promised to cut that budget." "But now that he is the president,"

b. Nick and Sue were listening to Jackson Browne on the radio. "All Jackson Browne songs sound alike." Sue Said. "Now isn't that the same song we heard him do on TV recently."
"No." Nick replied;

c. "He is singing a different tune."

(3) a. I want your promise documented
    b. This cheese cake with chocolate coating is exactly what you wanted:
    c. *black on white*

(4) a. *The Comprehensive Lexicon* will teach you whatever you are interested in
    b. Buy *The Comprehensive Guide for the Political Factions in Israel*
    c. so that you won't feel *you don't know your right from left.*

Why would speakers make use of utterances that might endanger coherence (even if only momentarily) and involve complex processes when less costly utterances are at hand? The explanation we intend to put forward and test here concerns speakers' pursuit of aesthetic effects. Speakers resort to innovativeness because they wish to disturb without repelling, to attract rather than detract listeners' attention. Apparently, the text in (1) does not resort to any aesthetic device in spite of its occasional figurative language. We claim here that it takes innovativeness rather than figurativeness to affect pleasure.

2 Optimal innovation and affect

Would any innovation be engaging? What kind of innovation will induce highly pleasurable effects? Earlier research (Giora 2003; Giora et al. 2004) demonstrates that it is *optimal innovation* that has the largest affective ratings (Hekkert et al. 2003; for a somewhat different view, see Brône and Coulson 2010).

To be optimally innovative, a stimulus should invoke

(5) a. a novel – less or nonsalient – response to a familiar stimulus, alongside
    b. a salient response from which, however, it differs (both quantitatively and qualitatively), so that both make sense (e.g., their similarity and difference can be assessable).

For example, in the Tel Aviv streetart (Know Hope 2006) in (6), the recognition of the salient ("No hope") in the novel (*KNOW HOPE*) makes the (literal) novel highly meaningful, despite its contextual incompatibility – invoking hopefulness in the midst of total destruction. It is this relation between the salient and the novel – de-automatizing the familiar pessimism by highlighting the optimism inherent in it – that is pleasing:

(6)

Similarly, labeling as "the ultimate form of greenwashing" (Blumenthal 2010) the practice, which included planting pine trees on the sites of the hundreds of Palestinian villages the Zionist militias evacuated and destroyed in 1948, must evoke the more salient "whitewashing" for the novel coin to make sense.

Along the same lines, in the contexts of (2b, 3b, 4b), the familiar expressions (2c, 3c, 4c) have an optimally innovative interpretation; in the context of (2a, 3a, 4a), they do not. The contexts of (2b, 3b, 4b) evoke a low-salience sense of the familiar expressions without blocking a salient response (Giora et al. 2004). In contrast, the contexts in (2a, 3a, 4a) are compatible with only the salient sense; the low-salience sense, it seems, does not reach sufficient levels of activation before integration gets underway. (If, however, it does, it would also make up an optimal innovation).

Optimal innovations are most pleasing primarily because of the (surprising) recognition of the salient in the novel (and also the novel in the familiar, Freud 1905). The familiar on its own would thus be less pleasing, because it has little or no novelty about it, but it will be quite pleasing on account of its familiarity; the novel on its own, however, would rank lowest on the aesthetics scale, because it involves little or no familiarity (for somewhat similar and yet different views, see Berlyne 1960, 1971; Miall and Kuiken 1994; Mukařovský 1964, 1978; Schopenhauer 1969; Shklovsky 1917, 1965; Townsend 1997).

Indeed, in Giora et al. (2004), we have shown that optimally innovative stimuli occupied mid position on the familiarity scale but scored most highly on the liking scale. Familiar stimuli came second. Least pleasurable were unfamiliar stimuli. Furthermore, optimally innovative stimuli took longer to read than their associated salient meanings, which they also primed; equivalent novel stimuli did not prime these meanings (Giora et al. 2004. Such findings demonstrate that, as assumed, stimuli rated as somewhat familiar and most pleasing indeed involved processing the salient meaning, which required reinterpretation.

In this chapter, we aim to show that (a) it is not figurativeness that hampers coherence, as would be deduced from the Standard Pragmatic Model. Instead, it is optimal innovativeness that obstructs smooth integration with prior context; (b) it is not figurativeness that induces pleasure, as would be expected from traditional views of 'poetic' language (see Steen, 1994 for a review), but rather optimal innovativeness. Both these predictions do not follow from the Direct Access View, which predicts that a constraining context may bypass contextually inappropriate interpretations (such as the literal interpretation of metaphors) and blur possible differences both in coherence and pleasure appreciation.

To test our hypotheses, we used high and low familiar metaphors and their literal interpretations. The set of items used in our experiments are those used in Giora and Fein (1999a). Although the items were measured only for degree of familiarity of their metaphoric interpretation (see also Experiment 1 below), reading times reassured us of the relative familiarity of their literal interpretations. Thus while equal reading times were found for the familiar metaphors and their literal interpretations, faster reading times were found for the literal interpretation of the novel metaphors compared to their metaphorical interpretation (Giora and Fein 1999a).

In this study, we intend to show that familiar items, whether metaphorical or literal (7a, 8b and 7b below) would be viewed as more coherent with prior context than less familiar items (8a) which would affect lower coherence ratings (2.1. Experiment 1). In addition, however, low coherence but innovative items would be rated as more engaging than equivalent, familiar, high coherence items, regardless of figurativeness (2.2. Experiment 2).

2.1 Experiment 1

The aim of Experiment 1 is to show that coherence is related to degree of salience: familiar targets whose salient meaning or salience-based interpretation (interpretation depending on the salient meanings of the utterance components) is related to prior context would be rated as more coherent with prior context than targets whose low-salience/innovative meaning or interpretation is related to prior context. Specifically, we aimed to show that similarly familiar items would be rated as equally coherent with prior context, regardless of figurativeness. In contrast, novel items would score lower on the coherence scale compared to their more conventional uses.

To be able to test these predictions, we first aimed at reestablishing degrees of salience in a pretest. The pretest involved 21 native speakers of Hebrew, graduates and undergraduates of Biology and Social Sciences at Tel Aviv University, aged 18–32. They were asked to rate the prospective materials of Experiments 1 and 2 (taken from Giora and Fein 1999a) on a 7 point familiarity scale. They were told that the items, which also have a literal interpretation, were metaphors and that their ratings should reflect the extent to which they were familiar with their metaphorical sense. In addition, they were asked to write down the meaning of each item. The written responses served to confirm that the familiar metaphorical sense of the familiar items was indeed recognized. Items scoring above 5 were considered familiar; items rated below 5 were considered less familiar/innovative. This rating test resulted in 20 innovative items (novel metaphors) and 16 familiar items (familiar metaphors). This division into familiar and novel metaphorical items closely overlaps the division we obtained in Giora and Fein (1999a) in which we found 18 familiar metaphors and 18 less and unfamiliar metaphors. As mentioned earlier, on the basis of the reading times obtained for these items in Giora and Fein (1999a), we assume here similar familiarity of literal and metaphorical meanings of familiar metaphors (which took equally long to read) and higher familiarity of literal interpretations of novel metaphors (which were faster to read than their metaphorical interpretation).

2.1.1 Method

Participants. Fifty-four volunteers served as participants. They were all native speakers of Hebrew, Natural Sciences and Social Sciences graduates and undergraduates of Tel Aviv University, aged 18–32.

Materials. Materials were the items rated for degree of metaphorical familiarity in the pretest (reported above). They were embedded at the end of a context biasing each of them either toward the literal or toward the metaphorical interpretation. They, thus, made up a set of 72 items (see Giora and Fein 1999a). In terms of familiarity, they formed 2 groups. The familiar items consisted of 16 familiar metaphors (7a) and their 16 literal alternatives (7b); the set of unfamiliar items consisted of 20 metaphors (8a) and their 20 literal alternatives (8b):

(7) a. In order to solve the math problem, the student *broke her head* [equivalent to the English *racked her brains*].
   b. Because she was so careless when she jumped into the pool, the student *broke her head*.

(8) a. Mary: My husband is terribly annoyed by his new boss. Every day he comes home after work even more depressed than he has been the day before. Somehow, he cannot adjust himself to the new situation. Billie: *Their bone density is not like ours.*
   b. Our granny had a fracture from just falling off a chair and was rushed to the hospital. I told my sister I never had fractions falling off a chair. She explained to me about the elderly. She said: *Their bone density is not like ours.*

Two different booklets were prepared, each containing 36 items so that subjects saw only one version of the contextual bias of the target sentences. Only one text appeared on each page.

Procedure. Participants were each presented a booklet and were asked to rate the extent to which the last (target) sentence of each text coheres with prior context on a 7 point coherence scale (1 = incoherent; 7 = highly coherent).

2.1.2 Results

Findings are presented in Table 1. They are consistent with the Graded Salience Hypothesis. Although there was a main effect of sentence type (metaphor/literal) as evident by both subject, $F_1(1,53) = 15.87$, $p < 0.001$ and item $F_2(1,34) = 6.28$, $p < 0.05$ analyses, this effect was only due to the interaction pattern between sentence type (metaphor/literal) and familiarity, $F_1(1,53) = 31.48$, $p < 0.001$, $F_2(1,34) = 3.85$, $p = 0.058$. That is, the metaphoricity effect was produced by the group of unfamiliar metaphors. The unfamiliar metaphors were rated as significantly less coherent with prior context than their literal interpretation $F_1(1,53) = 115.90$, $p < 0.0001$; $F_2(1,34) = 11.23$, $p < 0.005$. However, the familiar metaphors and their literal interpretations did not differ significantly on the coherence scale, as predicted by the Graded Salience Hypothesis, $F_1(1,53) < 1$, n.s., $F_2(1,34) < 1$, n.s.

Table 1: Familiarity and coherence ratings (SD in parentheses)

Item type	Familiar metaphor		Unfamiliar metaphor	
Contextual bias	Literal	metaphorical	literal	metaphorical
Coherence	5.15 (1.08)	5.20 (1.01)	5.70 (0.77)	4.63 (0.83)

2.1.3 Discussion

As predicted by the Graded Salience Hypothesis, low familiar metaphors were rated as less coherent with prior context than their (more familiar) salience-based literal interpretations; in contrast, familiar metaphors and their (familiar) literal interpretations were rated as similarly coherent with their respective contexts. In addition, highly familiar metaphors were rated as more coherent than low familiar metaphors. Such findings cannot be accommodated by either the Standard Pragmatic Model or the Direct Access View. According to the Standard Pragmatic Model, familiar metaphors and their literal interpretations should be viewed as distinguished in terms of coherence. According to the Direct Access View, unfamiliar metaphors and their literal interpretation should be viewed as equivalent in terms of coherence with their biasing contexts. These predictions did not gain support here.

The factor that best accounts for the different degrees of the coherence ratings is the degree of salience of the related stimuli, irrespective of figurativeness. When relevant/related items (Giora 1985) differ in terms of familiarity, it is their degree of familiarity that affects their degree of coherence.

2.2 Experiment 2

Experiment 2 aims to test the Optimal Innovation Hypothesis, which predicts that familiar metaphors and their familiar literal interpretations, rated as similarly coherent, would be similarly pleasing; however, unfamiliar metaphors, rated as less coherent with prior context than their (more familiar) literal interpretations, would be rated as more pleasing than these literal interpretations.

2.2.1 Method

Participants. One hundred and fourteen Linguistics and Social Sciences undergraduates of Tel Aviv University volunteered to act as participants. They were all native speakers of Hebrew, aged 21–26.

Materials. Same as in Experiment 1.

Procedure. Participants were each presented a booklet and were asked to rate the extent to which the last (target) sentence in its given context induces pleasure on a 7 point liking/pleasurability scale (1 = least pleasing; 7 = highly pleasing).

2.2.2 Results

Findings are presented in Table 2. They are consistent with the Optimal Innovation Hypothesis. Indeed, familiarity affected pleasurability. Familiar items were rated as more pleasing than unfamiliar items, $F_1(1,113) = 42.00$, $p < .0001$, $F_2(1,34) = 9.29$, $p < .005$. On the other hand, figurativeness, on its own, had no effect, $F_1(1,113) = 2.62$, n.s., $F_2(1,34) < 1$, n.s. Importantly, however, there was an interaction between sentence type (metaphor/literal) and familiarity, $F_1(1,113) = 7.61$, $p < .01$, $F_2(1,34) = 2.66$, $p = .11$. This interaction was due to the fact that unfamiliar metaphors were significantly more pleasurable than their (more familiar) literal interpretations $F_1(1,113) = 10.75$, $p < 0.005$, $F_2(1, 34) = 3.15$, $p = 0.085$, as predicted. In contrast, the familiar metaphors and their familiar literal interpretations did not vary significantly on the pleasurability scale, neither by subject ($F_1 < 1$) nor by item analyses ($F_2 < 1$), as predicted.

Table 2: Familiarity and pleasure ratings (SD in parentheses)

Item type	Familiar Metaphor		Unfamiliar Metaphor	
Contextual bias	literal	metaphorical	literal	metaphorical
Pleasure	4.03 (0.87)	3.96 (0.98)	3.52 (0.93)	3.79 (0.49)

2.2.3 Discussion

Novel metaphors meet the requirements of optimal innovation (5): They involve a novel (metaphorical) response to a familiar (literal) stimulus, without blocking its salience-based (literal) interpretation, as can be also deduced from their longer reading times compared to their literal interpretations (Giora and Fein 1999a). Their literal interpretations, however, do not: They involve only their salience-based interpretation. Hence, the difference in pleasurability ratings found between novel and familiar interpretations of the same stimuli.

The familiar metaphors used in this study did not vary salience-wise from their literal interpretations (as can be deduced from their equal reading times shown in Giora and Fein 1999a) and could not be classified as optimally innovative. No wonder they did not vary on the pleasurability scale. Their high ratings (compared to similar ratings of novel metaphors), although, in fact, incomparable, may provide only partial support for the view that familiarity is a crucial factor in pleasurability. In this respect, our view differs from that of other models of pleasurability (Berlyne 1971; Bornstein and D'Agostino 1992; Giora et al. 2004; Harrison 1977; Kunst-Wilson and Zajonc 1980; Zajonc 1968, 1980, 2000). Although these models attribute to familiarity a role in pleasure, they predict low pleasure ratings for high (and low) familiar items. In contrast, the Optimal Innovation Hypothesis predicts moderate pleasure ratings for high familiar items (as shown by Giora et al. 2004).

Additional support for the view that it is not figurativeness that accounts for pleasurability but optimal innovativeness comes from findings in Giora et al. (2004). In Giora et al. (2004), we tested this assumption by using the 10 most familiar and the 10 most novel items of the set used here. We figured that since the most familiar metaphors will be more familiar than their literal interpretations, it is their literal interpretation that would meet the requirements for optimal innovativeness, involving both salient (metaphorical) and low-salience (literal) responses. In contrast, the most novel metaphors will be rated as more pleasing than their literal interpretations, since they involve both a familiar salience-based (literal) interpretation alongside a novel (metaphorical) interpretation, which their literal interpretations do not. Findings indeed show that while novel metaphors were rated as more pleasing than their literal interpretations (Figure 1), most familiar metaphors were rated as less pleasurable than their literal interpretations, which were found to be more pleasing. Increase in figurativeness, then, does not guarantee increase in liking (see Figure 2). Instead, it is optimal innovativeness that incurs pleasure regardless of figurativeness.

In all, these findings support the Optimal Innovation Hypothesis according to which optimally innovative rather than metaphorical interpretations of same stimuli account for pleasurability. Theories assuming that the salience-based (literal) interpretations of novel (metaphorical) stimuli need not be computed in the process of their interpretation and might be circumvented due to a strong context cannot account for these findings.

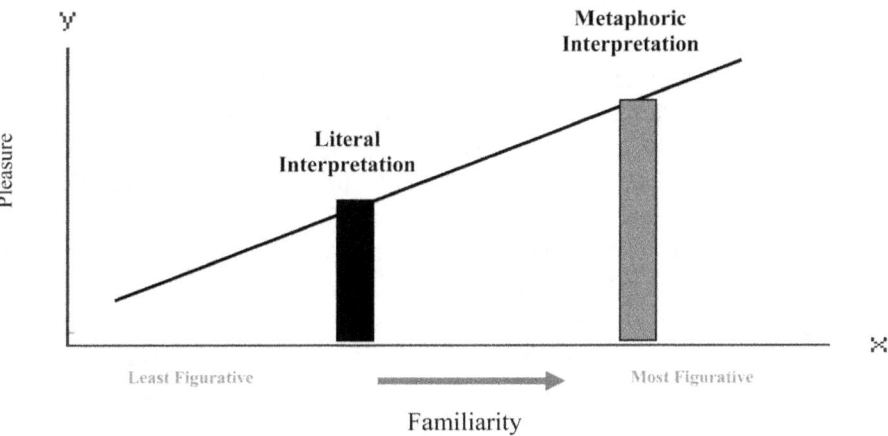

Figure 1: Pleasure ratings are a function of figurativeness

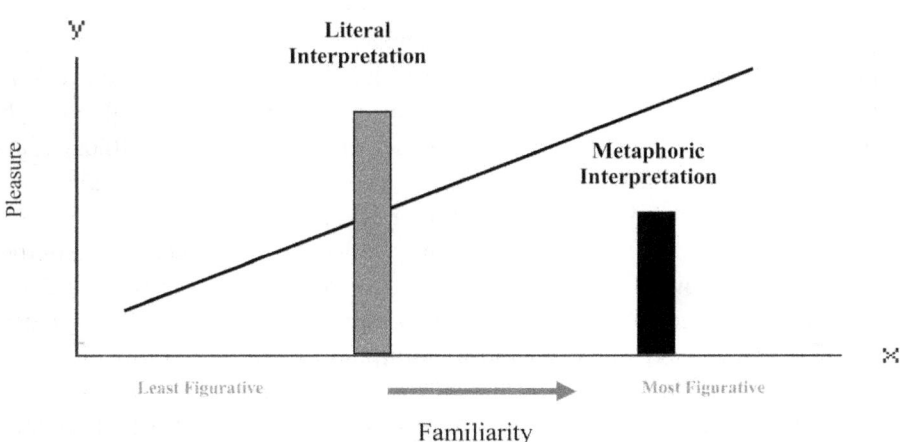

Figure 2: Pleasure ratings are not a function of figurativeness

3 General Discussion

Our studies show that, contrary to the Standard Pragmatic Model, metaphor does not hamper coherence; it is only novel metaphor that is viewed as hampering coherence (Experiment 1; Giora and Fein 1999a), as predicted by the Graded Salience Hypothesis. Complementarily, our studies show that, contrary to the Direct Access View, (given a highly informative prior context) metaphorical and literal interpretations of utterances are not equally coherent; it is only familiar metaphor and its familiar literal interpretation that cohere equally smoothly (Experiment 1; Giora and Fein 1999a), as predicted by the Graded Salience Hypothesis. Assuming similar relatedness to prior context and its discourse topic (Giora 1985), degree of coherence is sensitive to degree of salience rather than to degree of figurativeness. Compared to novel, nonsalient interpretations, salient meanings and salience-based interpretations are viewed as more coherent with prior context, regardless of figurativeness (Gibbs 1980).

Our studies further show that it is not metaphor that is pleasing; it is only novel metaphor that is viewed as likable; familiar metaphors are just as pleasing as their familiar literal interpretations (Experiment 2).

Our studies, thus, suggest that people might use utterances that hamper coherence in order to affect pleasure. Indeed, our studies demonstrate that pleasure ratings are induced by optimal innovation – innovation that allows the recoverability of a (familiar, conventional) response in the process of deriving a novel one, regardless of figurativeness (Giora et al., 2004).

Earlier research also suggests that people use language that hampers coherence in order to produce aesthetic effects. In Giora (1993), analogies were shown to interfere with comprehension. Notwithstanding, when scientific texts contained analogies, they were rated as more pleasing than when they did not.

At first blush, optimal innovations may seem more relevant (à la Sperber and Wilson 1986, 1995) than familiar expressions. Indeed, optimal innovations are rich in contextual effects. However, they are also highly taxing. And although familiar expressions are not as productive, they are still quite likable (Giora et al. 2004), while being less taxing. Contrary to appearances, then, both familiar and optimally innovative stimuli can be equally relevant.

In fact, what's likable about optimal innovativeness is the recognition of the familiar in the novel (Freud 1905; Giora et al. 2004), which is processed on account of its degree of saliency rather than due to its contextual (ir)relevance (e.g., the literal interpretation of novel metaphors; the metaphorical meaning of familiar metaphors and idioms intended literally). The Direct Access View, which assumes that contextually appropriate novel metaphors need not involve processing their irrelevant literal interpretations in highly supportive contexts and, likewise, that contextually appropriate literal interpretations of highly familiar metaphors embedded in highly supportive context need not involve processing their metaphorical interpretations (for evidence to the contrary, see Gibbs 1980; Giora et al. 2004), will have difficulties accounting for the aesthetic ratings of the optimally innovative stimuli.

Acknowledgement

This paper was supported by grants (No. 652/07 and No. 436/12) to the first author by THE ISRAEL SCIENCE FOUNDATION. We also deeply thank Gila Batori for her help with the statistics.

References

Anonymous. 2006. http://www.flickr.com/photos/idanska/247228762/ http://www.flickr.com/search/?q=%22Know+hope%22&page=3 http://www.sheinkinstreet.co.il/gallery/3254.image

Berlyne, Daniel E. 1960. *Conflict, arousal and curiosity.* New York: McGraw-Hill.

Berlyne, Daniel E. 1971. *Aesthetics and Psychobiology.* New York: Century Psychology Series.

Blumenthal, Max. December 8, 2010. The Carmel wildfire is burning all illusions in Israel http://www.huffingtonpost.com/max-blumenthal/the-carmel-wildfire-isbu_b_793484.html

Bornstein, Robert F., and Paul R. D'Agostino. 1992. Stimulus recognition and the mere exposure effect. *Journal of Personality and Social Psychology* 63: 545–552.

Brisard, Frank, Steven Frisson, and Dominiek Sandra. 2001. Processing unfamiliar metaphors in a self-paced reading task. *Metaphor and Symbol* 16: 87–108.

Brône, Geert, and Seana Coulson. 2010. Processing deliberate ambiguity in newspaper headlines: Double grounding. *Discourse Processes* 47(3): 212–236.

Duffy, Susan A., Robin K. Morris, and Keith Rayner. 1988. Lexical ambiguity and fixations times in reading. *Journal of Memory and Language* 27: 429–446.

Ferretti, Todd R., Christopher A. Schwint, and Albert N. Katz. 2007. Electrophysiological and behavioural measures of the influence of literal and figurative contextual constraints on proverb comprehension. *Brain and Language* 101: 38–49.

Fodor, Jerry A. 1983. *The Modularity of Mind.* Cambridge, Mass: MIT Press.

Freud, Sigmund. 1960. Reprint. *Jokes and their Relation to the Unconscious.* New York: Norton. Original edition, 1905.

Frisson, Steven, and Martin J. Pickering. 2007. The processing of familiar and novel senses of a word: Why reading Dickens is easy but reading Needham can be hard. *Language and Cognitive Processes* 22(4): 595–613.

Hekkert, Paul, Dirk Snelders, and Piet C. W. van Wieringen. 2003. 'Most advanced yet acceptable': Typicality and novelty as joint predictors of aesthetic preference in industrial design. *British Journal of Psychology* 94: 111–124.

Gibbs, Raymond W. Jr. 1980. Spilling the beans on understanding and memory for idioms in conversation. *Memory & Cognition* 8: 449–456.
Gibbs, Raymond W. Jr. 1994. *The Poetics of Mind*. Cambridge: Cambridge University Press.
Gibbs, Raymond W. Jr. 2001. Evaluating contemporary models of figurative language understanding. *Metaphor and Symbol* 16: 317–333.
Gibbs, Raymond W. Jr. 2002. A new look at literal meaning in understanding what is said and implicated. *Journal of Pragmatics* 34: 457–486.
Giora, Rachel. 1985. A text-based analysis of nonnarrative texts. *Theoretical Linguistics* 12: 115–135.
Giora, Rachel. 1993. On the function of analogies in informative texts. *Discourse Processes* 16: 591–611.
Giora, Rachel. 1997. Understanding figurative and literal language: The graded salience hypothesis. *Cognitive Linguistics* 7: 183–206.
Giora, Rachel. 1999. On the priority of salient meanings: Studies of literal and figurative language. *Journal of Pragmatics* 31: 919–929.
Giora, Rachel. 2002. Literal vs. figurative language: Different or equal? *Journal of Pragmatics* 34: 487–506.
Giora, Rachel. 2003. *On our Mind: Salience, Context and Figurative Language*. New York: Oxford University Press.
Giora, Rachel, and Ofer Fein. 1999a. On understanding familiar and less-familiar figurative language. *Journal of Pragmatics* 31: 1601–1618.
Giora, Rachel, and Ofer Fein. 1999b. Irony: Context and salience. *Metaphor and Symbol* 14: 241–257.
Giora, Rachel, Ofer Fein, Ronie Kaufman, Dana Eisenberg, and Shani Erez. 2009. Does an "ironic situation" favor an ironic interpretation? In: Geert Brône and Jeroen Vandaele (eds.) *Cognitive Poetics: Goals, Gains and Gaps*, 383–399. (Applications of Cognitive Linguistics series). Berlin/New York: Mouton de Gruyter.
Giora, Rachel, Ofer Fein, Ann Kronrod, Idit Elnatan, Noa Shuval, and Adir Zur. 2004. Weapons of mass distraction: Optimal innovation and pleasure ratings. *Metaphor and Symbol* 19: 115–141.
Giora, Rachel, Ofer Fein, Dafna Laadan, Joe Wolfson, Michal Zeituny, Ran Kidron, Ronie Kaufman, and Ronit Shaham. 200. Expecting irony: Context vs. salience-based effects. *Metaphor and Symbol* 22: 119–146.
Giora, Rachel, Ofer Fein, and Tamir Schwartz. 1998. Irony: Graded salience and indirect negation. *Metaphor and Symbol* 13: 83–101.
Glucksberg, Sam. 1995. Commentary on nonliteral language: Processing and use. *Metaphor and Symbolic Activity* 10: 47–57.
Glucksberg, Sam. 1998. Understanding metaphors. *Current Directions in Psychological Science* 7: 39–43.
Glucksberg, Sam. 2001. *Understanding Figurative Language: From Metaphors to Idioms*. New York: Oxford University Press.
Glucksberg, Sam, Patricia Gildea, and Howard B. Bookin. 1982. On understanding nonliteral speech: Can people ignore metaphors? *Journal of Verbal Learning and Verbal Behavior* 21: 85–98.
Grice, Herbert Paul. 1975. Logic and Conversation. In: Peter Cole and Jerry L. Morgan (eds.) *Speech Acts. Syntax and Semantics* Vol. 3: 41–58. New York: Academic Press.

Harrison, Albert A. 1977. Mere exposure. In: Leonard Berkowitz (ed.) *Advances in Experimental Social Psychology* Vol. 10: 610–646. New York: Academic Press.
Janus, Razi A., and Thomas G. Bever. 1985. Processing of metaphoric language: An investigation of the three stage model of metaphor comprehension. *Journal of Psycholinguistic Research* 14: 473–487.
Katz, Albert N., and Todd R. Ferretti. 2001. Moment-by-moment comprehension of proverbs in discourse. *Metaphor and Symbol* 16: 193–221.
Katz, Albert N., and Todd R. Ferretti. 2003. Reading proverbs in context: The role of explicit markers. *Discourse Processes* 36: 19–46.
Keysar, Boaz. 1989. On the functional equivalence of literal and metaphorical interpretations in discourse. *Journal of Memory and Language* 28: 375–385.
Keysar, Boaz. 1994. Discourse context effects: Metaphorical and literal interpretations. *Discourse Processes* 18: 247–269.
Kunst-Wilson, William Raft, and Robert B. Zajonc. 1980. Affective discrimination of stimuli that cannot be recognized. *Science* 207: 1019–1024.
Miall, David S., and Don Kuiken. 1994. Foregrounding, defamiliarization and affect response to literary stories. *Poetics* 22: 389–407.
Mukařovský, Jan. 1964. Standard language and poetic language. In: Paul L. Garvin (ed.) *A Prague School Reader on Esthetics, Literary Structure and Style*, 17–30. Washington, DC: Georgetown University Press. Original edition, 1932.
Mukařovský, Jan. 1978. *Structure, Sign and Function*. New Haven, CT: Yale University Press.
Ortony, Andrew, Diane L. Schallert, Raplh E. Reynolds, and Stephen J. Antos. 1978. Interpreting metaphors and idioms: Some effects of context on comprehension. *Journal of Verbal Learning and Verbal Behavior* 17: 465–477.
Peleg, Orna, and Zohar Eviatar. 2007. Hemispheric sensitivities to lexical and contextual information: evidence from lexical ambiguity resolution. *Brain and Language* 105(2): 71–82.
Peleg, Orna, Rachel Giora, and Ofer Fein. 2001. Salience and context effects: Two are better than one. *Metaphor and Symbol* 16: 173–192.
Peleg, Orna, Rachel Giora, and Ofer Fein. 2004. Contextual strength: The whens and hows of context effects. In: Iran A. Noveck and Dan Sperber (eds.) *Experimental Pragmatics*, 172–186. Palgrave: Basingstoke.
Rayner, Keith, Jeremy M. Pacht, and Susan A. Duffy. 1994. Effects of prior encounter and global discourse bias on the processing of lexically ambiguous words: Evidence from eye fixations. *Journal of Memory and Language* 33: 527–544.
Shopenhauer, Arthur. 1969. The world as will and representation. In: David E. Cooper (1997), (ed) *Aesthetics: The Classical Readings*, Ch.10. Oxford, England: Blackwell Publishers.
Searle, John. 1979. *Expression and meaning*. Cambridge, England: Cambridge University Press.
Shklovsky, Viktor. 1965. Reprint. Art as technique. In: Lee T. Lemon and Marion J. Reis (eds. and trans.) *Russian formalist criticism: Four essays*, 3–57. Lincoln, NE: University of Nebraska Press. Original edition, 1917.
Sperber, Dan, and Deirdre Wilson. 1995. Reprint. *Relevance: Communication and Cognition*. Oxford: Blackwell. Original edition, 1986.
Steen, Gerard J. 1994. *Understanding Metaphor in Literature: An Empirical Approach*. London: Longman.
Swinney, David A. 1979. Lexical access during sentence comprehension: (Re)consideration of context effects. *Journal of Verbal Learning and Verbal Behavior* 18: 645–659.
Townsend, Dabney. 1997. *An introduction to aesthetics*. Oxford, England: Blackwell Publishers.

Zajonc, Robert B. 1968. Attitudinal effects of mere exposure. *Journal of Personality and Social Psychology* 9: 1–27.
Zajonc, Robert B. 1980. Feeling and thinking: Preference need no inferences. *American Psychologist* 35: 151–175.
Zajonc, Robert B. 2000. Closing the debate over the independence of affect. In: Joseph P. Forgas (ed.) *Feeling and Thinking: The Role of Affect in Social Cognition*, 31–58. Cambridge: Cambridge University Press.

Gregory A. Bryant and Raymond W. Gibbs Jr.
8 Behavioral complexities in ironic humor

When do we judge what someone says as being humorous? Our aim in this chapter is to examine this question by considering contemporary empirical research on irony and laughter. Studying ironic humor requires multiple behavioral methods to assess the ways that humor may arise in spontaneous speech. Most importantly, understanding the humor in ironic speech demands explicit consideration of the complete repertoire of bodily actions that create any ironic event in conversational interaction. We will argue that the complex, highly varied nature of ironic talk makes it difficult to assume that humor in irony resides in any single cognitive or affective process. Consider the following exchange between two college students as they ironically complain about some guests visiting one of their housemates (Gibbs 2000a: 6):

(1) Anne: "By the way, were our wonderful guests still here when you came out and ate lunch?"
Dana: "I had a sandwich and ..."
Anne: "Isn't it so nice to have guests here?"
Dana: "Totally!"
Anne: "I just love it, you know, our housemates. They bring in the most wonderful guests in the world and they can totally relate to us."
Dana: "Yes, they do."
Anne: (laughs) "Like I would just love to have them here more often (laughs) so I can cook for them, I can prepare (laughs) ..."
Dana: "to make them feel welcome?"
Anne: "Yeah, isn't this great, Dana? Like today I was feeling all depressed and I came out and I saw the guests and they totally lightened up my mood. I was like the happiest person on earth."
Dana: "Uh huh."
Anne: "I just welcome them so much, you know, ask them if they want anything to drink or eat" (laughs).

Simply reading this transcript of the conversation, without auditory information, suggests that the participants found great humor in each other's comments. Anne and Dana employ different forms of ironic language (e.g., sarcasm, jocularity, rhetorical questions, hyperbole) to indirectly convey their mutual displeasure about the people staying as guests in their apartment. Much of the irony appears humorous, despite its implied criticism of the visitors (and the roommate who invited them), and observers/readers of this exchange may take humorous pleasure in the students' mockery of the visiting guest situation.

But how do we know that the speakers in this exchange experienced both irony and humor when interpreting what each other said? One clue to the participants' ironic understandings is the fact that both speakers produced different kinds of irony in response to what the other ironically said. Thus, Anne and Dana adopted an ironic mode of speaking that signaled their recognition of each other's ironic intent. Past studies have shown that speakers sometimes create "ironic chains" in conversation anywhere from 7% to 33% of the time (Eisterhold, Attardo and Boxer 2006; Gibbs 2000a; Whalen and Pexman 2010).

On the other hand, the easiest way of detecting humor is to examine whether, and how often, the participants laughed. Anne and Dana laughed on several occasions, not only in response to what the other speaker said, but also while each of them produced their utterances (e.g., Anne laughing at the start, middle, and end of her contribution beginning, "Like I would just love to have them here more often...."). At the same time, Anne and Dana were not merely laughing at what each other said (i.e., an individual cognitive event), but appeared to be sharing laughter itself (i.e., a joint product of their social interaction).

Laughter highlights the non-serious nature of their Anne and Dana's talk, which may facilitate their collective, humorous, understandings about the visiting guests. Anne and Dana may be seriously upset about the visiting guests, but their laughter and irony suggests that dealing with a more serious way (e.g., complaining directly to the guests or their other housemate) would be counterproductive (cf. Chafe 2007). In other circumstances, listeners may generate laughs only to mimic actual understanding, forcing all parties to assess listeners' behavioral responses. Similarly, speakers may laugh with the intention of inviting others to laugh with them, which listeners may decline for any number of social reasons.

1 Incongruity and Frame-Shifting

One reason Anne and Dana laughed is because they each recognized the incongruity between what each speaker said and what they really meant. Irony is famous for its apparent disparity between what is said and implied, which explains why much ironic speech and writing conveys humor, even if, especially with sarcasm, the humor is frequently dark and critical of others. One classic theory asserts that humor is most likely to be perceived whenever there is some realization and resolution of incongruity between what is being overtly expressed and what a speaker alternatively means (Attardo 2001; Ritchie 2001). For instance, Anne's rhetorical question, "Isn't it so nice to have guests here?" conveys an implied assertion about having guests as being "so nice" and making her "like the happiest person on earth." But in context of this specific conversation, what the speakers say momentarily creates incongruities given the difficulty of having to live with another housemate's visiting friends. We presumably resolve these incongruities by drawing inferences that Anne and Dana were really complaining about the guests, and did so in a way that seemed funny (at least for the speakers, if not for the missing victims of Anne and Dana's sarcastic barbs).

Not all incongruities in conversational exchanges are humorous, of course, and many scholars see humor as a specific mental contrast between the first, obvious meaning of what someone says and a listener's final, humorous, reinterpretation. Humor is most likely to arise when something violates one's sense of how things in the world should work, where the violation is relatively benign, and an audience is capable of simultaneously understanding both interpretations (McGraw and Warren 2010). The most humorous incongruities elicit a pleasurable feeling of non-seriousness, when acting serious would be less appropriate (Chafe 2007). Some evolutionary psychologists have argued that humor is the product of sexual selection, particularly in cases where the humor reveals traits, such as creative intelligence, that may indicate good genes (Miller 2001). As humor evolved over evolutionary time, situations that were most likely to evoke humorous responses extended from physical threats to violations of personal dignity (i.e., slapstick, teasing), linguistic expectations (e.g., puns, malapropisms), social norms (e.g., risqué jokes), and moral behaviors (e.g., disrespectful behavior) (McGraw and Warren 2010). For instance, the humor in Anne and Dana's conversation emerges from the apparent violations of social and moral norms given the intrusion of the unwanted guests into their home. Yet, once again, the students' comments about these violations were performed in playful manner, in part because of their laughter, which is a well-known marker of play (Vettin and Todt 2005).

These observations about the origins and functions of humor underlie the idea that why and when language is deemed funny involves several social, cognitive, and linguistic factors. Cognitive linguistic researchers have claimed that the basic cognitive operation of frame-shifting underlies the process of incongruity resolution, and is critical to people's interpretation and appreciation of humor. Frame-shifting involves a mental reorganization of the message-level aspects of a speaker's utterance. Although frame-shifting is seen in many different meaning construction processes, it is most immediately applicable to the analysis of linguistic humor. Various linguistic analyses of humorous discourse, especially puns and jokes, affirm the relevance of frame-shifting in understanding and appreciating verbal humor (Brone, Feyaerts and Veale 2006). Frame-shifting may be especially relevant to ironic humor when a culturally licensed perspective on some situation (e.g., acting gracious to visiting houseguests) is rejected in favor of an alternative, subversive view (e.g., mocking the houseguests outside their presence) (Ritchie 2005).

Experimental studies have gone on to show that frame-shifting processes can require additional cognitive effort. Thus, readers take more time to process linguistic expressions whose endings create jokes rather than straight, non-joke endings (Coulson and Kutas 1998). These longer reading times to comprehend jokes likely reflect the complexity of high-level processing of meaning where incongruities are noted and then resolved. Neurophysiological studies demonstrate that jokes elicit larger amplitude N400 waves than do non-joke controls (Coulson and Stevens 2007). People also make regressive eye-movements toward earlier parts of statements more so when reading jokes than non-jokes (Coulson et al. 2006). Regressive eye movements in these cases may reflect attempts to create alternative interpretations of what the speaker may actually mean given what they originally said (e.g., "I tried to snort Coke, but the ice cubes got stuck in my nose").

2 Is Frame-Shifting Sufficient?

We agree that basic cognitive operations such as frame-shifting and incongruity resolution may be important facets of understanding linguistic humor. Cognitive linguistic research is particularly critical for describing some of the linguistic properties of humorous speech, and inferring possible cognitive and experiential motivations for humorous language and behavior. But understanding how humor arises in interpersonal interaction requires a more extensive, quantitative behavioral analysis of the ways people spontaneously act funny, and give indications of their own possible humorous reactions to others, as well as themselves. Different methods are needed to appropriately evaluate if and when humor arises, and what functions humor may have in conversational interactions.

For example, one difficulty with purely linguistic analyses of humor is their inability to determine whether humor is noted, and when this may occur. Linguists may apply their own intuitions to judge something as being funny or not, yet scholarly impressions may be theory-driven, and not representative of what ordinary speakers do in naturalistic interaction (Gibbs 2006). Psycholinguistic and neuropsychological experiments are useful for assessing the degree of cognitive effort needed to interpret linguistic statements as humorous, especially in comparison to non-humorous control statements. But these different empirical methods suffer from their own limitations. First, measures of reading time and specific brain activity are indicators of overall mental effort; but global differences in reading time or greater brain activations do not necessarily imply that specific cognitive processes must be operating when humor is understood. The extra time needed to read jokes, as opposed to non-jokes may reflect various other cognitive operations, such difficulty in integrating the joke interpretation with previous discourse, or listeners assessing how to now view the speaker given that he or she just made a humorous remark that are not relevant to frame-shifting per se.

One reason to question the "extra processing time = frame-shifting" explanation in some humor studies is because other experiments have demonstrated how many forms of indirect and figurative meaning, including instances of humorous irony such as sarcastic indirect requests (e.g., "Why don't you take your time washing the dishes?"), can be understood quite quickly, requiring no more mental effort over that needed to interpret more direct, non-figurative meaning (Gibbs 1994). The issue of whether indirect and figurative language generally takes extra time to process is still widely debated in psycholinguistics and elsewhere (Giora 2003; Giora et al. 2009; Gibbs 2001). But the significant research showing easy processing of some humorous statements is at odds with claims that frame-shifting is necessary for humor understanding or, at the very least, requires extra mental effort.

A second concern with the psycholinguistic research is that it mostly focuses on the linguistic processing and not the products of humor understanding. What meanings, thoughts, and feelings do listeners experience when they interpret humorous irony? Consider again the conversation between Anne and Dana about their visiting guests. Each of their utterances does not simply communicate specific, single ironic meanings that in turn evoke a unitary, humorous response. Thus, when Anne said, "I just welcome them so much" in reference to the houseguests, she is not simply communicating that she does not welcome the guests, a meaning that she hopes will somehow evoke a single humorous response. Instead, each utterance conveys multiple cognitive, social, and affective meanings – a whole complex configuration of thoughts and feelings that are often impossible to neatly individuate and count. Indeed, people employ different forms of ironic talk on varying occasions to communicate different, complex pragmatic goals (Colston 2005), and to evoke different emotional reactions in listeners (Leggitt and Gibbs 2000). For instance, sarcasm, rhetorical questions, and hyperbole all frequently evoke similar, negative emotional reactions in listeners, whereas understatement and satire typically evoked more neutral reactions. People tend to experience greater degrees of emotional involvement having heard different forms of irony than when they encountered literal statements, a finding that contradicts the idea that irony mutes speakers' intended messages (Dews and Winner 1995).

Listeners also attribute different intentions to speakers depending on which form of irony they use (e.g., criticism when using sarcasm, and affiliation when using jocularity). Irony is routinely used in the ongoing flow of conversation between group members to affirm their solidarity by directing comments at individuals who are not group members and not deemed worthy of group membership. Some forms of irony, like sarcasm, may promote group solidarity, indicate the boundaries of acceptable behavior, and "reign in" normative transgressions (Ducharme 1994). Sarcasm, in particular, is often used to vent frustration when an individual finds some situation or object offensive, or sees a group's normative standards violated. A good illustration of this venting is seen in Anne and Dana's conversation. Sarcastic comments may also be self-directed and thus affirm the speaker's allegiance to the group and the prescribed behavioral norms.

Irony's capacity to convey different emotions and evoke various affective states in listeners, depending on the exact form of irony that is used, illustrates irony's important role in helping speakers negotiate social relationships, including who is, and who is not, a friend (Gibbs 2000). Studies also show that speakers with different occupations (Katz and Pexman 1997) and different genders (Colston and Lee 2004) are expected to speak ironically with varying degrees, information that listeners use to draw ironic inferences in some situations but not others, and judge whether a speaker's utterance is humorous or not. Adults' recognition and understanding of verbal irony depends on several factors, including the perceived personality characteristics of the conversationalists (Pexman and Olineck 2002), the degree of contrast between situational factors and ironic statements (Colston 2002; Kreuz and Glucksberg, 1989; Kreuz and Roberts 1995), and whether the contrast is a matter of kind or magnitude (Colston and O'Brien 2000).

3 Laughter and Voice in Humor and Irony

The complexity of factors shaping irony use and understanding underscore our concern with standard linguistic and psycholinguistic methods for assessing when people interpret different aspects of ironic meaning and whether they also appreciate any humor in what was said. We argue that more elaborate behavioral studies are needed to explore the range of ironic actions people engage in, both verbally and non-verbally. One psychological perspective emphasizes that irony is based on speakers pretending to be certain people or have certain views (a kind of "staged communicative act", Clark 1996; Gibbs 2000b). These kinds of staged communicative acts are not merely verbal, but involve a number of different bodily actions which both enact irony and humor and possibly elicit humorous responses in others. For instance, when Anne says "Isn't it so nice to have guests here?" she is taking action at two levels. First, she is asking a rhetorical question, one that is not meant to be literally answered. Second, she is pretending to embrace the idea conveyed by her questions, namely that it must be nice to have guests visiting. By highlighting the contrast between these two levels of meaning, the speaker can efficiently communicate a variety of social and affective meanings. Layering reflects metarepresentational reasoning because a speaker is, once more, alluding to, or echoing, some attributed utterance or thought of another person (i.e., people who really do like to have guests visiting), thus creating a representation of a representation (i.e., a second-order belief). Understanding ironic utterances, therefore, requires people to recognize the second-order nature of the speaker's beliefs if they are to correctly infer that individual's intended meaning (Bryant 2012; Colston and Gibbs 2002; Sperber and Wilson 1995).

Metarepresentational reasoning sounds very cognitive, and disembodied, but actually involves many non-linguistic actions that help create staged personas. Even if ironic speakers are pretending to act in certain ways, and indeed pretending to be other people, their actions, including non-linguistic ones such as laughing and tone of voice, are often critical to understanding the nature of ironic meaning and humor. Ironic speakers are not saying things to be funny; they are performing irony with humor and often expect listeners to co-participate in their "on stage" performances by adopting similar forms of pretense. Once again, speakers together adapt an "ironic mode" of not just speaking, but acting that includes various behaviors.

For example, empirical studies clearly demonstrate how laughter is often associated with humor and irony in combination. For example, Bryant (2010a) found that over half of all ironic utterances in spontaneous conversations between friends were closely associated with laughing. When used with irony, laughter may help listeners recognize an ironic intention, although to our knowledge, this has never been demonstrated empirically. Conversely, it is easy to imagine how laughter could be used to create ambiguity in meaning when used with irony. For instance, if a speaker intended to humiliate a victim through sarcasm, it might not be clear if laughter produced before, during, or just after the ironic utterance was intended to amplify the humiliation, or signal innocent play. Particular acoustic features of the laughter might be critical. Noisy, atonal features often associated with aggression and strength (e.g., Morton 1977) might facilitate antagonistic sarcasm, for example. Moreover, if irony is used as a means to sort social alliances, only those who are in on the joke might engage in laughter, and this could reveal a prevailing social network.

Most research on laughter examines people's reactions to humorous videos and comics. But people also laugh when they are not being humorous (Provine 2000). One analysis of over 1000 laughs in various natural contexts revealed that speakers were much more likely to laugh than listeners, suggesting that others' humor production is not the predominant trigger for laughter (Provine 1993). Many of the comments immediately preceding spontaneous laughter were not obviously funny. Given this observation, laughter may best be understood as a stereotyped, social vocalization not necessarily linked to humor. But many of the seemingly mundane utterances happening just before speakers laugh are probably actually often funny to those involved. There is no way to know why people laugh when they do without asking them, and even then, many people would have difficulty articulating exactly why they laughed (Provine 2000).

A recent theory of humor describes why people laugh when they do. Flamson and Barrett (2009) proposed that humor is often a form of encryption in which people signal honestly the possession of certain knowledge that requires specific implicit knowledge to recognize (i.e., a key). When this recognition occurs, it is subjectively experienced as funny, and often results in some indicator of that (e.g., a laugh). Flamson and Barrett manipulated the level of encryption in presented jokes, tested for prior relevant knowledge, and examined the effect of the variables on funniness. For example, consider the following headline taken from the satirical newspaper The Onion: "Frank Gehry no longer allowed to make sandwiches for grandkids." This line appeared with a picture of an abstract and oddly stacked assemblage of bread and lunch meat on a plate. Headlines and pictures like this were presented along with high encryption and low encryption paragraphs. In this example, the high encryption information provided basic biographical information of Frank Gehry such as when he was born, where he went to college, and where he currently lives. The low encryption paragraph was matched in length but instead included information about his architectural career and fame for designing curved and uneven buildings. Participants were also tested for their background knowledge. As expected, high encrypted jokes were generally judged as being significantly funnier, with people having prior background knowledge of the joke topics more likely to judge jokes as being funny, especially when that knowledge was needed to actually "get" the jokes.

To a large extent, people's production and understanding of laughter follows general principles that have previously been outlined for irony (Kaufer 1977). First, some people recognize the irony and understand what the speaker/author intends to communicate, and because of their wisdom may be called "wolves." People who fail to recognize the irony mistake what the speaker/author appears to say for what he or she intends to say. For their gullibility, these people may be called "sheep." Audiences who agree with the speaker/author's intended meaning are "confederates" and those that disagree are "victims." These two groups are not the same as wolves and sheep, because understanding what the author intends to say and agreeing with it are distinct aspects of communication. Overall, irony divides the audience into four groups: (1) those who recognize the irony and agree with the author's intended message (i.e., wolf-confederates), (2) those who recognize the irony but disagree with the author's intended message (i.e., wolf-victims), (3) those who do not recognize the irony but would agree with the author's message if they had correctly understood it (i.e., sheep-confederates), and (4) those who do not recognize the irony and would not accept the author's communicative message (i.e., sheep-victims). The main job of an ironic speaker is to create as many wolf-confederates as possible while keeping to a minimum the number of sheep-confederates who wrongly believe themselves opposed to the creator's position (Kaufer 1977).

Our suggestion is that laughter too may be divided into the same four categories (e.g., wolf-confederates, wolf-victims, sheep-confederates, and sheep-victims), and thus serve different purposes depending on the kind of encrypted information shared between conversational participants. If laughter indicates the recognition of some encrypted information, it is important to know whether the listener actually got the joke, or they merely recognized the presence of a joke and produced a laugh to pretend understanding. This effort is motivated by the desire for accessing the many possible benefits of sharing a joke with someone – a potentially costly kind of deception for joke producers. Scholars have distinguished between different kinds of laughs, designating some as deliberate as opposed to spontaneous (Keltner and Bonanno 1997). This distinction relates closely to "fake" versus "real" smiles, or Duchenne smiles (Ekman, Davidson and Friesen 1990). Laughter generated during the production of different kinds of smiles have been labeled similarly, and some research has explored the difference between real and fake laughs, though no acoustic data as of yet exists. One possibility is that the production and perception of different laughs and smiles emerge as a kind of co-evolutionary arms race. From this perspective, laughing is manipulative, and people must mind read laughers to assess a person's real intention when laughing. Is the laugher actually revealing the possession of a "key" and generating a spontaneous laugh motivated by the

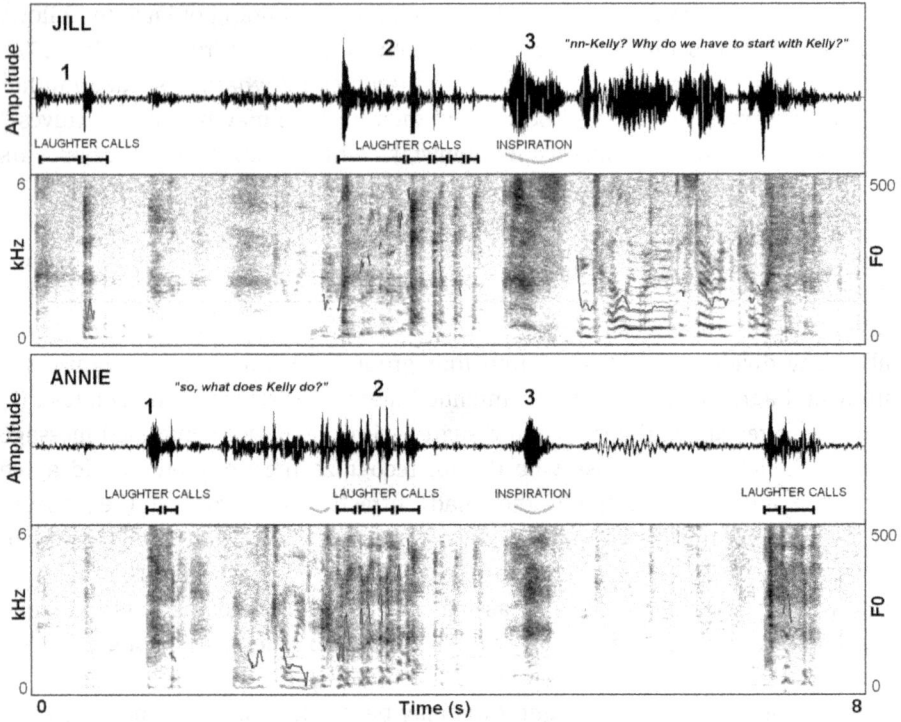

Figure 1: Spectrogram (FFT method, window length – 0.005 s., Gaussian window shape, dynamic range – 50 dB) and wave form of conversation segment containing antiphonal laughter. Lines in spectrogram indicate fundamental frequency (pitch). Straight lines underneath waveform indicate laughter calls, and curved lines indicate inspiration. 1. First antiphonal laugh sequence where each speaker produced a two-call bout with the first call unvoiced, and the second call voiced. 2. Second antiphonal laugh sequence with bottom speaker (Annie) producing initial inspiratory call, then four expiratory calls, each with two microelements. Top speaker (Jill) produced an initial long antiphonal call in synch with Jill's second call (first expiratory call), and proceeds with four short calls. 3. Simultaneous inspiration revealing synchronized breathing and speech rates.

pleasure of decryption? Or is the laugher generating a deliberate laugh in an effort to align strategically with the speaker without the requisite knowledge that reveals insider status, or some other relevant dimension?

Recent research has examined the acoustic features of laughing in spontaneous conversation (Bryant 2010b). People often engage in shared laughter (also called antiphonal laughter), and researchers are just beginning to distinguish this behavior from other forms of laughter (Smoski and Bachorowski 2003a,b; though see Jefferson 1979 for an early exception). Consider the example illustrated in Figure 1. Jill and Annie are 18 year-old women who have been friends for about four months. As in the earlier example, these friends were discussing roommate experiences, and began laughing together immediately. In the figure, laughs are designated by straight lines with end points, inspiratory (inhaling) elements are indicated by curved lines, and the text of the speech is provided for an eight-second period. First note that there is much laughter here even though nothing funny is being said. More interesting is the way these speakers laugh together. They began by producing quite similar laughs (Annie after Jill) where the first part was unvoiced, and the second half was voiced. When Annie suggested that Jill talk about her roommate, she laughed again, triggering Jill to laugh along in close synchrony. The two ended this antiphonal laugh bout with simultaneous inhalations likely indicating their mutually entrained speech production and breathing (Wilson and Wilson 2006). This lead Jill to ask why she must go first, that caused Annie to laugh again. The conversation continued on like this for ten minutes with much shared laughing. There are at least two adaptive reasons why interacting speakers might laugh simultaneously. First, laughing can mutually signal affiliative intentions. Voiced laughter is associated with greater friendliness, higher interest in meeting, and positive emotions (Bachorowski and Owren 2001) that can contribute to cooperative behavior, and can also signal sexual interest (Grammer 1990). Laughing is associated with endogenous reward, generally inferred from research identifying brain areas linked to laughter that have known mesolimbic dopamine pathways (Dunbar 2002; Panksepp 2007), and might offer other physiological benefits as well, including helping the immune system (Hasan, and Hasan, 2009). By laughing together, conversationalists can jointly communicate a willingness to pursue a relationship and/or continue to cooperate. If people signal to each other the possession of mutual unspoken knowledge, they are assorting themselves socially – laughter can operate as a type of social glue in such contexts (thus opening up a niche for social exploitation described above). This coordinated shared laughing constitutes the second potential function. Antiphonal laughter generates a signal that is broadcast to those outside of the interaction, so listeners can infer relevant relationship information by hearing others laugh together. A group of people laughing in concert can quickly signal to others a whole range of information, including but not limited to normative expectations, current alliances, sources of potential conflict, and various aesthetic preferences. In this way, laughter can be a powerful social group communication device.

Given these two possible functions of antiphonal laughter, laughing should possibly have specific acoustic properties that assist others in recognizing the laughter as such. For example, the effort to broadcast affiliation to outsiders might be enhanced if the antiphonal laughter was longer, louder, and less acoustically variable – all features that facilitate signal transmission in noisy environments. An analysis of over 2000 laughs taken from 40 natural conversations between friends and strangers, in all gender combinations, indicated that antiphonal laughs between friends possess many of the predicted differences from individual laughs (Bryant 2010b). When laughing antiphonally, a speaker generates the first laugh, an "initiation," and their partner produces a "response" laugh. This study isolated laughs, extracted them acoustically, and then coded for various features and subjected to acoustic analysis. Not surprisingly, friends laughed more than strangers, and women laughed more than men. Friends and females also produced more voiced laughs (i.e., laughter with tonal properties) relative to unvoiced laughs. As mentioned earlier, voiced laughter has been judged emotionally as relatively more positive (Bachorowski and Owren 2001). Friends also produced significantly more antiphonal laughs than strangers, but did so with much more variable timing. In Bryant (2010b), a response laugh needed to occur within one-second of the initiation in order for the pair to be categorized as antiphonal. The time from the onset of the initiation laugh to the onset of the response laugh was measured, and an unexpected difference was revealed between friends and strangers. The average latency for a response in all antiphonal laughs within one-second was about 400ms, with friends being slightly, although not significantly longer. But the variation between these groups was radically different. Using a bootstrap analysis, distributions of the standard deviations of the latencies were generated, and strangers were much less variable, with very little overlap between distributions. This suggests that strangers responded to antiphonal laughs in a much more regimented manner, possibly as a reflexive laugh reflecting an early relationship negotiation tactic (and/or manipulative social strategy). Friends, conversely, produced much more variable laugh responses, perhaps reflecting the tremendous diversity of familiar interactive behavior. If laughers are signaling something about their relationship to others outside the interaction, we might expect that the coordinated signals would be quite varied given that more variable (although still coordinated) signals honestly reflect the investment of time friends must spend to organize complex behavior (Hagen and Bryant 2003).

This type of analysis speaks to the long standing conflict between examining actual communication-in-action and experimental control. If one is interested in how laughs manifest themselves during real interaction, it is necessary to retrieve the behavior of interest from the wild, so to speak. Most researchers studying laughter use various stimuli to elicit laughter in experimental contexts, but there is good reason to suspect that the acoustic properties of this kind of laughter might be different from more natural, spontaneous laughter. Moreover, these studies do not address the crucial issue of how laughter functions in normal conversation. Studying conversational laughter, however, presents researchers with difficult methodological problems associated with the messiness of spontaneous communicative behavior. Laughs often co-occur with talk and overlap with other speakers, as well as manifest with incredible phonetic variation. One simple criterion researchers often use is to rely on subjective judgment of what "sounds like a laugh" to decide on whether a laugh is present. But there are basic acoustic features that often distinguish laughs from other vocalizations, such as short (~500 ms) and often successive expiratory elements that are similar within individual bouts, and generally either tonal (i.e., vowel-like), or if nonvoiced, have clear onsets (Bachorowski, Smoski and Owren 2001; Vettin and Todt 2004). Even with these relatively specific features, deciding on the acoustic boundaries of laughs in speech can be extremely difficult, and somewhat subjective. Speakers blend speech into laughs both at onset and offset, and many unvoiced laughs are barely more than a 100 ms puff of air. While laughter punctuates speech in what appears to be rule-governed ways (Provine 1993), it does so with extreme complexity – certainly a contributing factor in the paucity of detailed acoustic and pragmatic analysis of laughter in the wild. Laughter can often mark humorous interaction and utterances, but how and when people signal they are being funny is clearly not so simple. One question of recent interest is whether speakers mark their humor prosodically. For example, irony is frequently assumed to have a special "tone of voice" that makes it uniquely identifiable as conveying ironic meaning and perhaps humor. For instance, a sarcastic speaker might lower his pitch, speak louder, and slow down his speech rate relative to his baseline speech. These particular adjustments are often found with actors (Rockwell 2000). But in spontaneous conversations, the acoustic patterns are not at all consistent, except that speakers quite often slow down (Bryant 2010a). Consider the following exchange between two housemates discussing past roommate experiences:

(2) Kristen: "My side of the room would always be messy."
    Shayna: "You the messy? Ha."
    Kristen: "Hah ha ha, I know, can you believe it?"

Kristen explains that in a past living situation her side of the room would be messy, and this comes as no surprise to Shayna, her current roommate. Shayna responds with an ironic rhetorical question that elicits ironic jocularity, and in it she exaggerates particular prosodic features associated with interrogatives. She also laughs immediately after, clearly marking her ironic intention. Kristen responds with exaggerated surprise signaling her participation in the irony, especially with shared laughter following Shayna's laugh. These vocal features not only contrast from baseline speaking patterns in the current conversation, but also sound over-the-top for ordinary speech. Functionally, these vocal signals serve to mark play, and make this part of the interaction distinct from other talk in the immediate communicative context.

One study of spontaneous ironic speech isolated the specific instances of irony, and then compared those utterances acoustically to speech immediately preceding them by the same speaker (Bryant 2010a). This method quantitatively measures how particular vocal changes manifest themselves in discourse. Not only do speakers change vocal dimensions in significant and perceptible ways, they do so in a manner reflecting the particular emotional content of their speech. Thus, Shayna's ironic rhetorical question contained exaggerated features of questions, not some stereotyped form such as low pitch and nasalization – speech characteristics commonly associated with verbal irony (Cutler 1974; Rockwell 2000). Interrogatives have greater pitch range than complementary declaratives, and have a distinctive rise-fall pattern in the pitch and amplitude as well as stress on specific parts of the sentence. Shayna's question contained these exaggerated features relative to her speech immediately preceding it.

Of course, context drives a good deal of the comprehension process as well. Prosody is not always necessary for accurate understanding but can serve to highlight various aspects of the intention, including the humor. Kristen signals her understanding of Shayna's intention, as well as her willingness to participate in the play by also contrasting several acoustic dimensions in her statement of pretended surprise. But if her statement was another ironic utterance, her vocal features likely would have been quite different. For example, if she has instead said, "I know, I'm a bad person" with exaggerated features of shame and sadness (e.g., higher, descending pitch, and lowered, descending amplitude), then the contrast from her previous speech would still be noticeable, but the actual form would have better reflected the quite different emotional connotation.

In all kinds of speech communication, prosodic contrasts can manifest in a variety of ways depending on the affective and intentional goals of the speaker and the communicative context. Flamson, Bryant and Barrett (2011) examined the vocal features of humor in a natural context amongst rural Brazilian farmers. Five hours of speech were recorded during two community meetings where landowners discussed matters of business – not a time for joking in the traditional sense, but certainly a time when speakers use various communicative tactics to highlight alliances. If speakers are signaling encrypted knowledge as a means for highlighting the depth of similarity with those audience members who manage to detect the encryption (i.e., think an utterance is funny), then we should not expect very much explicit marking.

A similar methodology was used in this study as in the research described earlier examining prosodic contrasts in verbal irony (Bryant 2010a). Humorous speech was first identified based on the presence of audience (and sometimes speaker) laughter. Following this, the speech was then divided into two segments based on the sentence structure and content: set-up, and punch line. The punch line speech was the utterance that concluded the immediate talk just before the laughter. This is not a punch line in the traditional sense of a joke, but rather the final statement in a series. The set-up speech was always related in content to the punch line, and immediately preceding it. Separating these segments can prove difficult, and is generally not obvious. Often times the whole segment was divided based on intonational phrasing. The speech immediately preceding these pairs of segments was then extracted to get comparison baseline speech. These segments were comparable in length to the set-up segments, and occurred anywhere from immediately preceding the set-up speech to up to five seconds before. Here is an example of one trio of utterances (in Portuguese with English translation in italics):

(3) Baseline: *Poluicão, era poluicão, né?*
                  'Pollution, it was pollution, right?'
     Set-up: *Aí se outro acende um fogo*
                  'Then, if someone else starts a fire'
     Punch line: *eu posso acusar ele, né?*
                  'I can accuse him, right?'

These three segments were then analyzed within speakers to check for prosodic contrasts in the acoustic dimensions of vocal pitch, loudness, and duration. If speakers were marking humorous utterances, this analysis should reveal it, especially between baseline segments and the other two. In this sample of 24 trios of segments, there were no differences in the rate of contrasts between any of the segment types indicating that speakers were not contrasting their prosody differently when they were using humor. But only a between speaker analysis can reveal systematic marking in any one dimension. The acoustic data were analyzed between speakers, and only a difference in overall loudness was found between baseline speech and the other two segments. Baseline speech was lower in amplitude suggesting that when speakers began saying something intended to be funny, they increased their loudness. But this is not likely due to explicit marking of humor. The room where the meetings took place was loud, given the large number of people participating (~25), the acoustic properties of the space, and the laughter often erupting as the punch line approached. The increased loudness of the set-up and punch line segments is likely due to an effort toward being heard, and not for prosodic marking of humor. Of course, this effort could be used potentially as a cue to humor, although not a particularly reliable one given the many reasons (not related to humor) speakers raise their voices. There was also a trend of speakers reducing the range of their pitch in set-up and punch line speech, further supporting the interpretation of the speech differences as effort toward increasing the signal-to-noise ratio rather than marking humor specifically. These findings are consistent with other research examining the production of punch lines in scripted jokes. Pickering et al. (2009) found that when speakers told jokes, their punch lines were not different from the speech leading up to them. There was a general decline in vocal pitch, but this was not considered to be beyond what one would expect from ordinary pitch declination in sentence production.

In the example above, it is not difficult to imagine how this could be funny to the people involved, but it certainly is not obvious to outsiders. Audience members began laughing during the set-up portion of the speech, as they likely had some idea what the speaker was going to say. But the speaker was likely communicating encrypted information that solicited the laughter from certain target audience members. Flamson (2010) found that social network proximity was related to judgments of humor in jokes – they tended to find funny the same things their friends did. So why laugh? As mentioned before, laughter could be serving multiple functions simultaneously including helping cooperators sort themselves and mutually communicate their intentions, as well as signal to others information about their bond. Studies in the field that examine not only acoustic features of real speech interactions, but also social network analyses that explore the relationships between interlocutors, can help illuminate the complex and dynamic patterns in ordinary talk. This approach provides insight into these communicative processes that traditional linguistic analyses could easily miss. Using mixed methods (e.g., acoustic analysis, social network analysis, and conversational analysis) in combination allows researchers to identify interactions that one-dimensional analytic techniques would be unable to measure.

4 Conclusion

The study of ironic humor often seeks broad principles that can explain people's understanding of ironic intent and their possible humorous reactions to what others say. Cognitive linguistic methods have allowed scholars to explore different conceptual and experiential aspects of meaning constructions that often appear to play important roles in the communication and understanding of humorous language. Our suggestion is that other methods are also required to better characterize some of the rich variation in how both ironic speech is used and understood, as well as when people are likely to show humorous appreciation of irony via laughter. The main lesson from our review of contemporary research on laughter, tone of voice, and ironic meaning is that when people laugh, and give indications that they have, or have not understood humorous intent, depends on many complex factors such that no simple theory can adequately explain the diversity of humorous ironic situations. Knowing when a speaker intends his or her utterance to be ironic is not merely a matter of adopting a specific tone of voice, which is conventional to use in all ironic contexts. Instead, speakers employ a variety of contrastive strategies to set off what they are saying, and the tone of voice in which they do so, to alert listeners to their possible ironic intent. Speaking ironically is also not a linguistic matter per se, but involves a wide range of possible bodily actions that essentially enact irony as part of a speaker's "staged communicative act." Laughter, for example, can be used in different ways, and expressed differently, depending on the context, and what speakers and addressees mutually know about the topic being discussed.

Teasing apart the different ways that ironic humor is enacted demands behavioral studies that examine larger corpora of what people do and say in conversation, and which also, critically, quantitatively analyze various metrics of what people are doing beyond the mere words they utter. Scholars have long noted different social and affective reasons for using ironic speech, including humor, yet many of these observations have not been empirically verified through experimental study, especially in relation to subtle changes in laughter and tone of voice that are often key to signaling different kinds of ironic intent. Yet even doing behavioral studies along the lines described in this article requires that scholars not overgeneralize their findings into simple theoretical conclusions. Just as irony differs depending on its form (e.g., sarcasm, jocularity, rhetorical questions, hyperbole, understatement) and the contexts in which it is used, so too do accompanying bodily actions also take on different forms and have different meanings depending on the precise interpersonal situation. The methodological trick for humor studies is to find sufficient quantitative behavioral evidence regarding some way that humor is enacted and then explore various motivations for why people are speaking and acting as they are in those contexts.

References

Attardo, Salvatore. 2001. *Humorous texts: A semantic and pragmatic analysis.* Berlin: Mouton de Gruyter.
Bachorowski, Jo-Anne, and Michael J. Owren. 2001. Not all laughs are alike: Voiced but not unvoiced laughter readily elicits positive affect. *Psychological Science*, 1: 252–257.
Bachorowski, Jo-Anne, Smoski Moria J., and Michael J. Owren. 2001. The acoustic features of human laughter. *Journal of the Acoustical Society of America*, 110: 1581–1597.
Brône, Geert, Feyaerts Kurt, and Tony Veale (eds.). 2006. Cognitive linguistic approaches to humor (thematic issue). *Humor: International Journal of Humor Research*, 19: 203–228.
Bryant, Gregory A. 2010a. Prosodic contrasts in ironic speech. *Discourse Processes*, 47(7): 545–566.
Bryant, Gregory A. 2010b. *Acoustic features of conversational laughter.* Paper presented at the 19th Annual Meeting of the Human Behavior and Evolution Society, Eugene, OR.
Bryant, Gregory A., and Jean E. Fox Tree. 2002. Recognizing verbal irony in spontaneous speech. *Metaphor and Symbol*, 17(2): 99–117.
Bryant, Gregory A., and Jean E. Fox Tree. 2005. Is there an ironic tone of voice? *Language and Speech*, 48(3): 257–277.
Bryant, Gregory A. 2012. Is verbal irony special? *Language and Linguistics Compass*, 6(11): 673–685.
Chafe, Wallace. 2007. *The importance of not being earnest: The feeling behind laughter.* Amsterdam: Benjamins.
Clark, Herbert H. 1996. *Using language.* Cambridge: Cambridge University Press.
Clark, Herbert H. 2002. Contrast and assimilation in verbal irony. *Journal of Pragmatics*, 34: 111–142.
Clark, Herbert H. 2005. Social and cultural influences on figurative and indirect language. In: Colston H., and Albert Katz (eds.), *Figurative language comprehension: Social and cultural influences*, 99–130. Mahwah, NJ: Erlbaum.
Colston, Herbert L., and Raymond W. Gibbs. 2002. Are irony and metaphor understood differently? *Metaphor and Symbol*, 17: 57–80.
Colston, Herbert L., and Shyh-Yuan Lee. 2004. Gender differences on verbal irony use. *Metaphor and Symbol*, 19(4): 289–306.
Colston, Herbert L., and J. O'Brien. 2000. Contrast of kind versus contrast of magnitude: The pragmatic accomplishments of irony and hyperbole. *Discourse Processes*, 30 (2): 179–199.
Coulson, Seana, and Marta Kutas. 1998. *Frame-shifting and sentential integration.* University of California San Diego Cognitive, Science Technical Report 98-03.
Coulson, Seana, and Els Severens. 2007. Hemispheric asymmetry and pun comprehension: When cowboys have sore calves. *Brain & Language*, 100: 172–187.
Coulson, Seana, Thomas P. Urbach, and Marta Kutas. 2006. Looking back: Joke comprehension and the space structuring model. *Humor: International Journal of Humor Research*, 19: 229–250.
Cutler, Anne. 1974. *On saying what you mean without meaning what you say.* Papers from the 10th Regional Meeting of the Chicago Linguistics Society, 117–127. Chicago: Department of Linguistics, University of Chicago.
Dews, S., and Ellen Winner. 1995. Muting the meaning: A social function of irony. *Metaphor and Symbolic Activity*, 10: 3–19.

Ducharme, Lori J. 1994. Sarcasm and international politics. *Symbolic Interaction*, 17: 51–62.
Dunbar, Robin I. 2002. Language, music and laughter in evolutionary perspective. In D. Kimbrough Oller and Ulrike Griebel (eds.), *Evolution of communication systems: A comparative approach*, 257–273. Cambridge, MA: MIT Press.
Eisterhold, Jodie, Salvatore Attardo, and Diana Boxer. 2006. Reactions to irony in discourse: Evidence for the least disruption principle. *Journal of Pragmatics*, 38: 1239–1256.
Ekman, Paul, Richard J. Davidson, and Ward Friesen. 1990. The Duchenne smile: Emotional expression and brain physiology II. *Journal of Personality and Social Psychology*, 58: 342–353.
Flamson, Thomas. 2010. *Conversational humor and social networks in rural Brazil*. Doctoral Dissertation, Department of Anthropology, University of California, Los Angeles.
Flamson, Thomas, and H. Clark Barrett. 2008. The encryption theory of humor: A knowledge based mechanism of honest signaling. *Journal of Evolutionary Psychology*, 6(4): 261–281.
Flamson, T., Bryant, G. A., & Barrett, H. C. 2011. Prosody in spontaneous humor: Evidence for encryption. Pragmatics and Cognition, 19(2): 248–267.
Gibbs, Raymond W. 1994. *The poetics of mind: Figurative thought, language, and understanding*. New York: Cambridge University Press.
Gibbs, Raymond W. 2000a. Irony in talk among friends. *Metaphor and Symbol*, 15, 5–27.
Gibbs, Raymond W. 2000b. Metarepresentations in staged communicative acts. In Dan Sperber (eds.), *Metarepresentations*, 389–410. New York: Oxford University Press.
Gibbs, Raymond W. 2001. Evaluating contemporary models of figurative language understanding. *Metaphor and Symbol*, 16: 317–333.
Gibbs, Raymond W. 2006. Introspection and cognitive linguistics: Should we trust our own intuitions? *Annual Review of Cognitive Linguistics*, 4: 133–152.
Giora, Rachel. 2003. *On our mind: Salience, context, and figurative language*. New York: Oxford University Press.
Giora, Rachel, Ofer Fein, Ronie Kaufman, Dana Eisenberg, and Shani Erez. 2009. Does an "ironic situation" favor an ironic interpretation? In Geert Brône and Jeroen Vandaele (eds.), *Cognitive poetics. Goals, gains and gaps*, 383–399. Berlin: Mouton de Gruyter.
Grammer, Karl. 1990. Strangers meet: Laughter and nonverbal signs of interest in opposite sex encounters. *Journal of Nonverbal Behavior*, 14: 209–236.
Hagen, Edward H., and Gregory A. Bryant. 2003. Music and dance as a coalition signaling system. *Human Nature*, 14: 21–51.
Hasan, H., and T. F. Hasan. 2009. Laugh yourself into a healthier person: A cross cultural analysis of the effects of varying levels of laughter on health. *International Journal of Medical Sciences*, 6(4): 200–211.
Jefferson, Gail. 1979. A technique for inviting laughter and its subsequent acceptance/declination. In George Psathas (ed.), *Everyday language: Studies in ethnomethodology*, 79–211. New York, NY: Irvington Publishers.
Katz, Albert N., and Penny M. Pexman. 1997. Interpreting figurative statements: Speaker occupation can change metaphor into irony. *Metaphor and Symbol*, 12: 19-41.
Kaufer, David S. 1977. Irony and rhetorical strategy. *Philosophy and Rhetoric*, 10(2): 90–110.
Keltner, Dacher, and George A. Bonanno. 1997. A study of laughter and dissociation: The distinct correlates of laughter and smiling during bereavement. *Journal of Personality and Social Psychology*, 73: 687–702.
Kreuz, Roger James, and S. Glucksberg. 1989. How to be sarcastic: The echoic reminder theory of verbal irony. *Journal of Experimental Psychology: General*, 118: 374–386.

Kreuz, Roger James, and R. Michael Roberts. 1995. Two cues for verbal irony: Hyperbole and the ironic tone of voice. *Metaphor and Symbolic Activity*, 10: 21–31.

Leggitt, J. S., and Raymond W. Gibbs. 2000. Emotional reactions to verbal irony. *Discourse Processes*, 29: 1–24.

McGraw, A. Peter, and Caleb Warren. 2010. Benign violations making immoral behavior funny. *Psychological Science*, 21(8): 1141–1149.

Miller, Geoffrey. 2001. *The mating mind: How sexual choice shaped the evolution of human nature*. New York: Anchor.

Morton, Eugene S. 1977. On the occurrence and significance of motivation-structural rules in some bird and mammal sounds. *The American Naturalist*, 111: 855–869.

Panksepp, Jaak. 2007. Neuroevolutionary sources of laughter and social joy: Modeling primal human laughter in laboratory rats. *Behavioral Brain Research*, 182: 231–244.

Pexman, Penny M., and K. M. Olineck. 2002. Understanding irony: How do stereotypes cue speaker intent? *Journal of Language and Social Psychology*, 21(3): 245–274.

Pickering, Lucy, M. Corduas, Jodie Eisterhold, B. Seifried, A. Eggleston, and Salvatore Attardo. 2009. Prosodic markers of saliency in humorous narratives. *Discourse Processes*, 46: 517–540.

Provine, Robert R. 1993. Laughter punctuates speech: Linguistic, social and gender contexts of laughter. *Ethology*, 95: 291–298.

Provine, Robert R. 2000. *Laughter: A scientific investigation*. New York: Viking.

Ritchie, David. 2005. Frame-shifting in humor and irony. *Metaphor and Symbol*, 20: 275–294.

Ritchie, Graeme. 2001. *The linguistic analysis of jokes*. London: Routledge.

Rockwell, P. 2000. Lower, slower, louder: Vocal cues of sarcasm. *Journal of Psycholinguistic Research*, 29(5): 483–495.

Smoski, Moria J., and Jo-Anne Bachorowski. 2003a. Antiphonal laughter between friends and strangers. *Cognition and Emotion*, 17: 327–340.

Smoski, Moria J., and Jo-Anne Bachorowski. 2003b. Antiphonal laughter in developing friendships. *Annals of the New York Academy of Sciences*, 1000: 300–303.

Sperber, Daniel, and Deirdre Wilson. 1995. *Relevance: Communication and cognition*. Cambridge: Harvard University Press.

Vettin, J, and D Todt. 2005. Human laughter, social play and play vocalizations of non-human primates: An evolutionary approach. *Behaviour*, 142: 217–240.

Whalen, J, and Penny M. Pexman. 2010. How do children respond to verbal irony in face-to-face communication? The development of mode adoption across middle childhood. *Discourse Processes*, 47: 363–387.

Wilson, Margaret, and T. P. Wilson. 2005. An oscillator model of the timing of turn-taking. *Psychonomic Bulletin and Review*, 12(6): 957–968.

Seana Coulson
9 Frame-shifting and frame semantics: Joke comprehension on the space structuring model

Consider how one might understand the following ad, "For Sale, Parachute. Used once; never opened; small stain." Although there are no explicit cues to do so, the reader naturally recruits knowledge about how and why parachutes are normally used in order to construe the listed features of this chute as being causally related to one another. Empirical support for the importance of such causal and relational information in language comprehension comes from the consistent finding that memory for short texts includes inferred material (Sanford 1981). Further, computational considerations imply that language comprehension involves a capacity for dynamic inferencing based on general knowledge represented as frames (Lange 1989).

Invented somewhat independently by researchers in the field of linguistics (Fillmore 1968), psycholinguistics (Sanford 1981), artificial intelligence (Minsky 1975), and natural language processing (Schank 1977), frame-type data structures are often invoked to account for inferential aspects of language comprehension (Fillmore 1982). As used here, frames are representations with slot/filler structure, default values, and weak constraints on the type of fillers for a given slot (Barsalou 1992). Frames contain causal and relational information, are organized hierarchically so as to allow recursive embedding of frames within frames, and can be used to represent knowledge about a wide variety of objects, actions, and events.

In linguistics, frame semantics is a research program in which a word's semantic properties are described with respect to the way that they highlight aspects of an associated frame (Osswald & Van Valin 2014). For example, *buy* and *sell* both evoke the Commercial Transaction frame. But *buy* highlights the buyer and the goods, while *sell* highlights the seller and the money. Background knowledge thus figures prominently in the establishment of meaning, as language functions against the backdrop of conceptual structure. Below we examine the utility of frame semantics for models of language comprehension, and focus on its capacity to explain the sorts of inference needed to understand the parachute joke.

In section 1, we consider the role that pragmatics plays in on-line meaning construction, contrasting the view that context-independent meaning is *supplemented* with background and contextual knowledge with the view that background and contextual knowledge is *essential* for the construction of meaning.

Although most people working in pragmatics subscribe to varying versions of the latter, these portraits of the semantics/pragmatics interface have had very limited on language researchers in psychology, computer science, and cognitive science (c.f. Hagoort & vanBerkum 2007). One exception to this trend is the space structuring model (Coulson 2001), a model of language comprehension inspired by ideas in cognitive linguistics. Section 2 outlines some assumptions of the model, and sections 3 and 4 describe experimental work on joke comprehension designed to test some of those assumptions. Section 5 reviews the adequacy of some frame-based models in cognitive science, and offers some speculations about the future of this approach.

1 Pragmatics: What's that?

On the classical approach to language, pragmatics is defined largely by what semantics leaves out (Gazdar 1979). This definition involves positing an implicit model of comprehension in which purely linguistic knowledge of meaning is used to determine sentence meaning. To determine *utterance* meaning, all that remains is to bring background knowledge and contextual information to bear on sentence meaning. Indeed the core phenomena in pragmatics are deixis, speech acts, and implicature – all topics in which the primary concern is how contextual factors modulate interpretation.

One problematic aspect of the classical view of meaning is that it relegates pragmatics to the role of disambiguator. Katz and Fodor (1963), for example, argued that a viable theory of semantics would require a theory of pragmatics that would disambiguate sentences vis-à-vis their contexts of utterance. In a sentence about a pawn in a chess game, pragmatics is supposed to answer the question "Which pawn?" Similarly, a prominent function of pragmatics on the traditional view is to give content to indexicals. Thus, on such an account, pragmatics is what answers questions such as "Who are *you*?" and "Where is *here*?"

Although few people working in pragmatics are likely to agree to exactly this characterization, unfortunately, it still captures the way that many linguists and psycholinguists think about language in context. In psycholinguistics, in particular, context is understood almost exclusively in terms of its role in the resolution of ambiguities in lexical meaning (Duffy et al. 2001; Sheridan & Rheingold 2012) and syntactic structure (Clifton and Staub 2008; Frazier 1995; Spivey-Knowlton 1994; Spivey-Knowlton, Trueswell & Tanenhaus 2013). To the psycholinguist, then, pragmatics is what answers the question, "Is that *funny* 'haha' or *funny* 'weird'?" Similarly, when confronted with the statement "Tonight we'll discuss sex with the President," pragmatics is what tells us whether the President will be the *topic* of discussion, or a *participant* in it.

While these are all valuable contributions, and disambiguator is a perfectly respectable occupation, it is not (I believe) the role that background and contextual knowledge in fact plays in meaning construction. Though presumably motivated by the observation that many words have many meanings, the pragmatics as disambiguator model is ultimately undermined by careful consideration of the way in which word meaning changes from context to context. Although *tomato* is not ambiguous in the examples below, Johnson-Laird has pointed out that different features of tomatoes are salient in (1) than in (2) (Johnson-Laird 1993).

(1) The tomato rolled across the floor.

(2) He accidentally sat on a tomato.

Examples such as this would seem to argue against a view in which the speaker's knowledge of the context of utterance helps her to adjudicate between a finite set of determinate meanings. Rather, background knowledge about tomatoes is used to enrich the cognitive models constructed to represent the referential situation depicted in the sentences. Moreover, various pragmatic functions are available that allow any noun to refer to an infinite set of related phenomena. For example, *BMW* can be used to refer to all sorts of BMW-related things, including stock in the company, as in (3), the building that houses the company, as in (4), or shattered BMW car parts as in (5).

(3) He bought 6,000 shares of BMW.

(4) He works next door at BMW.

(5) My ex- planted a bomb in my car and I've been cleaning up BMW ever since.

Similarly, Clark has pointed out that these sorts of mechanisms allow speakers to improvise word meanings ad infinitum (Clark 1983). For example, in an article about choosing a college roommate based on the appliances she owns, "computer" can mean roommate who owns a computer, as in (6).

(6) Our computer fell in love and left school.

The problem with the pragmatics as disambiguator model is that while it presumes that computing utterance meaning is difficult because language is semantically *ambiguous*, the difficulty really lies in the fact that language is semantically *indeterminate*. Rather than helping to adjudicate between pre-specified meanings, it would seem that context plays a constitutive role in the construction of meaning (Coulson 2006; Frisson 2009). Moreover, any mechanism that can account for the way that people can deal with semantic indeterminacy, ought to account quite trivially for semantic ambiguity as well. Rather than attempting to explain how pragmatic factors disambiguate a fully specified meaning constructed by semantics, then, it makes more sense to explore how pragmatic mechanisms contribute to the specification of meaning in the first place.

2 Space structuring model

On the space structuring model (Coulson 2001), a model of language comprehension motivated by ideas in mental space theory (Fauconnier 1994), conceptual blending theory (Fauconnier and Turner 1998; Fauconnier and Turner 2002), and cognitive grammar (Langacker 1987), perceptual input, language input, social context, and the speaker's current cognitive state all contribute to the construction of cognitive models of the discourse situation. This can include models of the referential aspects of sentences as well as models relevant to the agent's social and material goals. Both linguistic and non-linguistic cues prompt the retrieval of frames from long-term memory, and these frames are exploited in the construction of cognitive models of the message-level representation.

Three assumptions of the model include:
(i) *the embodiment assumption*, that the structure of language at least partially reflects bodily constraints on perception and action;
(ii) *the immediacy assumption*, that the integration of linguistic and non-linguistic information occurs rapidly, and does not (necessarily) require the prior construction of a propositional representation of sentence meaning;
(iii) *the elaboration assumption*, that language comprehension involves animating the cognitive models constructed by the listener.

In traditional frame-based approaches (Schank 1977), comprehension requires frames to be bound to contextually available elements. However, in the space structuring model, this need not be the case. At times comprehension can proceed by binding slots or attributes in the activated frame. However, often the frame serves only to constrain the construction of a cognitive model that is particularized to the discourse situation. Like the frames that inform them, these cognitive models are hierarchically organized, have attribute/value structure, and a mechanism that assigns default values for unspecified attributes. Though schematic and partial, these models are detailed enough to enable small-scale simulations of the scenarios they represent (as in the mental models described by Norman 1974; see also, Singer 2012).

For example, if a listener heard the sentence in (7), she might, at one level at least, respond by constructing a model of the referential situation described by the speaker.

(7) When I asked the bartender for something cold and full of rum, he recommended his daquiri.

Of course, at other levels the listener might be building models related to why the speaker might make this particular statement, what the speaker's attitude is toward her, or many other things. Nonetheless, at the referential level, the listener combines linguistic information with background knowledge to build a cognitive model of an interaction between a customer and a bartender.

The fact that speakers build models like this, and the extent to which those developing models guide their expectations is perhaps best appreciated by examining examples in which those expectations are violated. For example, (8) is very similar to (7) but prompts the construction of a very different cognitive model.

(8) When I asked the bartender for something cold and full of rum, he recommended his wife.

Rather than recommending a drink, the bartender in (8) has just insulted his wife. The semantic and pragmatic reanalysis that reorganizes existing elements in the message-level representation is known as *frame-shifting* (Coulson 2001). With the activation of background knowledge and the establishment of mappings between counterpart structure in the old frame and in the new one, the bartender's wife is accused of being a frigid lush.

In fact, jokes are deliberately constructed to suggest one frame while evoking elements consistent with another. While frame-shifting is not unique to jokes, jokes differ from more 'everyday' examples in the extent to which the need to shift is clearly demarcated. For example, in (9) the reader begins by evoking a frame in which a busy professional pays an accountant to do his taxes.

(9) I let my accountant do my taxes because it saves time: last spring it saved me ten years.

The disjunctor *years*, however, forces the reader to go back and reinterpret *time* to evoke a frame where a crooked businessman pays an accountant to conceal his illegal business dealings. The word *time* is called a *connector* because it serves as a bridge between the two frames. Merely knowing that *time* refers to time in prison does not in and of itself explain why the accountant is doing the man's taxes, or how doing so will prevent a prison sentence. A full understanding of (9) requires recruitment of background knowledge about the particular sorts of relationships that can obtain between business people and their accountants so that the initial busy professional interpretation can be mapped into the crooked-businessman frame.

Frame-shifting involves a dramatic reorganization of the message-level aspects of the utterance, most of which can't be attributed to compositional mechanisms of reanalysis. For example, most examples of frame-shifts in jokes don't require the listener to instantiate a new structural analysis of the sentence. Though the listener is led down a pragmatic garden path, it is often the case that pragmatic reanalysis proceeds without syntactic reanalysis. In (8), for example, *wife* is the object of *recommended* just as *daquiri* is in (7), the straight version of (8). In (9), the joke interpretation actually requires the reader to abandon the fully grammatical reading of "saved me ten years" for something akin to "saved me jail time," which is questionable at best.

Further, such cases of frame-shifting frequently require the creation of nonce senses. For example, in the accountant joke in (9) "saves time" is re-interpreted as meaning "prevents me from having to do time." In the case of the bartender's wife, "full of rum" comes to mean "alcoholic." However, the construction of these somewhat novel phrasal meanings is as much the *effect* of frame-shifting as the *cause*. That is, it seems likely that understanding the novel reading of "full of rum" at least partially depends on the construal of the bartender's speech act as an insult. Moreover, the adaptation of the idiomatic meaning of *time* in (9) as in ("do time") is only congruous because of a stereotyped scenario that involves accountants obscuring illegal business dealings.

3 The psychological reality of frame-shifting

Demonstration of the psychological reality of frame-shifting, then, would suggest a role for pragmatics that goes beyond pragmatics the disambiguator. In particular, frame-shifting suggests that lexical processing does not simply benefit from context, but actively contributes to it. Moreover, background and contextual knowledge do not merely help the listener to specify the meaning of indexicals and disambiguate the meaning of lexical items, but, rather, are crucial for the construction of the message-level representation. Below we discuss the results of studies using three different techniques that establish the psychological reality of frame-shifting: self-paced reading times, eye movement registration, and event-related brain potentials.

3.1 Self-paced reading times

To demonstrate the psychological reality of frame-shifting, Coulson and Kutas (1998) conducted a variety of experiments using the self-paced reading time technique. In this experimental paradigm, the task is to read sentences one word at a time, pressing a button to advance to the next word. As each word appears, the preceding word disappears, so that the experimenter gets a record of how long the participant spent reading each word in the sentence.

Stimuli for this experiment were comprised of one-line jokes that required frame-shifting for their comprehension, and straight versions of the same sentences that did not require a frame-shift. Moreover, because we wanted to be able to detect the effect of frame-shifting on the processing of a single word, the *disjunctor*, or frame-shifting trigger, was always a sentence-final noun. In order to find out what sort of non-joke frames people constructed for these sentences, we performed a norming task in which people were given the jokes minus the last word and asked to complete the sentence with the first word or phrase that came to mind. This is known as a *cloze task*, and the percentage of people who offer a given word in a given sentence context is known as the *cloze probability* of that word in that particular sentence context.

Results of the cloze task enabled Coulson and Kutas to ascertain readers' default (non-joke) interpretation for the sentences. However, it also revealed a disparity in the cloze probability of the most popular response for the items, suggesting that some of the sentence fragments provided a more constraining context than others. For example, (10) elicited a similar response from 81% of the participants, while (11) elicited many different responses, albeit mostly from the gambling frame.

(10)   I asked the woman at the party if she remembered me from last year and she said she never forgets a (face 81%).

(11) My husband took the money we were saving to buy a new car and blew it all at the (casino 18%).

As a result, two types of jokes were tested: high constraint jokes like (10) which elicited at least one response with a cloze probability of greater than 40%, and low constraint jokes like (11) which elicited responses with cloze probabilities of less than 40%. To control for the fact that the joke endings are (by definition) unexpected, the straight controls were chosen so that they matched the joke endings for cloze probability, but were consistent with the frame evoked by the context. For example, the straight ending for (10) was *name* (the joke ending was *dress*); while the straight ending for (11) was *tables* (the joke ending was *movies*). The cloze probability of all four ending types (high and low constraint joke and straight endings) was equal, and ranged from 0% to 5%.

Given the impact of frame-shifting on the interpretation of one-line jokes, one might expect the underlying processes to take time, and, consequently result in increased reading times for jokes that require frame-shifting than "straight" versions of the same sentences. Coulson and Kutas (1998) found that readers spent longer on the joke than the straight endings, and that this difference in reading times was larger and more robust in the high constraint sentences. This finding suggests there was a processing cost associated with frame-shifting reflected in increased reading times for the joke endings, especially in high constraint sentences that allow readers to commit to a particular interpretation of the sentence.

3.2 Eye movement registration

The self-paced reading paradigm is a good technique for establishing that one kind of sentence requires more processing time than another (presumably very comparable) type of sentence. However, one drawback to this technique is its lack of ecological validity. In contrast to normal reading, participants in a self-paced reading task are permitted to see only one word at a time, and moreover, are not permitted to look back at earlier regions of the sentence. In contrast, in free reading, people frequently move their eyes leftward (or *regress*) to re-examine earlier parts of the text. Another deficit of the self-paced reading paradigm is that it provides little information about the *nature* of the processing difficulty that readers encounter. For example, longer reading times for sentences that ended as jokes than straight controls in Coulson and Kutas (1998) suggests the jokes engendered more processing difficulty. However, reading time data do not indicate whether this difficulty occurs in the initial stages of word processing, or later as the reader moves on to inferential aspects of processing.

To address these questions, Coulson, Urbach and Kutas (2006) conducted an eye movement study comparing reading times for sentences that ended as jokes to reading times for the same sentences with the unexpected straight endings (Coulson and Kutas 1998). They found that just as in the reading time study, readers spent reliably longer on the joke endings, and that this difference was far more pronounced for the high constraint sentences. Moreover, this effect arose in the later stages of processing associated with subsequent fixations of the sentence final word (rather than in the initial phase of processing). Further, in both high and low constraint sentences, participants were more likely to regress when they encountered joke endings than straight ones. This finding is consistent with the psychological reality of frame-shifting, suggesting readers literally revisit aspects of the preceding context in order to get the jokes.

3.3 Event-related brain potentials

Another way of assessing readers' on-line comprehension of language materials is to use event-related brain potentials (henceforth ERPs). ERPs provide an on-going record of brain activity related to various kinds of sensory, motor, and cognitive processing events. The physical basis of the ERP signal is the fact that when large groups of neurons (on the order of tens of thousands) fire simultaneously, they create an electrical field in the brain that can be detected with electrodes at the scalp via the electroencephalogram (henceforth EEG). The ERP is obtained by applying electrodes to the scalp, recording participants' EEG, and averaging across events within experimental categories. Because the averaging process presumably cancels out the EEG that is not related to the experimenter's categories, the remaining signal represents the brain activity related to the processing of the experimental stimuli. By comparing the ERPs to different sorts of stimuli, the researcher can assess how changing the nature of the cognitive task modulates the brain response.

Because eye movements necessary for normal reading produce artifacts in the EEG, ERP reading experiments typically involve presenting sentences one word at a time in the center of a computer monitor. EEG can thus be time-locked to the onset of each word on the monitor, and the resultant ERP represents brain activity associated with reading a particular category of words (i.e., the last word of an incongruous sentence). The ERP is a waveform with a series of positive and negative peaks (often called *components*) that can be correlated with various types of processing. Components are generally labeled by reference to their polarity (P for positive-going and N for negative-going activity), and their latency, or when they occur relative to either the onset of the stimulus event or to other ERP components.

In a classic ERP language experiment, Kutas and Hillyard (Kutas and Hillyard 1980) contrasted ERPs elicited by visually presented sentences that ended congruously, as in (12), with ERPs elicited by sentences that ended incongruously, as in (13).

(12) I take my coffee with cream and sugar.

(13) I take my coffee with cream and socks.

They found a negativity in the brainwaves that was much larger for incongruous sentence completions than the congruous ones. Because it peaks about 400 milliseconds after the onset of a visually presented word, this negativity is called N400.

Over forty years of research have revealed reliable relationships between the nature of various stimulus and task manipulations designed to alter participants' cognitive state, and corresponding modulations of ERP components. For example, the P1 component is the first positive deflection in the ERP elicited by visually presented words. This component, evident 70–100 milliseconds after the word is shown (or post-word onset), reflects early sensory and vision-related attentional processing. Mangun, Hillyard and Luck (Mangun 1993) have proposed that the P1 component reflects a gating mechanism responsible for modulating the width of the attentional spotlight. P1, N1, and P2 components elicited during reading probably reflect the visual feature extraction necessary to relate the visual stimulus to information in memory (Kutas and King 1996).

Most ERP studies of language processing have focused on longer latency components, such as the N400. Because the N400 was initially reported as a brain response to incongruous sentence completions (Kutas and Hillyard 1980), many people mistakenly believe it is only elicited by semantic anomalies. However, research indicates it is a far more generally elicited ERP component associated with semantic retrieval prompted by a the stimulus (see Kutas & Federmeier, 2011 for a review). In fact, N400 is elicited by *all* words, spoken, signed, or read, and its size, or amplitude, is an index of the difficulty of semantic activation. The best predictor of N400 amplitude is a word's cloze probability in a particular sentence: N400 is small for high cloze expected completions like *sugar* in (12), large for low cloze completions like *socks* in (13), and intermediate amplitude for sentence final words of intermediate cloze probability.

Besides providing an on-going record of brain activity during language processing, ERP data can complement reaction time data such as that collected in the self-paced reading and eye movement registration paradigms discussed above. These two kinds of data are often complementary as reaction time data can provide an estimate of how long a given processing event took, while ERP data can suggest whether distinct processes were used in its generation. An experimental manipulation that produces a reaction time effect might produce two or more ERP effects, each of which is affected by different sorts of manipulations. To the extent that ERP effects can be identified with specific cognitive processes (i.e., the N400 and semantic retrieval), they provide some evidence of *how* processing differs in the different conditions (King 1995).

With this in mind, Coulson and Kutas (2001) recorded participants' brainwaves as they read sentences that ended either as jokes or with unexpected straight endings (Coulson and Kutas 1998). In an ERP study of the brain response to jokes like those discussed in the previous section, Coulson and Kutas found that ERPs to the joke endings differed in several respects from those to the straight endings, depending on contextual constraint as well as participants' ability to get the jokes. In poor joke comprehenders, jokes elicited a negativity in the ERPs between 300 and 700 milliseconds after the onset of the disjunctor. In good joke comprehenders, high but not low constraint endings elicited a larger N400 (300–500 ms post-onset) than the straights. Also, in this group, both sorts of jokes (high and low constraint) elicited a positivity in the ERP (500–900 ms post-onset) as well as a slow, sustained negativity over left frontal sites. Multiple ERP effects of frame-shifting suggest the processing difficulty associated with joke comprehension involves multiple neural generators operating with slightly different time- courses.

3.4 Summary

Taken together, these three studies of frame-shifting in jokes are far more informative than any one study alone. The self-paced reading time studies suggested that frame-shifting needed for joke comprehension exerts a processing cost that was especially evident in high constraint sentence contexts (Coulson 1998). The eye movement study of the same stimulus set confirmed that the processing cost of frame-shifting was evident under more natural reading conditions, and replicated the finding that differences between reading times for joke and straight endings were much larger for high constraint sentences. Moreover, the eye movement study suggested that the processing cost was not at the level of word recognition (indexed by the length of a reader's initial fixation of a word), but was related to higher-level processing indexed by the total amount of time spent looking at the word (that is the sum of the time that elapsed during the initial fixation as well as all subsequent fixations). Coulson, Urbach and Kutas (2006) also found that people were more likely to make regressive eye movements when they read the joke than the straight endings, suggesting they wanted to re-examine earlier parts of the sentence for clues to which alternative frames should be retrieved.

ERP results from the study by Coulson and Kutas (2001) also suggest the processing cost associated with frame-shifting is related to higher-level processing. In the case of the high constraint jokes, the difficulty includes the semantic retrieval process indexed by the N400, as well as the processes indexed by the late-developing ERP effects. In the case of the low constraint jokes, the difficulty was confined to the processes indexed by the late-developing ERP effects. The added difference in semantic retrieval indexed by the N400 may explain why the joke effects on both reading times and gaze durations were more pronounced for high constraint sentences than for low. Because the late developing ERP effects were only evident for good joke comprehenders who successfully frame-shifted, they are more likely to be direct indices of the semantic and pragmatic reanalysis processes involved in joke comprehension. The temporally extended nature of these effects – lasting at least 400 ms – is also consistent with the idea that they index the construction of the message-level representation.

4 The neural substrate of frame-shifting

Another way of exploring the computational demands of frame-shifting is to look at the overlap in the brain regions underlying joke comprehension and those invoked for comparable language comprehension tasks. Interestingly, joke comprehension is thought to recruit brain regions above and beyond the set of left hemisphere (henceforth LH) areas thought to underlie core language abilities. Neuropsychologists have suggested that joke comprehension is particularly compromised in patients with right hemisphere (henceforth RH) lesions, especially when there is damage to the frontal lobe (Brownell et al. 1983; Shammi and Stuss 1999). Classic studies have assessed patients' ability to choose the punch line for a joke from an array that includes both straightforward and non sequitur endings as distracter items. On such tests, right hemisphere damage (RHD) patients have tended to choose the non sequitur endings, suggesting they understood that jokes involve a surprise ending, but had difficulty with the frame-shifting process required to re-establish coherence (Brownell et al. 1983).

The pattern of deficits in RHD patients differs dramatically from those evidenced by LHD patients whose communicative difficulties are seemingly more severe. To compare the performance of LHD and RHD patients on joke comprehension, Bihrle and colleagues used both verbal (jokes) and nonverbal (cartoons) materials with the same narrative structure (Bihrle et al. 1986). Patients were asked to pick the punch-line (or punch frame) from an array of four choices: a straightforward ending, a neutral non sequitur, a humorous non sequitur, or the correct punch-line. Though both LHD and RHD groups were impaired on this task, their errors were qualitatively different. RHD patients showed a consistent preference for humorous non sequitur endings over straightforward endings and correct punch-lines; in contrast, LHD patients more often chose the straightforward endings than either of the non sequitur endings (Bihrle et al. 1986). RHD patients displayed preserved appreciation of the slapstick depicted in the humorous non sequitur endings, but were impaired at the frame-shifting needed to understand the correct punch lines.

One attempt to link the deficits observed in RHD patients to hemispheric asymmetries evident in healthy adults is Beeman's coarse coding hypothesis (Beeman and Chiarello 1998; Beeman et al. 1994). According to this hypothesis, words in the RH are represented by means of wide semantic fields, while words in the LH are represented via a narrow range of features relevant to the immediate discourse context. Because jokes frequently require the integration of novel information, the reinterpretation of a word or phrase, and the reinterpretation of the scenario depicted by the preceding context, diffuse RH activation might provide additional information that makes joke processing easier. Similarly, Coulson and Wu (2005) have suggested that semantic activations in the RH include causal and relational information crucial for frame-shifting. Reduced access to these semantic activations in RH damaged patients could result in joke comprehension deficits.

Several studies in our laboratory have addressed whether hemispheric differences in semantic activation are relevant for joke comprehension. In one study, we recorded ERPs as healthy adults read laterally presented "punch words" to one-line jokes (Coulson and Williams 2005). Lateral presentation of critical words was intended to affect which cerebral hemisphere received the initial information from the stimulus, and to increase the participation of that hemisphere in the processing of the stimulus. The organization of the visual system is such that words presented in the left visual field (henceforth LVF) are initially processed in the RH, while words presented in the right visual field (henceforth RVF) are initially processed in the LH. In healthy adults, the visual information is rapidly transferred to the other hemisphere. Nonetheless, lateral presentation shifts the balance of processing to favor the hemisphere that initially received the visual information, and as such can give us clues to processing differences between the two halves of the brain.

In our study of how lateral presentation impacts ERPs to jokes, the N400 component was of particular interest, as its amplitude indexes the difficulty of retrieving semantic information appropriate for the discourse context (Kutas & Federmeier, 2011; Kutas & Van Petten, 1994). As noted above, the critical word in a joke often elicits a larger N400 than a similarly unexpected "straight" ending for the same sentence: the N400 joke effect (Coulson and Kutas 2001). We reasoned that if hemispheric differences in semantic activation are relevant for joke comprehension, lateral presentation of joke (GIRL) versus straight (BALL) endings for sentences such as "A replacement player hit a home run with my" would result in different N400 joke effects as a function of visual field of presentation.

In this sentence comprehension paradigm, the difficulty of joke comprehension is indexed by the size of the N400 joke effect with larger effects pointing to relatively more processing difficulty. In fact, N400 joke effects were smaller when the critical words were presented to the LVF/RH than the RVF/LH, suggesting joke comprehension was easier with LVF presentation and consistent with the claim that coarse coding in the RH facilitates joke comprehension (Coulson and Williams 2005).

In a similarly motivated study, we measured ERPs elicited by laterally presented probe words that were preceded either by a joke, or by a non-funny control (Coulson and Wu 2005). Since all jokes turned on the last word of the sentence, control sentences were formed by replacing the sentence final word with a "straight" ending. For example, the straight ending for "Everyone had so much fun diving from the tree into the swimming pool, we decided to put in a little water," was "platform." Probes (such as *crazy*) were designed to be related to the meaning of the joke, but unrelated to the meaning of the straight control. In this sentence prime paradigm, the activation of information relevant to joke comprehension was signaled by differences in the size of the N400 elicited by related versus unrelated probes. The more active joke-related information was, the larger the N400 relatedness effect could be expected to be. Consistent with the coarse coding hypothesis, we found larger N400 relatedness effects with LVF/RH presentation suggesting joke-related information was more active in the RH (Hull, Chen, Vaid and Martinez 2005 for comparable evidence using behavioral measures).

The importance of the RH in understanding narrative jokes, however, contrasts with its importance in understanding the word play in puns. Coulson and

Severens (2007) addressed hemispheric sensitivity to the different meanings of a pun using a sentence prime paradigm with puns and pun-related probe words. We recorded ERPs as healthy adults listened to puns and read probe words presented in either participants' left or right visual fields. Probe words were either highly related to the pun that preceded them, moderately related to the pun that preceded them, or were unrelated to the pun that preceded them. For example, the highly related probe for "During branding cowboys have sore calves," was "cow" and the moderately related probe was "leg".

The activation of pun-related information was assessed by the presence of relatedness effects on the N400 component of the ERP and on positive waveforms that frequently follow the N400 such as the late positive complex (henceforth LPC). With an ISI of 0ms, we observed similarly sized priming effects for both the highly and moderately related probes with RVF/LH presentation; with LVF/RH presentation, we observed priming for the highly but not the moderately related probes. With an ISI of 500 ms, we observed similarly sized N400 relatedness effects for highly and moderately related probes with presentation to the RVF/LH as well as the LVF/RH. In addition, RVF/LH, but not LVF/RH presentation, resulted in a larger centro-parietally distributed LPC for related probes. In sum, these results suggest that initially both meanings of a pun were equally active in the LH while only the highly related probes were active in the RH. By 500 ms after the offset of the pun, both meanings were available in both hemispheres.

The importance of the LH for pun comprehension thus contrasts with the role of the RH in understanding simple narrative jokes of comparable complexity in terms of vocabulary and grammar. Presumably this relates to the relative import of the retrieval of word meanings in puns versus frame semantic information involved in narrative jokes. While narrative jokes begin by suggesting one interpretation of the discourse situation only to replace it with another at the punch line (Giora 1991, 2003), the point of puns is simply to promote both meanings of an ambiguous word or phrase. The LH advantage observed in Coulson and Severens (2007) may reflect the importance of this hemisphere (especially the left frontal lobe) in coding the association between a word's form and its meaning.

In fact, a neuroimaging study that compared narrative jokes with non-funny controls revealed bilateral temporal lobe activations, while an analogous comparison using puns revealed left frontal activations (Goel and Dolan 2001). Whereas the frontal activations to puns were consistent with the need to retrieve word meanings, the temporal lobe activations in both the left and the right hemispheres presumably reflect memory processes important for frame-shifting.

5 Integration

The research reviewed above suggests that the relationship between a word and its surrounding context is multifold. This relationship involves both the way that individual words add to the cognitive models active in working memory, and the way that individual words can prompt the construction of new models. Of course, the experiments reviewed above do not substantiate all of the theoretical claims we have made. They merely establish that people spend longer reading jokes than straight versions of the same sentences, that jokes prompt more regressive eye movements, that jokes elicit slightly different brainwaves, and that the recruitment of right hemisphere brain regions is more important for jokes that rely on frame-shifting, than for puns which do not. These findings are, however, consistent with the psychological reality of frame-shifting, and highlight the importance of this process for any comprehensive account of meaning construction.

Frame-shifting seems to occur whenever it is necessary to represent the relationship between two or more objects, actions, or events. If the disjunctor, or frame-shifting trigger, cannot be sensibly incorporated into existing structure, the words that served to evoke that structure are reanalyzed to provide a coherent bridge between the initial and the revised representations. The relationship between the disjunctor and the connector can be suggested by grammatical clues, conceptual relationships, or a combination of the two.

Interestingly, frame-shifting presents a bit of a paradox for traditional frame-based models of language comprehension. On the one hand, the computational challenge of connecting an initial interpretation to the reinterpretation seems to require essential properties of frames, including the representation of causal and relational information, attribute/value (or slot/filler) organization, and the existence of default values. On the other hand, given the rigidity of the frame as a data structure (e.g. Allen 1987; Wilensky 1986), it is highly questionable as to whether frame-based models can accommodate the demands of frame-shifting.

5.1 Traditional implementations of frames

Wilensky (1986), for example, has argued that scripts are rigid data structures that cannot accommodate events that are out of the ordinary. While knowledge of typical scenarios represented in scripts and frames is necessary for understanding narrative jokes, it is far from sufficient. For example, in (14), the word water is surprising, not because it is unusual to put water in a swimming pool, but because it would be unusual not to.

(14) Everyone had so much fun diving from the tree into the swimming pool we decided to put in a little water.

Presumably, the swimming pool frame constructed to understand (14) has a *Contains(x)* slot that has been filled by its default value *water*. Interpretation of (14) indeed relies on knowledge of the typical backyard swimming pool. The first clause ("Everyone had so much fun diving from the tree into the swimming pool,") evokes a model of people having fun diving from a tree into a backyard swimming pool. Moreover, cloze data collected by Coulson and Kutas (1998) suggests the second clause ("we decided to put in a little...") is initially interpreted as referring to the owner's decision to install a piece of equipment commonly found near backyard swimming pools that might function in an analogous way to the tree (e.g. a diving board).

The disjunctor *water* prompts the reader to revise a default assumption of the *Backyard swimming* frame, namely that there was water in the pool. Revising this simple assumption has substantial implications for the consequences of diving from the tree into the pool, and for the mindset of those who enjoy such activities. However, it is unlikely that these implications are represented in generic frames for *Backyard Swimming Pools*, and less likely that these implications can be logically derived from them.

The challenge of frame-shifting is to create a new super-frame and to adapt previously created structure accordingly. While a traditional script- or frame-based system can generate a new slot in response to an unexpected event, it is unable to compute the relationship between unexpected and normal events, because its inferencing capacity is based on knowledge represented in the frame itself. In many cases, there is simply no frame that can be recruited to relate events to one another. Ironically, traditional implementations of frames are completely inadequate for modeling the semantic reorganization involved in frame-shifting.

5.2 Sub-symbolic implementations of frames

The need for a sufficiently flexible implementation of frames has driven some researchers to explore the adequacy of sub-symbolic processing in neural networks (McClelland 1986). The propensity of these networks to display (a) graceful degradation, viz. arriving at a best guess given imperfect information, (b) spontaneous generalization, that is, accommodating inputs that do not conform to previously instantiated schemas, and (c) the ability to arrive at a compromise solution to mutual constraint satisfaction problems is compatible with the flexibility people show in their interpretation of jokes.

The early promise of this approach can be seen in a model proposed by Rumelhart and colleagues (Rumelhart 1986) that classifies rooms in a house based on their contents (e.g. whether they have beds, chairs, refrigerators, and so on). Units in the network represent semantic micro-features, and the weights between units encode correlations between those micro-features. The network is set up to promote excitatory weights between micro-features that co-occur, and inhibitory weights between features that do not. If the network has experienced a high correlation between the mutual activations of stove, refrigerator, and counter, when the stove unit is activated, the network (using a gradient descent algorithm) activates correlated micro-features (e.g., refrigerator, counter) until it settles into a kitchen frame.

While the model by Rumelhart and colleagues reveals the flexibility of probabilistic approaches, it is incapable of representing information needed to get the jokes discussed above. This is because it contains no mechanisms for generating the high-level inferences that relate frames to one another. A more sophisticated model by St. John is able to use co-occurrence frequencies in its input to infer default information, and to modify its predictions about upcoming events in a way that is sensitive to context (St. John 1992). However, St. John's model is limited in much the same way as symbolic implementations: information that deviates too much from stored frames cannot be accommodated. Because it is unable to compute the relationships between different higher-level representations, St. John's (1992) model is incapable of combining information from different scripts in any sensible way.

Lange and Dyer (1989) propose a structured connectionist model called ROBIN (role-binding network) that explicitly attempts to capture inferential revisions in frame-shifting. ROBIN uses connections between nodes to encode semantic knowledge represented in a frame type data structure. Each frame has one or more slots, and slots have constraints on the type of fillers to which they can be bound. The relationships between frames are represented by excitatory and inhibitory connections between nodes and the pathways between corresponding slots. Once initial role assignments have been made, ROBIN propagates evidential activation values in order to compute inferences from the information the programmers have given it.

Inference is understood as resulting from the spread of activation across the connections between related frames and competing slot-fillers. For example, connections between frames for *Transfer-Inside* and *Inside-of* allow the system to 'infer' *Inside-of (Pizza, Oven)* from *Transfer-Inside (Seana, Pizza, Oven)*. In this model, frame selection is entirely a matter of spreading activation. Because each slot has a number of binding nodes, all of the meanings of an ambiguous word can serve as candidate bindings. Candidate bindings can be activated simultaneously, and the binding node with the greatest evidential activation eventually wins out. Because multiple frames are activated in parallel, contextual information can further activate an already highly activated node (or set of nodes), thus confirming an initial interpretation. Alternatively, contextual information can activate a previously less-active interpretation, thus implementing frame-shifting.

The neurally inspired architecture of these models contributes important advances over traditional, symbolic implementations of frames. Advances include probabilistic representations, parallel activations, and the use of spreading activation mechanisms. However, none of these models have the capacity to creatively combine frames, to draw inferences that require an understanding of the relationship between frames, or to construct novel frames in response to contextual demands. While sub-symbolic implementations of frames represent an improvement over traditional frame-based models, they share many of the same limitations.

5.3 Grounded frames

The best way to achieve the flexible interpretative capacity needed for frame-shifting may be to adopt an empirically inspired architecture that is based on dynamic internal imagery (Bergen and Coulson 2006). In such models, language interpretation involves the creation of internal simulations of events that include sensory, motor, and affective dimensions. Barsalou (1999) has suggested that background knowledge is stored as perceptual symbols, schematic representations of perceptual experience stored around a common frame that promotes schematized simulations. Perceptual symbols are thus grounded in experience as the brain captures states across modalities and integrates them into a multi-modal representation stored in memory. This multi-modal representation is later reactivated to simulate relevant aspects of perception, action, and introspection.

Whereas frames have traditionally been understood as amodal knowledge structures that result from a distillation of experience, perceptual symbols are understood as having modal characteristics. Perceptual symbols recruit brain areas involved in the acquisition of the relevant concepts, and have some characteristics of analogue representations. However, perceptual symbols have also been argued to be schematic enough to implement standard symbolic functions, such as type-token relationships, recursion, and inference (Barsalou 1999).

As in traditional implementations of frames, perceptual symbols capture causal and relational information needed for frame-shifting. Moreover, because they are the product of neural learning mechanisms, perceptual symbols incorporate many of the features of sub-symbolic frames, such as partial and probabilistic activation patterns. Perhaps most importantly, the analogue character of perceptual symbols allows for novel combinations based on the affordances of the constituent concepts (Glenberg and Robertson 2000).

This model is supported by research indicating that the neural systems responsible for performing actions or perceiving percepts are also recruited for linguistically inspired simulations (Barsalou 2008). Consistent with the embodiment and elaboration assumptions in the space structuring model, recent findings suggest that language processing utilizes the perceptual and motor systems as internal models that allow for the construction of subjective experiences in the absence of motor action or perceptual input (Pecher and Zwaan 2005).

Bergen and Coulson (2006) argue that a simulation based model might account for the joke about the pool in (14). Because our experiences with pools almost without exception include water, water will automatically be activated in mental simulations that involve pools. Our experience with diving, by contrast, presumably involves some cases of landing on a solid surface, thus enabling us to viscerally imagine diving into a pool with water.

5.4 Conclusion

In accordance with the frame semantics program, we have argued that linguistic utterances cue the retrieval of abstract grammatical frames which speakers unify with frames evoked by lexical and contextual information. Meaning construction thus involves assembling a series of simple cognitive models while keeping track of common elements and relations. But, rather than just retrieving and instantiating frames, speakers are continuously and creatively building and blending cognitive models to yield new concepts and construals.

This view correctly predicts that scenarios which occasion frame-shifting present a challenge to the processor that differs from that presented by lexical violations consistent with the currently active frame. In contrast to the impoverished notion of context in psycholinguistics as something that is important only insofar as it facilitates processes that are clearly linguistic, the difficulty of frame-shifting in jokes demonstrates the need for a model of message-level processing prompted by language. Moreover, it suggests that message level representations are amenable to fairly substantive changes with minimal linguistic input.

Indeed the demands of joke comprehension suggest the models we build and revise so quickly derive from perceptual symbols, schematic representations of perceptual experience stored around a common frame that promotes schematized simulations (Barsalou 1999). We suggest that with frames built from perceptual symbols, one could maintain the representational advantages of hierarchically organized slot-filler structures, as well as explaining how speakers might construct a simulation of a parachute that was used, but never opened, in order to infer the origin of its stain.

References

Allen, James. 1987. *Natural Language Processing*. Philadelphia, PA: Benjamin/Cummings Publication.
Barsalou, Lawrence W. 1992. Frames, concepts and conceptual fields. In: A. L. E Feder Kittay (ed.) *Frames, Fields and Contrasts: New Essays in Lexical and Semantic Organization*. Hillsdale, NJ: Erlbaum.
Barsalou, Lawrence W. 1999. Perceptual symbol systems. *Behavioral and Brain Sciences* 22: 577–609.
Barsalou, Lawrence W. 2008. Grounded Cognition. *Annual Review of Psychology* 59: 617–645.
Beeman, Mark Jung, Rhonda Friedman, Jordan Grafman, Enrique Perez, Sherri Diamond, and Miriam Beadle Lindsay. 1994. Summation priming and coarse coding in the right hemisphere. *Journal of Cognitive Neuroscience* 6: 26–45.
Bergen, Benjamin, and Seana Coulson. 2006. Frame-shifting humor in simulation-based language understanding. *IEEE Intelligent Systems* 21(2): 59–62.
Bihrle, Amy M., Hiram H. Brownell, and Howard Gardner. 1986. Comprehension of humorous and nonhumorous materials by left- and right- brain damaged patients. *Brain and Cognition* 5: 399–411.
Brownell, Hiram H., Dee Michel, John A. Powelson, and Howard Gardner. 1983. Surprise but not coherence: Sensitivity to verbal humor in right-hemisphere patients. *Brain and Language* 18: 20–27.
Clark, Herbert H. 1983. Making sense of nonce sense. In: Robert J. Jarvella (ed.) *The Process of Language Understanding*, 297–332. Chichester: John Wiley and Sons.
Coulson, Seana, and Marta Kutas. 1998. *Frame-shifting and Sentential Integration*. (Cognitive Science Technical Report No. 98.02). UCSD.
Coulson, Seana. 2001. *Semantic Leaps: Frame-shifting and Conceptual Blending in Meaning Construction*. Cambridge, UK: Cambridge University Press.
Coulson, Seana. 2006. Constructing meaning. Metaphor and symbol, 21(4), 245–266.
Coulson, Seana, and Robert F. Williams. 2005. Hemispheric asymmetries and joke comprehension. *Neuropsychologia* 43:128–141.
Coulson, Seana, and Ying Choon Wu. 2005. Right hemisphere activation of joke-related information: An event-related brain potential study. *Journal of Cognitive Neuroscience* 17: 494–506.
Coulson, Seana, Thomas P. Urbach, and Marta Kutas. 2006. Looking back: Joke comprehension and the space structuring model. *Humor* 19(3): 229–250.

Coulson, Seana, and Els Severens. 2007. Hemispheric asymmetry and pun comprehension: When cowboys have sore calves. *Brain and Language* 100: 172–187.
Fauconnier, Gilles. 1994. *Mental Spaces: Aspects of Meaning Construction in Natural Language.* Cambridge: Cambridge University Press.
Fauconnier, Gilles, and Mark Turner. 1998. Conceptual integration networks. *Cognitive Science* 22: 133–187.
Fauconnier, Gilles, and Mark Turner. 2002. *The Way We Think.* New York: Basic Books.
Fillmore, Charles J. 1968. The case for case. In: E. B. R. T. Harm (ed.) *Universals of Linguistic Theory*, 1–90. New York: Holt, Rinehart and Winston.
Fillmore, Charles J. 1976. The need for frame semantics within linguistics. *Statistical Methods in Linguistics* 12(5): 5–29.
Fillmore, Charles J. 1982. Frame Semantics. In: Linguistic Society of Korea (ed.) *Linguistics in the Morning Calm*, 111–137. Seoul: Hanshin.
Fillmore, Charles J. 1988. The mechanisms of construction grammar. In: A. J. Shelley Axmaker, and Helen Singmaster (eds.) *Proceedings of the Fourteenth Annual Meeting of the Berkeley Linguistics Society*, 35–55. Berkeley: Berkeley Linguistics Society.
Frazier, Lyn. 1995. Issues in representation in psycholinguistics. In: Peter D. Eimas (ed.) *Speech, Language and Communication: Handbook of Perception and Cognition*, 1–27. San Diego: Academic Press.
Frisson, S. 2009. Semantic underspecification in language processing. *Language and Linguistics Compass*, 3(1), 111–127.
Gazdar, Gerald. 1979. *Pragmatics: Implicature, Presupposition and Logical Form.* New York: Academic Press.
Giora, Rachel. 1991. On the cognitive aspects of the joke. *Journal of Pragmatics* 16, 465–485.
Giora, Rachel. 2003. *On Our Mind: Salience, Context and Figurative Language.* New York: Oxford University Press.
Glenberg, Arthur M., and David A. Robertson. 2000. Symbol grounding and meaning: A comparison of high-dimensional and embodied theories of meaning. *Journal of Memory and Language* 43: 379–401.
Goel, Vinod, and Raymond J. Dolan. 2001. The functional anatomy of humor: Segregating cognitive and affective components. *Nature Neuroscience* 4: 237–238.
Hagoort, P., & van Berkum, J. 2007. Beyond the sentence given. *Philosophical Transactions of the Royal Society B: Biological Sciences*, 362(1481), 801–811.
Hull, R., Chen, H.-C., Vaid, J. and Martinez, F. 2005. Great expectations: Humor comprehension across hemispheres. *Brain and Cognition* 57: 281–282.
Johnson-Laird, Philip N. 1993. The mental representation of the meaning of words. In: A. I. Goldman (ed.) *Readings in Philosophy and Cognitive Science*, 561–584. Cambridge, MA and London: MIT Press.
Katz, Jerrold J., and Jerry A. Fodor. 1963. The structure of a semantic theory. *Language* 39: 170–210.
King, Jonathan W., and Marta Kutas. 1995. Who did what and when? Using word- and clause-level ERPs to monitor working memory usage in reading. *Journal of Cognitive Neuroscience* 7(3): 376–395.
Kutas, Marta, and Steven A. Hillyard. 1980. Reading senseless sentences: Brain potentials reflect semantic incongruity. *Science* 207: 203–205.
Kutas, Marta and Cyma K. Van Petten. 1994. Psycholinguistics electrified. In: M. Gernsbacher (ed.) *Handbook of Psycholinguistics*, 83–143. San Diego, CA: Academic Press.

Kutas, M., & Federmeier, K. D. 2011. Thirty years and counting: Finding meaning in the N400 component of the event related brain potential (ERP). *Annual review of psychology*, 62, 621.
Langacker, Ronald W. 1987. *Foundations of Cognitive Grammar: Theoretical Prerequisites*. Stanford, CA: Stanford University Press.
Lange, Trent E., and Michael G. Dyer. 1989. High-level inferencing in a connectionist network. *Connection Science* 1: 181–217.
Mangun, George R., Steven A. Hillyard, and Steven J. Luck. 1993. Electrocortical substrates of visual selective attention. In: D. E. M. S. Kornblum (ed.) *Attention and Performance 14: Synergies in Experimental Psychology, Artificial Intelligence and Cognitive Neuroscience*, 219–243. Cambridge, MA: MIT Press.
McClelland, James L., and David E. Rumelhart (eds.). 1986. *Explorations in Parallel Distributed Processing: A Handbook of Models, Programs and Exercises* .Cambridge, MA: MIT Press.
Minksy, Marvin. 1975. Frame system theory. In: P. Wason (ed.) *Thinking: Readings in Cognitive Science*, 355–376. Cambridge: Cambridge University Press.
Minksy, Marvin. 1980. *Jokes and the logic of the cognitive unconscious* (AI Memo No. 603). MIT.
Norman, Donald A. 1974. Some observations on mental models. In: D. G. A. Stevens (ed.) *Mental Models*, 7–14. Hillsdale, NJ: Lawrence Erlbaum Associates.
Osswald, R., & Van Valin Jr, R. D. 2014. FrameNet, frame structure, and the syntax-semantics interface. In *Frames and Concept Types*, 125–156. Springer International Publishing.
Pecher, Diane, and Rolf A. Zwaan. 2005. *Grounding Cognition: The Role of Perception and Action in Memory, Language and Thinking*. Cambridge and New York: Cambridge University Press.
Rumelhart, David E., Paul Smolensky, James L. McClelland, and Geoffrey Hinton. 1986. Schemata and sequential thought processes in PDP models. In: D. E. R. J. L. McClelland (ed.) *Parallel Distributed Processing: Explorations in the Microstructure of Cognition* Vol. 2: 7–57. Cambridge, MA: MIT Press.
Sanford, Anthony J., and Simon C. Garrod. 1981. *Understanding Written Language: Explorations Beyond the Sentence*. Chichester: John Wiley and Sons.
Schank, Roger C., and Robert P. Abelson. 1977. *Scripts, Plans, Goals and Understanding: An Inquiry into Human Knowledge Structures*. Hillsdale, NJ: Lawrence Erlbaum Associates.
Shammi, Pratibha, and Donald T. Stuss. 1999. Humour appreciation: A role of the right frontal lobe. *Brain* 122: 657–666.
Sheridan, H., & Reingold, E. M. 2012. The time course of contextual influences during lexical ambiguity resolution: Evidence from distributional analyses of fixation durations. *Memory & cognition*, 40(7), 1122–1131.
Shastri, Lokendra, and Venkat Ajjanagadde. 1993. From simple associations to systematic reasoning: A connectionist representation of rules, variables and dynamic bindings using temporal asynchrony. *Behavioral and Brain Sciences* 16(3): 417–494.
Simpson, Greg B. 1994. Context and the processing of ambiguous words. In: E. Morton Ann Gernsbacher (ed.) *Handbook of psycholinguistics*, xxii, 1174. Academic Press, Inc.
Singer, M. 2012. Psychological Studies of Higher Language Processes: Behavioral and Empirical. *Higher level language processes in the brain: Inference and comprehension processes*, 9–46.
Spivey-Knowlton, Michael J., and Michael K. Tanenhaus. 1994. Referential context and syntactic ambiguity resolution. In: A. L. F. Charles Clifton and Keith Rayner (eds.) *Perspectives on Sentence Processing*. Hillsdale, NJ: Lawrence Erlbaum.

Spivey-Knowlton, M. J., Trueswell, J. C., & Tanenhaus, M. K. 2013. 8 Context Effects in Syntactic Ambiguity Resolution: Discourse and Semantic Influences in Parsing Reduced Relative Clauses. *Reading and language processing*, 148.

St. John, Mark F. 1992. The story gestalt: A model of knowledge intensive processes in text comprehension. *Cognitive Science* 16: 271–306.

Wilensky, Robert. 1986. Points: A theory of the structure of stories in memory. In: K. S. J. B. J. Grosz and B. L. Weber (eds.) *Readings in Natural Language Processing*, 459–473. Los Altos, CA: Morgan Kaufman Publishing.

Margherita Dore
10 Metaphor, humour and characterisation in the TV comedy programme *Friends**

1 Introduction

The recent surge of interest in the application of Cognitive Linguistics (CL) theories to humour research has produced a fair amount of literature (Giora 1991, 2001; Coulson 2001, 2003; Brône and Feyaerts 2004; Kyratzis 2003 just to name a few). The lively debate between some of these CL scholars and Salvatore Attardo, the proponent of the General Theory of Verbal Humour (hence, GTVH), has certainly contributed to the ongoing research in this sense (cf. the 2006 special issue of *Humor: International Journal of Humor Research*). In particular, Brône et al. (2006: 217) argue that CL theories can offer a better explanation of the inferential process involved in humour creation and interpretation as opposed to linguistic theories of humour such as GTVH. Although in partial agreement, Attardo (2006: 356) urges these scholars and in general all those interested in the application of CL theories to humour to develop a precise formulation that can account for the mechanism at the root of this phenomenon.

This study attempts to bring together two influential approaches in CL (Conceptual Metaphor Theory, or CMT, and Blending Theory, or BT) and the GTVH. These theories are used to examine the production of humour via metaphor ('metaphor' is used here as an umbrella term to include phenomena based on cross-domain mapping, be they pure metaphors or similes; cf. Semino 2008: 16–17) in some instances taken from the first series of the North American TV comedy programme *Friends*, (M. Kauffman, D. Crane, 1994). This eclectic approach seeks to demonstrate how the scriptwriters exploit metaphors in conversation within the fictional world to convey humour and, at the same time, to reinforce some of the six main character's specific traits and idiosyncrasies (e.g., Joey is simple minded, Rachel is a spoilt young woman, etc.). CMT can help to understand the underlying conceptual metaphor that given sets of linguistic expressions entail, which are also a sign of our conventional ways of perceiving the world and making sense of it (cf. next section). In contrast, BT can explain how central (i.e. most relevant) inferences are produced while we speak or write in a given context or situation (cf. Section 3 for a detailed explanation).

---

* I am particularly grateful to Elena Semino, for her guidance as PhD Supervisor and while I was writing this paper. I would also like to thank Salvatore Attardo who helped me improve my work with his paper in this volume.

The relation between metaphor and humour is obviously central to this work as it addresses the question why some metaphors are humorous while others are not. In this regard, the general points of oppositeness and overlapping postulated by the GTVH for other types of humorous creations hold for humorous metaphors as well. However, the creative and interpreting process seems to vary for this type of humour triggers. As suggested in Attardo (this volume), potentially humorous metaphors do not seem to resolve the incongruity they imply, thus adding to the effect the text conveys. This incongruous tension can be visualised by means of the BT model that shows how the elements that are part of the source and target domain are projected into the same space (i.e. the blend).

2 Conceptual Metaphor Theory (CMT)

Metaphors have been traditionally defined as a linguistic tool mainly used for artistic or rhetoric purposes (e.g.,: poetry, oratory). Therefore, the approach to the study of this phenomenon has usually been linguistic-oriented. However, theorists in the field of Cognitive Linguistics proposed a new way to explain it. In their view, the creation of a metaphor starts at a cognitive level and it is subsequently lexicalised via a linguistic expression. Lakoff and Johnson's (1980) influential books on metaphor has aimed to demonstrate that this phenomenon is an integral part of our conceptual system and explored its pervasive nature in everyday human life, including language, thought and action (1980: 3). Lakoff and Johnson's observation is that among the various ways of understanding and talking about the reality that surrounds them, human beings tend to use metaphors more often than they think and mostly unconsciously. For example, a concept such as 'argument' in English is often expressed in terms of 'war' with entrenched lexical expressions such as "I demolished her argument" or "he shot down all of my arguments". Linguistic metaphorical expressions are therefore the manifestation of a conceptual process in our mind that is based on the projection of some structure from one domain (source) in to another (target) (1980: 4–5). The examples above are therefore linguistic realisations of the conceptual metaphor "argument is war".

Lakoff and Johnson also highlight the fact that conceptual metaphors are created according to our physical, cultural and social experience; therefore, they may vary across culture. Some of them may be present in many cultures while others may be peculiar to a given culture (1980: 23–24). Subsequent studies have confirmed that some metaphors are shared by many cultures, especially of those based on bodily experience (Lakoff 1987; Lakoff and Johnson 1999; Kövecses 2000, 2002 on 'universal' conceptual metaphors). However, other studies have focused on the diachronic and synchronic nature of metaphorical expressions. For example, Kövecses (2005: 233) demonstrates that universal conceptual metaphors can present some 'cultural variation' within a given culture, which depends on many factors, such as social context, communicative situation, topic etc. (Deignan 2003).

Most importantly, Kövecses (2002: 242; 2005: 106–111) puts forward the idea that individuals have the ability to shape metaphors according to their peculiar way of perceiving the external world or their personal experiences in life (i.e. as a child, teenager, student, etc.). In other words, they tend to create a metaphor by means of one source domain that is part of their concerns or interests ('human concern'), which belong to their 'personal history'. This concept can be applied to the investigation of online metaphor both in the real world and in fiction. On the one hand, it can reveal how authors can create their characters' metaphorical patterns in an unconscious way as the result of the author's 'personal history' (cf. Kövecses ibid. ch. 8). On the other hand, it can be a fruitful tool to show how repeated idiosyncratic metaphors may be used in order to project the peculiarities of a character, their mind style (Semino and Swindlerhurst 1996; Semino 2002). I will apply the concepts of 'human concern' and 'personal history' during the data analysis, which demonstrates how the scriptwriters of *Friends* make use of online metaphorical expressions to convey specific characterisation cues.

It can be certainly argued that CMT has been a real breakthrough in the field of metaphor research, opening new avenues for the analysis and understanding of this phenomenon. However, CMT seems to lack suitable methodology for extrapolating conceptual metaphors from linguistic evidence. Therefore, it is sometimes difficult categorising linguistic expressions under one or the other conceptual metaphor. A more precise model and further analyses based on data other than linguistic patterns have also been advocated (cf. Murphy 1996). More importantly, CMT cannot fully account for all the processes involved in creating and understanding metaphors, especially the online production and reception of novel ones (Kövecses 2002: 233; 2005: 267). Conversely, Blending Theory (BT) and its model seems more adequate to explain specific interpretations of particular metaphorical expressions.

3 Blending Theory (BT)

In their comprehensive exposition of BT, Fauconnier and Turner (1996, 1998, 2002) claim that many cognitive operations, including metaphors, involve the integration of different mental structures into a single representation. They call this process 'blending' and the resulting representation 'blend'. According to these scholars, the human mind organises new information in mental spaces, which are:

> [S]mall conceptual packets constructed as we think and talk, for the purpose of local understanding and action. They are very partial assemblies containing elements, structured by frames and cognitive models (...). Mental spaces are interconnected in working memory, can be modified dynamically as thought and discourse unfold, and can be used generally to model dynamic mappings in thought and language (2002: 102).

Each space contains some elements taken from 'frames', or 'schemata', which are stored in our long-term memory. Mental spaces are constructed for specific purposes of understanding and are modified by individual situations. As mentioned in the quotation above, spaces are dynamic and can establish connections with other spaces, thus creating networks. If exposed to new external stimuli, our mind will initially activate a default mental space based on entrenched associations. However, it will also be ready to integrate dynamically this default mental space with the elements from other spaces as new information is processed. The set of correspondences created between the elements of the two spaces will produce a new mental space that fits the new given scenario, or experience (2002: 102–103).

This general process can be fruitfully used to explain metaphors whose understanding is mainly based on inferential reasoning. For instance, if we consider the metaphor 'This surgeon is a butcher' discussed by Grady et al. (1999: 103–105; cf. Figure 1), we soon realise that it cannot be explained by approaches that treat metaphor as a uni-directional process, that is a mapping from the source into the target domain (as in the CMT model).

The problem here lies in the fact that neither the source domain (butchery) nor the target one (surgery) of this metaphor contains the feature of 'incompetence' within their organising frame. Rather, its central inference (the surgeon is incompetent) results from merging elements, or structures, of the two domains together. The BT model can account for the inferential process created by this metaphor.

Fauconnier and Turner's basic model of blending, or 'integration network', consists of four main spaces that are hierarchically connected (cf. Figure 1). There is a 'generic' space that contains the elements that the two input spaces share. In the specific example of the metaphor above, Grady et al. list elements such as 'agent', 'undergoer', 'sharp instrument' and so on (cf. Figure 1). Nowadays some scholars tend not to reproduce this space because its constituent elements are already present in the input spaces (i.e. Kövecses 2005: 269). I will do the same during my data analysis.

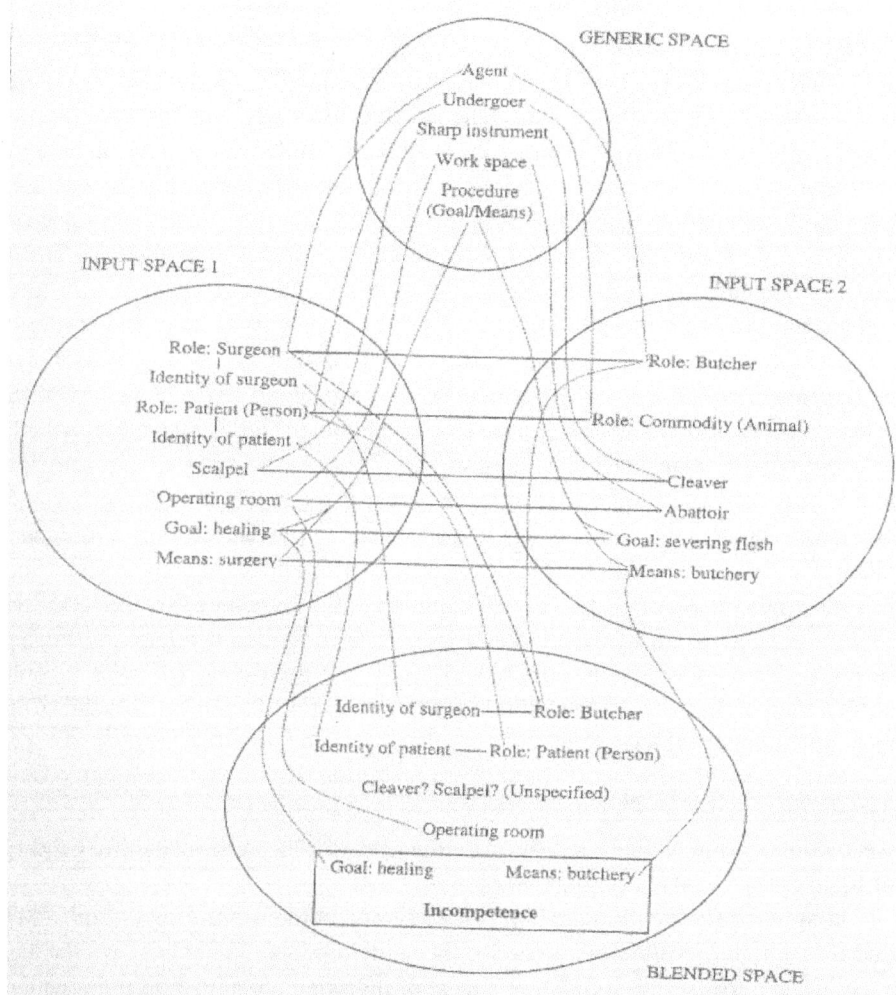

Figure 1: Grady et al.'s (1999: 105) conceptual integration network: surgeon as butcher

The composing elements of the two input spaces derive from the domains activated by the relevant linguistic expressions. In the example above, the two (mental) input spaces (surgery and butchery) draw their structure, or elements, respectively from the source and the target domain that are relevant to the local situation presented in it (i.e. 'surgeon', 'butcher', 'scalpel', etc.). It is also possible to establish a set of correspondences between the counterparts in each space (i.e. 'operating room' correspond to 'abattoir', 'surgery' corresponds to 'butchery').

The forth space is called 'the blended space', or 'the blend' and it is where some elements from each input are projected (i.e. 'scalpel', 'healing', 'cleaver' 'butchery', etc.). Projection is selective, which means that not all the elements in the inputs reach the blend. Only relevant or central elements for understanding are projected. These elements then integrate and form a new 'emergent structure' (in our case, 'incompetence'). This process is based on *composition* (new connections are created between the elements of the inputs once projected in the blend), *completion* (addition of structures not present in the inputs but deriving directly from our knowledge of the elements that shape them) and *elaboration* (addition of extra structures that might logically fit in the scenario presented in the blend. This process is also called 'running the blend'). Fauconnier and Turner (2002: 42–44) also remind us that the blend never detaches itself from the other spaces. On the contrary, the blend is an important tool by which it is possible to map back the relations between the counterparts in the two inputs and the features they share in the generic space (Coulson 2001: 178–196 on retrospective projection). In their discussion of the 'surgeon is a butcher' metaphor, Grady et al. (2001: 106) show how the notion of incompetence is the result of the composition process that combines the butcher's 'means' and the surgeon's 'goals'. Clearly, the blending process is context-dependent and highly selective. Even though it is possible to create multiple compatible or incompatible spaces from the same domain, the context will help us to select the most adequate or relevant.

Throughout their work, Fauconnier and Turner offer some compelling evidence of the validity of BT. However, the high flexibility of this model may cast some doubts on its validity (cf. for example Gibbs 2000 on the scientific validity of BT in terms of falsifiability).

In spite of the methodological issues I have pointed out above, both CMT and BT seem to be valid approaches to the study of metaphors. More specifically, each of them focuses on a different aspect of the same phenomenon (entrenched metaphors for the former and novel metaphors for the latter). Therefore, it is not surprising that some scholars have suggested their combined use, as discussed in the next section.

4 Complementary use of CMT and BT

CMT and BT have gathered a wealth of research on their application. In particular, some scholars have studied the feasibility of using the BT model and CMT together (Grady et al. 1999; Semino 2002).

As mentioned above, CMT and BT share salient aspects in the analysis of conceptual metaphors but they also reveal some important differences. According to Grady et al., the former is concerned with the way fixed, conventional metaphors in a language are composed and how their two domains are cognitively connected. The latter instead deals with the online processing of mostly novel metaphors and with the inferences stemming from them, which cannot be captured only by means of CMT (Grady et al 1999: 101). Nevertheless, the two theories, rather than being considered mutually exclusive, can be seen as complementary. Grady et al. demonstrate how CMT can account for the way receivers easily understand apparently novel metaphors when they are based on entrenched relations between two domains in a given language and culture. For example, a sentence like "you'd need an electron microscope to find the point of this article" can be understood in terms of the established correlation between the domain of visual perception and the one of intellectual activity (1999: 102). Entrenched metaphors can be retrieved from long-term memory to make sense of new cognitive associations. However, when the central inference of the metaphor cannot be explained simply in terms of a mapping between the source and target domain, BT comes into play including a feature that the CMT does not, that is the emergent structure (1999: 103). In this way BT fills the gap left by CMT, as we have seen in the example referring to the surgeon's incompetence.

Unlike Grady et al. who discuss examples mainly taken from everyday language, Semino (2002) concentrates on the exploitation of metaphors in fictional texts. By means of examples taken from John Fowles's novel *The Collector*, Semino shows how CMT and BT can be usefully combined to explain the construction of a character's mind style (and 'ideological point of view') through metaphor. In this novel, a young man, Frederick Clegg, is a butterfly collector who kidnaps a woman, Miranda. She dies of pneumonia while kept in captivity. According to Semino, on the one hand, the CMT can demonstrate that the protagonist's (obsessive) application of the (source) butterfly domain to different target domains ('the scope of metaphor', Kövecses 2002: 108) does not correspond to any entrenched conceptual metaphor in English. Therefore, this can be said to represent his idiosyncratic way to see and deal with the external world (1999: 109). On the other hand, however, CMT cannot account for the interpretation of particular instances of this metaphor (i.e. the specific scenarios deriving from the source and target domain; 1999: 114). For this reason, Semino suggests that BT can be applied to describe the online production and comprehension of those specific cases.

In a similar vein, I make a combined use CMT and BT during the investigation of my data. CMT demonstrates how novel metaphor can be processed easily because based on entrenched conceptualisations in English. BT shows how online metaphor are processed and how they can be exploited in order to convey the characters' mind styles for humorous purposes. The linguistic analysis of each example is also supported by the GTVH since it can isolate pragmatic factors at work in the creation of humorous texts. Hence, a brief summary of this theory follows below.

5 GTVH

The General Theory of Verbal Humour (Attardo and Raskin 1991; Attado 1994, 2001) is a linguistic theory of humour developed on the basis of Raskin's (1985) Semantic Script Theory of Humour (SSTH). The latter postulates two fundamental conditions that a text has to satisfy in order to be humorous:
1. The text is compatible, fully or in part, with two different scripts;
2. The two scripts with which the text is compatible are in opposition (ibid. 99).

A 'script' is defined as "an organized chunk of information about something [...]. It is a cognitive structure internalized by the speaker which provides the speaker with information on how things are done, organized, etc." (Attardo 1994: 199). As can be noted, the notion of script does not differ substantially from that of 'frame' or 'schema'[1] developed in Linguistics and Cognitive Linguistics and derives, among others, form Schank and Abelson's (1977: 41) seminal work on Artificial Intelligence, which defined a script as "a structure that describes appropriate sequences of events in a particular context".

Raskin's empirical investigation on a corpus of jokes demonstrates that scripts undergo a process of partial or total 'overlapping', which produces ambiguity and possible incongruity. However, this overlapping condition is not sufficient for the creation of humorous texts. Indeed, humour is the result of both overlapping and opposition of scripts (1977: 104–114).

Unlike Raskin, Attardo (1994: 143) favours the Incongruity-Resolution (IR) model developed in Psychology to explain the interpretative process of a humorous text. According to this model, the interpretation of a joke involves two steps. At first, the receiver interprets the text according to the linguistic cues and the

---

[1] Nonetheless, some scholars tend to use the terms script, frame and schema to refer to different types of background knowledge (cf. for instance Bartlett 1932 for an in-depth discussion on the concept of script, Rumelhart 1980 on schema and Goffman, E. 1974 on frame).

script they activate. Subsequently, the punch line forces the receiver to detect the incongruity and then reinterpret the linguistic cues in the text according to another script, which is in opposition to the one activated previously. This step is called the 'Resolution' phase.

Although retaining the main tenets of SSTH (overlapping and oppositeness of scripts), Attardo (1994: 208, 217–219) also notices that this theory focuses on short humorous texts such as jokes. Yet, humour is also known to be present in longer texts (e.g., short stories, novels or, for the purpose of this study, TV comedy). In addition, it is unable to distinguish between *verbal humour* (based on language, i.e. puns) and *referential humour* (based on non-linguistic humour, i.e. ethnic jokes). Conversely, the GTVH is a full-fledged theory of humour comprising six Knowledge Resources (KRs), including the already established features of script opposition. These six KRs are conceived according to a hierarchical structure, at the top of which is the script opposition (SO). The following KR is called logical mechanism (LM) and it is the parameter that explains how the two scripts are brought together (i.e. by juxtaposition, ground reversal, etc.; cf. Attardo et al. 2002: 18 for a list of known LMs). According to the IR model mentioned above, the SO is the parameter that reveals the incongruity while the LM is the parameter that resolves it. The situation (SI) describes the context (e.g., objects, participants, activities, etc.) while the target (TA) defines the 'butt' of the joke. The narrative strategy (NS) is responsible for the organisation of the text (e.g., a dialogue, narrative, figure of speech, etc.). At the bottom, we find the KR called language (LA), which contains the information regarding the verbalisation of the text (Attardo 1994: 223–227). The advantages of the GTVH are that it can tackle different text types and that the analyses are easily comparable (1994: 227–229; cf. also Ruch et al. 1993 for the empirical application of the GTVH to demonstrate joke similarity).

In his subsequent studies, Attardo (1998, 2001, 2002) has further developed the GTVH and its applicability to texts longer than jokes. In particular, Attardo (2001: 38) argues that jokes and some longer humorous texts seem to have a common compositional structure with a build up and a punch line. However, while jokes are likely to have only one script opposition, longer texts may have several. Hence, Attardo (ibid. 82-85) distinguishes between the well known *punch lines* (humorous triggers at the end of the text), and what he names as *jab lines* (humorous triggers that occur within the body of the text).

Several scholars in different fields have successfully applied the GTVH to various instances of humorous texts (i.e. Ritchie 2000 on computational humour, Antonopoulou 2004 on the translation of proper names, Archakis and Tsakona 2005 on humour and identity, just to name a few). Some of them have focused in particular on the distinction between jab and punch line and their function in the text (cf. Tsakona 2003, 2007; Antonopoulou and Sifianou 2003). The GTVH has also attracted some criticism. For instance, Cłopicki (2003: 157) highlights the fact that the GTVH does not seem to account fully for other entities in the text such as characters, places, objects and events. Moreover, he remarks that the application of the GTVH seems to overlook the process of reception of the text by the 'ideal' audience. Müller (2007: 51) instead points out the difficulty of identifying jab lines within a text, which may differ importantly according to each analyst's approach. These areas clearly require further development in the future. Most importantly, as suggested in the introduction above, some scholars in CL have also debated the validity of the GTVH in the perception and interpretation of humorous metaphors. This will be also the subject of the next section.

6 Metaphor and Humour

The relationship between humour and metaphor has fascinated many scholars in various fields. Some of them have attempted to explain in what metaphor and humour differ. For example, Oring (2003: 5–6) sees both phenomena as involving a clash between conceptual categories, which he calls 'appropriate incongruity'. However, in his view, appropriate incongruity in metaphor is 'genuine' because it is ultimately perceived as legitimate. In contrast, in jokes (or humorous texts) the appropriateness is 'spurious' or illegitimate because they violates logic. Müller (2007: 47) has instead considered what ground both phenomena share. He suggests that both metaphor and several types of humour playfully combine thoughts or conceptual knowledge. However, neither of these authors addresses the issue regarding the potential funniness of some metaphorical expression.

Some scholars have attempted to explain why some metaphors are humorous using the 'distance theory' (Mio and Graesser 1991; Kyratzis 2003). However, as Attardo (in this volume) points out, the main problem with 'distance theory' lies in the fact that the distance between domains cannot be quantified and cannot be accepted as a discriminating parameter for the funniness of a metaphor. Tsur's (1992, 2003) studies in Cognitive Poetics tackle this problem suggesting that witty, ironic, paradoxical, and in some cases, emotionally disorientating metaphors are perceived as such because they have a 'split-focus'. In his view, a metaphor with a split-focus foregrounds the incongruous and discordant elements of source and target concepts. Hence, Tsur's work reconnects the funniness of some metaphors to the concept of incongruity in the text.

Brône and Feyaerts (2004) and Veale et al. (2006) have cast doubts on the possibility of applying the GTVH to the study of humorous texts that are based on the non-prototypical use of common organizational principles like (creative) metaphor or metonymy. In particular, they suggested that such texts may not have a LM, which drives the resolution of the incongruity in the IR model. As opposed to this, Attardo (2006: 356–357) states that metaphors and metonymies would instead be considered as complex LMs. Indeed, he remarks that Attardo et al. (2002) has proven that some logical mechanisms correspond to mapping, which is also the basis of cognitive phenomena such as blending. Although suggesting that it may be impossible to provide a unified theory that explains why some metaphors are humorous and others are not, Attardo (in this volume) ventures in the following suggestion. Drawing from Oring's (2003) idea of 'appropriate incongruity' and the IR model, he proposes that some metaphors are perceived as humorous because they are:

> [M]etaphors in which the incongruity of the mapping of different domains is not fully resolved by the interpretation (finding appropriateness/resolution) of the metaphor (Oring 2003). This explanation combines semantic and pragmatic factors: the incongruity of the mapping is a semantic fact, the research fro appropriateness a pragmatic one. It is obvious that is can be recast in blending terms without any loss of analytical power (p. 95 in this volume) (2003).

Humorous metaphors therefore involve detecting an incongruity that is only partially resolved. As Attardo emphasises in the quotation above, the IR model (and consequently GTVH) and BT can be equally apt to explain this process (cf. also Howell 2007 for an application of the GTHV metric and conceptual blending to Brussig's 1995 *Helden wie wir*).

In the analysis of the examples below, I will attempt to bring together all the points made above and make a combined use of CMT and BT, along with the GTVH metric.

7 Data Analysis

As anticipated above, I use CMT here to demonstrate how language can be exploited to create novel metaphors based of universal as well as culture-specific (e.g., Anglo-American culture) entrenched concepts. Moreover, I show how the scriptwriters select the domains of these novel metaphors so as to convey characterisation cues and develop the general topics of the series (interpersonal relationships, work, sex, friendship, etc.).

In the last subsection, the examination of a more complex novel metaphor developed during a conversational exchange among the six main characters will demonstrate that a combined use of both CMT and BT can explain the process at work better that the use of CMT alone. All examples are also discussed according to the script opposition (SO) and target (TA) Knowledge Resources, as proposed in the GTVH. I have chosen to concentrate in particular on these two KRs because the former helps to detect recurrent patterns in humour creation in the text whereas the latter can help to relate the humour and the characterisation patterns in the series.

Before proceeding with the data analysis, I will briefly introduce the TV comedy programme *Friends*. It revolves around the lives of six main young characters, namely Chandler, Joey, Ross, Monica, Phoebe and Rachel. They all live and work in New York, U.S.A. and the usual settings for the funny and sometimes grotesque situations involving them are their flats and a coffee shop called Central Perk where they meet on a regular basis. The first series sets the ground for the six main characters' idiosyncratic features, which seem to fit what Culpeper (2001: 88–89) names as 'exaggerated prototype' as they "fail to exhibit contextually sensitive behaviour" that "can become established as fictional stock figures in their own right". In the examples below, Rachel and Joey show such peculiar traits, which are often, *but not always*, conveyed by means of humorous metaphors, or similes that are extended via metaphorical expressions.[2] The last example instead demonstrates how exploiting a metaphor based on stereotyped ideological points of view can convey humour.

7.1 Rachel

Rachel is one of the three main female characters. She is introduced in the first episode as an old high-school friend of Monica's who (still wearing the wedding dress) has just run away from her wedding. Rachel comes from a rich family and has never worked in her life. Her father has always provided her with everything she needed and her not-to-be husband was supposed to continue on the same line. She seems to ignore the fact that people work and earn money in order to be able to buy goods. She loves shopping for clothes, shoes, accessories, etc. but she has never earned the money she spends. Most of this information is introduced in episode 1 and reinforced throughout the series.[3]

In example (1), taken from episode 1, Rachel is on the phone with her father and she uses the following metaphor in order to explain to him the reason why she left just before her wedding:

---

[2] Due to space limitation, I could not include the analysis of another character's (Ross's) use of idiosyncratic novel metaphors. It can be found in ch.7 of my PhD thesis.

[3] Episode 2 also contains instances of Rachel's shopaholic behavior. In this episode, Phoebe does not want 500 dollars that her bank added to her account by mistake. Rachel suggests: "Yeah, but if you spent it, it would be like shopping!". Similarly, in episode 18, Rachel is offered a job interview and comments: "Assistant buyer. Oh! I would be shopping... for a living!"

(1) Rachel: C'mon Daddy, listen to me! It's like, it's like, it's like all my life, everyone has always told me 'You're a shoe!

You're a shoe! You're a shoe! You're a shoe!' And today I just stopped and I said, 'What if I don't wanna be a shoe?

What if I wanna be a- a purse, y'know? Or a- or a hat!' No, I'm not saying I want you to buy me a hat I'm saying I am a ha- It's a metaphor, Daddy!

Ross: You can see where you have trouble.

Coherent with her character, personal history and interests, Rachel (or the scriptwriters for her) chooses the source domain of accessories to talk about her feelings regarding what others think of her and the new identity (target domain) she may be developing. Therefore, this metaphor can be conceptually translated as identities are accessories and generally linked to metonymic associations of women and commodities and/or sale products (cf. Hiraga 1991: 42–44). More specifically, Rachel uses a metaphor to express how she thinks others see her ("You're a shoe") and how she might want to see herself ("What if I don't wanna be a shoe? What if I wanna be a- a purse, y'know? Or a- or a hat!"). Clearly, Rachel uses the accessories as the source domain of her metaphor because of its relevance among her priorities and interests (human concern). The metaphor seems to reinforce the set of inferences that the audience is likely to draw about Rachel and her character (i.e. a rich and superficial young woman).

The humour of this example appears to work at several levels. Firstly, it seems to reside in the incongruity that Rachel's metaphor conveys. Most, if not all, cultures usually consider personality and material possessions at the opposite ends of a scale of values. Rachel gives the impression of sharing this moral value because she wants people to see her as a capable and thoughtful person. Nevertheless, she talks about her identity in terms of material possessions, thus acting superficially and incongruously.

The potential humour is reinforced by Rachel's father's reaction to her metaphor. Proposing to buy her a hat may lead the audience to infer that her father's reaction is due to his knowledge and expectations about his daughter. In other words, he does believe that Rachel is a material person. Ross's following turns ("You can see where you have trouble") underlines that both Rachel and the people around her are equally superficial. In GTVH terms, the semantic and conceptual clash can be seen by the SOs identity/accessories, and more in general human/non-human, or even money/no-money. In addition, the TA defines the disparaging function of this metaphor, which targets Rachel, and possibly her father.

7.2 Joey

Joey is a young man who wants to become an actor. He does not have a permanent job and occasionally performs in TV series or in theatres. He is rather simple minded and sometimes he cannot grasp implied meanings in conversation. However, he has his own interests and concerns, which mainly relate to sex (and consequently women) and food. Therefore, women and food function as metaphoric source domains in many of Joey's contributions[4] but the most striking and novel exploitation of both domains can be found in example (2) below, which is a simile that is extended via a metaphorical expression. In this example, taken from episode 1, Joey uses food as the source domain to talk about women. Interestingly, the exchange can be seen as a self-standing joke because it opens with Ross, Chandler and Joey in Ross's flat. Ross has just been left his lesbian wife and he is very upset. Joey tries to cheer him up by means of a metaphor and Chandler's punch line closes the scene. Hence, it can be analyzed according to Attardo's (1998, 2001) distinction between jab and punch lines:

(2) Ross: You know what the scariest part is? What if there's only one woman for everybody, y'know? I mean what if you get one woman- and that's it? Unfortunately in my case, there was only one woman- for her...

Joey: What are you talking about? 'One woman'? That's like saying there's only one flavor of ice cream for you. Lemme tell you something, Ross. There's [sic.] lots of flavors out there. There's Rocky Road, and Cookie Dough, and Bing!

Cherry Vanilla. You could get 'em with Jimmies or nuts, or whipped cream! This is the best thing that ever happened to you! You got married, you were, like what, eight? Welcome back to the world! Grab a spoon!

Ross: I honestly don't know if I'm hungry or horny.

Chandler: You stay out of my freezer!

---

4 Some examples of Joey's obsessive interest in sex: in episode 4 he says he could kill himself if he was unable to perform sexually. In episode 5 all six characters talk about the advantages of being a man or a woman. Joey's contribution is the following: "Ok, you know what blows my mind? Women can see breasts any time they want. You just look down and there they are. How you get any work done is beyond me". As for Joey's obsession with food, in episode 15, when Ross asks his friends if they know any nice restaurant to take a woman for a date, Joey suggests: "How about Tony's? If you can finish a 32-ounce [900 gr.] steak, it's free".

As in Rachel's metaphor, the scriptwriters seem to exploit this metaphor in order to associate the domains of women and food to Joey's persona and further reinforce the audience's inferences about him (and his 'human concern'). Describing women in terms of food is not novel in English as the application of CMT has demonstrated that the entrenched metaphors that define women as 'tarts' or 'cakes' are part of everyday language (cf. Goatly 1997: 155–156 on ideology and metaphor; cf. also Hiraga 1991: 44–46 for similar findings in Japanese). However, Joey's use of ice-cream flavours is very creative. His metaphor portrays a scenario where human features and objects (food) blend and clash in an unresolved tension that triggers humour. In addition, the mutual presence of both the literal (source domain) and the metaphorical reading (target domain) contributes to the humorous effect. Joey's reference to different types of ice-cream ("Rocky Road", "Cherry Vanilla", etc.) and toppings ("Jimmies", "nuts" and most importantly "whipped cream") evokes a sexual script and a scenario in which Ross can choose whatever type of woman he wants and have sex with them in whatever way he wants. The reference to whipped cream metonymically reinforces this point as whipped cream can stand for the process of what one can do with it in a sexual context.

This example can be seen as a clear cut case of humour because it is based on two clichés present in many Western societies. Firstly, men see women as objects (in this case ice-cream flavours) that they can obtain. Secondly, Joey subverts the cultural value of monogamy in the attempt of cheering Ross up. Since Ross does not have much experience with women (as we infer from Joey's hyperbole "You got married, you were like what eight?"), Joey points out that being single means to be able to have many new sexual experiences ("grab a spoon"). However, Joey soon forgets about the delicate topic of the conversation (Ross's sexual life) and offers and over detailed account that seems to go beyond its initial purpose (cf. comment on Culpeper's 2001 exaggerated prototypes reported above).

Ross's jab line and Chandler's punch line reinforce the humour of the metaphor. Interestingly, Ross processes both the literal and metaphorical meaning of Joey's utterance and replies exploiting both. From the literal point of view, Ross plays on Joey's metaphor implying that his detailed explanation of ice-cream flavours prevents him from going beyond the literal interpretation and makes him feel hungry (cf. Goatly 1997: 127–128 on asymmetric interpretation of metaphors for humorous purposes and Norrick 1993: 30 on the use of extended metaphors for punning in conversation, be it intentional or due to misunderstanding). From a metaphorical point of view, Ross's turn seems to indicate that Joey's metaphor creates such strong connections between the two domains (food and women) that Ross cannot help being aroused by it and fantasising about women. More interestingly, in BT terms Chandler's punch line seems to elaborate on both Joey's metaphor and Ross's jab line. Chandler's warning ("you better stay out of my freezer") may suggest that, after talking profusely with two men about sex, he needs to reaffirm his own sexual orientation. Hence, his "freezer" can be metaphorically understood as his sexual body parts that he tries to protect from other men. Alternatively, Chandler may be using "freezer" to refer to his girlfriend (or stock of girlfriends) he is not willing to share with Ross and Joey. According to the GTVH metric, the SOs in the exchange are food/women and more in general human/non-human but also sex/no-sex while the TAs are Joey and Ross.

7.3 Sex is a rock concert

The last example is a complex metaphor based on the exploitation of the stereotyped idea that men and women have opposing views about sex. This is a striking example of the way metaphors can be used in conversation for humorous purposes. It is also confirms the relevance of disparagement in humorous metaphors (Mio and Graesser 1991: 91). The conversational exchange in example (3) is taken from the opening scene of episode 2. Technically speaking, this particular scene is called a 'teaser', that is a humorous part that opens an episode and that may or may not be connected with the rest of the action (Attardo 1998: 241). In this scene, all six main characters are sitting in Central Perk. Their conversation revolves around the importance of kissing within sexual intercourse between men and women. The male and female characters take opposite sides in the discussion, thus creating the following humorous exchange:

(3) Monica: What you guys don't understand is, for us, kissing is as important as any part of it.
Joey: Yeah, right! Y'serious?
Phoebe: Oh, yeah!
Rachel: Everything you need to know is in that first kiss.
Monica: Absolutely.
Chandler: Yeah. I think for us, kissing is pretty much like an opening act, y'know? I mean it's like the stand-up comedian you have to sit through before Pink Floyd comes out.
Ross: Yeah, and-and it's not that we don't like the comedian, it's that- that... that's not why we bought the ticket.

Chandler: The problem is, though, after the concert's over, no matter how great the show was, you girls are always looking for the comedian again, y'know? I mean, we're in the car, we're fighting traffic... basically just trying to stay awake.

Rachel: Yeah, well, word of advice: Bring back the comedian. Otherwise next time you're gonna find yourself sitting at home, listening to that album **alone**. [Rachel and Monica give each other a five as a sign of agreement]

Joey: [pause, to Ross] Are we still talking about sex? [Ross rises his thumb as to confirm they are still talking about sex].

From its very beginning, the conversation polarises. Monica, Rachel and Phoebe support the importance of kissing within the whole sexual intercourse. In her first turn, Monica makes no explicit reference to sex, which is replaced by the pronoun 'it'. This linguistic strategy is commonly used in order to refer to taboo topics and all the other characters, apart from Joey who utters it in his punch line ('Are we still talking about sex?'), use it throughout the conversation. This may imply that they share the same set of values regarding sex as a taboo topic, which might be part of their 'ideological point of view' (Fowler 1986: 130, 1996: 16, quoted in Semino 2002: 96). Unlike the female characters, Chandler, Ross and Joey consider kissing irrelevant and/or superfluous. This point is put forward in Chandler's first turn by means of a simile and supported by Ross's following comment. In addition, they deem women's attitude towards kissing after the main sexual act as nonsensical. This idea is expressed in Chandler's second turn, which extends the simile via a metaphorical expression. Chandler's (or the scriptwriters') choice of the rock concert domain among various kinds of stage performances is pivotal. Indeed, at the beginning of a rock concert, an emergent and less popular band or singer (the opening act) usually performs before the main band. This allows the audience some time to find a place and enjoy the main event. Some people may like to attend this introductory part but most of the audience tends to pay little or no attention to it. Therefore, the supporting band is usually considered as superfluous. The same could not happen in other types of events. For example, if we want to go to the theatre and watch a play, we cannot attend the second act and miss the first one in order to enjoy it fully.

In CMT terms, Chandler's metaphor can be described as sex is a rock concert (cf. for Lakoff 1987; Murphy 2001 and Crespo Fernández 2008 for extensive analyses of metaphorical conceptualisations of sex according to the CMT). The elements of the source domain rock concert are mapped into the target sex

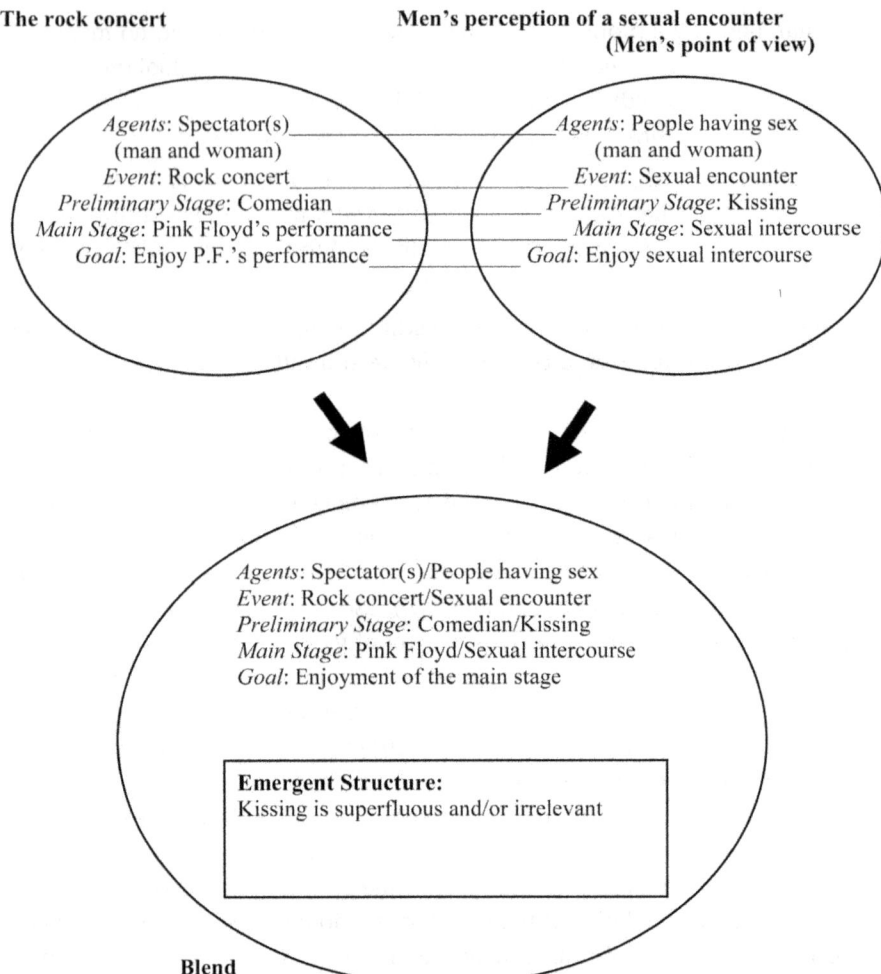

Figure 2: Conceptual integration network: Sex is a rock concert

domain. Therefore, the agents in the source domain are the 'spectators attending the concert', which correspond to 'people having sex (a man and a woman)'. The 'opening act (the comedian)' corresponds to 'kissing' while Pink Floyd corresponds to 'the sexual intercourse', etc. (cf. Figure 2 above and Figure 3 below). However, BT seems more suitable to explain the reason(s) why the male characters in this scene use a novel metaphor to convey the central inference that 'women's attitude to kissing makes no sense'. Figures 2 and 3 are visual representations of Chandler's metaphor. Both represent the conceptualisation of the target domain

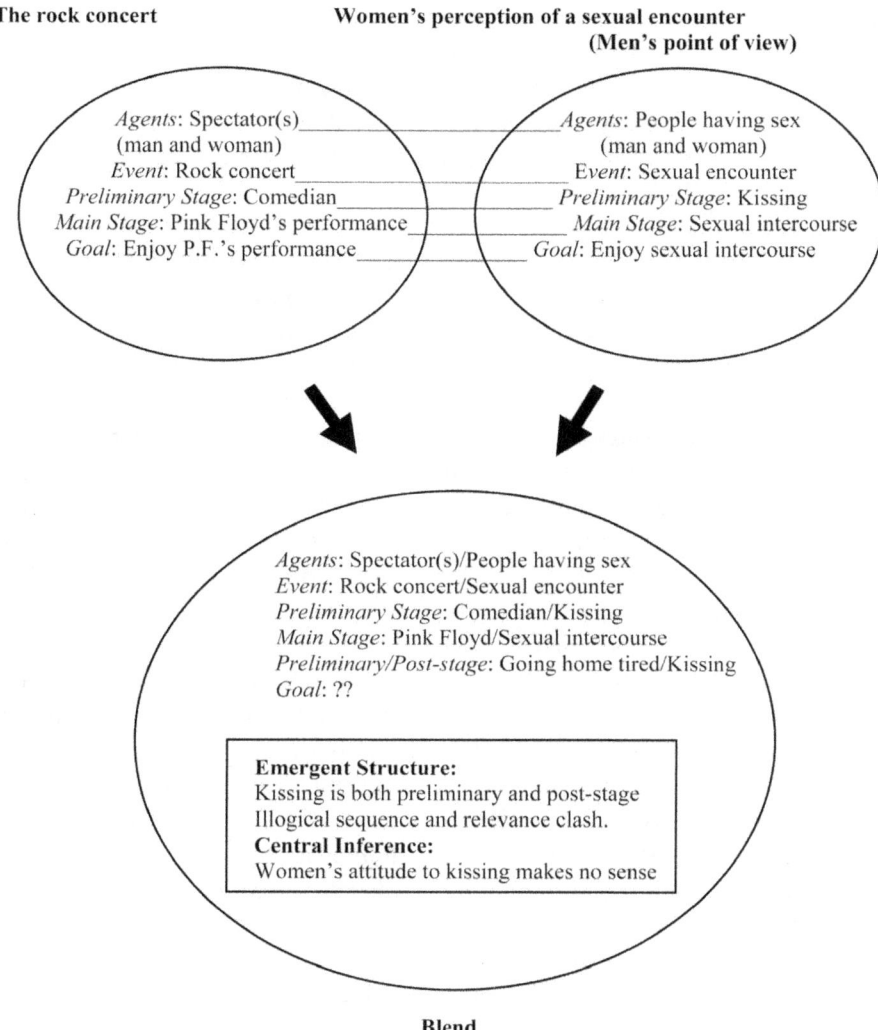

Figure 3: Conceptual integration network: Sex is a rock concert

(sex) according to the source one (rock concert). Figure 2 shows how men perceive a sexual encounter from their point of view (Chandler's first turn). Figure 3 shows how men think women perceive a sexual encounter (Chandler's second turn). As suggested earlier on, the 'generic space' is not reproduced here because its elements are already present in both input spaces (i.e. 'agents', 'event', etc.). In Figure 2, the mapping of the elements of the source domain (rock concert) onto the target domain (sex) and their projection into the blended space show that the logical sequences of both events match perfectly. In particular, the blend demonstrates that the main goal of attending a rock concert and engaging in a sexual encounter is to enjoy the event's main stage (Pink Floyd's performance, sexual intercourse). Hence, the emergent structure (logical sequence) leads to the central inference that the preliminary stage in both events (the comedian, kissing) is superfluous and/or irrelevant.

Figure 3 represents Chandler's elaboration of his metaphor in his second turn, which results in a new emergent structure (he is 'running the blend' in Fauconnier and Turner's 2002: 301 terminology). He aims to attack women's attitude towards kissing within the whole sexual encounter. In order to do so, Chandler adds new structure (the post-stage) to both the source and target domain. Thus, he shows that in the rock concert domain involves driving home tired after the main stage. Moreover, he points out that women's conceptualisation of the sex domain involves kissing as preliminary and post-stage (as the female characters also confirmed at the beginning of the exchange). Women's perception of a sexual intercourse cannot be deemed as incongruous *per se*. However, Chandler's use of a metaphor aims to demonstrate that in his (and generally men's) point of view, kissing after sex is as illogical as expecting another comedian's performance after Pink Floyd have played. Projecting the elements of both domains into the blend makes the clash between post-stages ('going home tired' vs. 'kissing') evident. This clash leads to the central inference that 'women's attitude towards kissing makes no sense'.

This example further confirms Attardo's suggestion above that the incongruity in humorous metaphors is not resolved. The interpretation process of this example does not lead to discard the first interpretation in favour of another. On the contrary, the interpretation is enriched by the cumulative blending process that produces a new clash. In GTVH terms the SO in this metaphor is generally sex/no-sex while the TAs are Monica, Rachel, Phoebe and women in general.

Rachel's second turn is also an interesting example of elaboration of the metaphor. Due to space constraints, I do not visually represent Rachel's run of the blend but I will attempt to explain it as clearly as possible. Rather than questioning or rejecting Chandler's (and Ross's) metaphor, Rachel chooses to exploit it. She makes use of the broader music industry domain, which includes elements such as 'band's (Pink Floyd's) album', 'agents purchasing and listening to the album at home', alongside with 'band's (Pink Floyd's) live performance', etc. This allows Rachel to subvert the initial metaphor. She implies that if men overlook the role of the comedian within the whole concert going experience in future they are likely to experience a less attractive substitute, which is listening to the album alone (corresponding to masturbation in the source domain). In this case the SOs can be: attending a concert/listening to an album, having company/being alone and more in general sex/no-sex (i.e. autoerotism or masturbation). The TA are Joey, Chandler, Ross and men in general.

As in example (2), the clear cut boundaries of the exchange above make it similar to a self-standing joke, which also offers a remarkable example of the relation between topics and characterisation. Clearly, Joey's concluding turn can be seen as the punch line of the humorous exchange among the other characters. Although the receivers of the text, or the audience, may not find it difficult to follow the flow of the characters' conversation and the metaphoric expression used, Joey does. Differently from example (2) in which Ross consciously exploits the literal and metaphorical meaning of Joey's metaphor, here Joey cannot grasp the intended meaning of Chandler's metaphor and its further elaborations. This reinforces the audience's inferences regarding Joey's (low) cognitive skills and makes them laugh at him.

8 Conclusion

Although based on a small number of cases, this study has hopefully shed some light on the debated relationship between metaphor and humour. The examples discussed above are often based on taboo topics that are exploited in order to make fun of stereotyped points of view and characters. Yet, their novelty lies in their creation process and purpose. The humour conveyed by these exchanges hinges on the main theme at a superficial level and on the idiosyncrasies associated to the main characters at a deeper one. The data analysis clearly shows that the scriptwriters exploited metaphor in order to produce humorous exchanges that also convey specific characterisation cues and develop the topics of the series. In particular, they reveal some of the characters' features and interests, their human concern and personal history. Sometimes the scriptwriters have creatively exploited the linguistic ambiguity of metaphors (literal and implied meaning). Other times, they have played with the image the metaphor conjures up. In all cases, the interaction between characters and their interpretation of the metaphor within the fictional world become the basis for the communication at the author-audience level. They serve the scriptwriters' objective to entertain their 'ideal' audience by playing with the latter's expectations and world knowledge.

The application of three theoretical frameworks proves their advantages and limitations. CMT has demonstrated how novel metaphors can be easily processed because they rely on the conceptual metaphors that are part of their receivers' background knowledge. However, it can only deal with metaphorical conceptualisations based on a uni-directional cross mapping. Conversely, the combined use of CMT and BT has shown that the latter can handle complex metaphor successfully because it takes into account the dynamic nature of conversational humour expressed via metaphor. Finally, the GTVH helps to analyse each metaphorical expression from both the linguistic and pragmatic point of view (script oppositions and targets). The combination of these theories confirms once again the multifaceted nature of humour and the benefits that an eclectic approach can offer. Clearly, further research in the complementary use of CMT and especially BT and the GTVH to other types of humorous texts is needed. This study has hopefully contributed in this direction.

References

Archakis, Argiris, and Villy Tsakona. 2005. Analysing conversational data in GTVH terms: A new approach to the issue of identity construction via humour. *Humor: International Journal of Humor Research* 18 (1): 41–68.

Antonopoulou, Eleni. 2004. Humor theory and translation research: Proper names in humorous discourse. *Humor: International Journal of Humor Research* 17(3): 219–255.

Antonopoulou, Eleni, and Maria Sifianou. 2003. Conversational dynamics of humor: The telephone game in Greek. *Journal of Pragmatics* 35(5): 741–769.

Attardo, Salvatore. 1994. *Linguistic Theories of Humour*. Berlin: Mouton de Gruyter.

Attardo, Salvatore. 1998. The analysis of humorous narratives. *Humour: International Journal of Humor Research* 11 (3): 231–260.

Attardo, Salvatore. 2001. *Humorous Texts: A Semantic and Pragmatic Analysis*. Berlin and New York: Mouton de Gruyter.

Attardo, Salvatore. 2002. Cognitive stylistics of humorous texts. In Semino, Elena and Jonathan Culpeper (eds.), *Cognitive Stylistics: Language and Cognition in Text Analysis*, Amsterdam: John Benjamins.

Attardo, Salvatore, Christian F. Hempelmann, and Sara Di Maio. 2002. Script opposition and logical mechanisms: Modelling incongruity and their resolutions. *Humor: International Journal of Humor Research* 15 (1): 3–46.

Attardo, Salvatore, and Victor Raskin. 1991. Script theory revis(it)ed: Joke similarity and joke representational model. *Humor: International Journal of Humor Research* 4 (3): 293–347.

Bartlett, Frederic C. 1932. *Remembering*. Cambridge: Cambridge University Press.

Brône, Geert, and Kurt Feyaerts. 2004. Assessing the SSHT and GTVH: A view from Cognitive Linguistics. *Humor: International Journal of Humor Research* 17 (4): 361–373.

Brône, Geert, Kurt Feyaerts, and Tony Veale. 2006. Introduction: Cognitive linguistic approaches to humor. In Brône, Geert, Kurt Feyaerts and Tony Veale (eds.), *Humor: International Journal of Humor Research* 19 (3): 203–228.

Crespo Fernández, Eliecer. 2008. Sex-Related Euphemism and Dysphemism: An Analysis in Terms of Conceptual Metaphor Theory. *Atlantis* 30 (2): 95–110.

Coulson, Seana. 2001. *Leaps. Frame-Shifting and Conceptual Blending in Meaning Construction*. Cambridge: Cambridge University Press.

Coulson, Seana. 2003. What's so funny?: Conceptual integration in humorous examples. Available at: http://cogsci.uscd.edu/~coulson/funstuff/funny.html.
Culpeper, Jonathan. 2001. *Language & Characterisation: People in Plays & Other Texts*. Harlow England and New York: Longman.
Deignan, Alice. 2003. Metaphorical Expressions and Culture: An Indirect Link. *Metaphor and Symbol*, 18 (4): 255–271.
Fauconnier, Gilles, and Mark Turner. 1996. Blending as a Central Process of Grammar. In Goldberg, Adele (ed.), *Conceptual Structure, Discourse, and Language*, Stanford: Center for The Study of Language and Information (CSLI): Cambridge University Press, 113–129.
Fauconnier, Gilles, and Mark Turner. 1998. Conceptual Integration Network. *Cognitive Science*, 22 (2): 133–187.
Fauconnier, Gilles, and Mark Turner. 2002. *The Way We Think: Conceptual Blending and the Mind's Hidden Complexities*. New York: Basic Books.
Giora, Rachel. 1991. On the cognitive aspects of jokes. *Journal of Pragmatics* 16, 465–485.
Giora, Rachel. 2003. *On our Mind: Salience, Context and Figurative Language*. New York: University Press.
Goatly, Andrew. 1997. *The Language of Metaphors*. London & New York: Routledge.
Goffman, Erving. 1974. *Frame Analysis*. Cambridge, Massachusetts: Harvard University Press.
Grady Joseph E., Todd Oakley, and Seana Coulson. 1999. Blending and metaphor. In Gibb, Jr., Raymond W. and Gerard J. Steen (eds.), *Metaphor in Cognitive Linguistics*, Amsterdam: John Benjamins, 101–24.
Hiraga, Masako. 1991. Metaphor Japanese women live by. *Working Papers on Language, Gender and Sexism*, AILA Commission on Language and Gender 1 (1): 38–75.
Howell, Tess. 2007. Two cognitive approaches to humorous narratives. In Popa, Diana and Salvatore Attardo (eds.), *New Approaches to the Linguistic of Humour*, Galati: Editura Academina, 55–71.
Kövecses, Zoltan. 2002. *Metaphor: a practical introduction*. New York and Oxford: Oxford University Press.
Kövecses, Zoltan. 2005. *Metaphor in Culture. Universality and Variation*. New York: Cambridge University Press.
Kyratzis, Sakis. 2003. Laughing Metaphorically: Metaphor and Humour in Discourse. Unpublished paper, presented at the Conference on 'Cognitive Linguistics Approaches to Humour', available online at: http://wwwling.arts.kuleuven.ac.be/iclc/Participants.htm.
Lakoff, George. 1987. *Women, fire, and dangerous things: what categories reveal about the mind*. Chicago and London: University of Chicago Press.
Lakoff, George and Mark Johnson. 1980. *Metaphors We Live By*. Chicago and London: The University of Chicago Press.
Lakoff, George and Mark Johnson. 1999. *Philosophy In The Flesh: the Embodied Mind and its Challenge to Western Thought*. New York: Basic Books.
Murphy, Gregory L. 1996. On metaphoric representation. *Cognition*, 60: 173–204.
Murphy, Gregory L. 2001. *Studs, Tools and the Family Jewels. Metaphors Men Live By*. Madison and Wisconsin: The U. of Wisconsin P.
Norrick, Neal R. 1993. Conversational Joking: Humor in Everyday Talk. Bloomington: Indiana University Press.
Raskin, Victor. 1985. *Semantic Mechanisms of Humour*. Dordrecht: D. Reidel.

Rumelhart, David E. 1980. Schemata: The Building Blocks of Cognition. In Spiro, Rand J., Bertram C. Bruce and William F. Brewer (eds.). *Theoretical Issues in Reading Comprehension*. Hillsdale, NJ: Erlbaum, 38–58.

Semino, Elena. 2008. *Metaphor in Discourse*. Cambridge: Cambridge University Press.

Semino, Elena. 2002. Stylistics and linguistic variation in poetry. *Journal of English Linguistics*, 30 (1): 28–50.

Semino, Elena, and Swindlerhurst. 1996. Metaphor and Mind Style in Ken Kesey's One Flew Over the Cuckoo's Nest. *Style* 30 (1): 143–166.

Tsakona, Villy. 2003. Jab lines in narrative jokes. *Humor: International Journal of Humor Research* 16 (3): 315–329.

Tsakona, Villy. 2007. Towards a revised typology of humorous texts and humorous lines. In Popa, Diana and Salvatore Attardo (eds.), *New Approaches to the Linguistics of Humor*. Galați: Academica, 35–43.

Veale, Tony, Kurt Feyaerts, and Geert Brône. 2006. The cognitive mechanisms of adversarial humour. In Brône, Geert, Kurt Feyaerts and Tony Veale. *Humor: International Journal of Humor Research* 19 (3): 305–339.

Kurt Feyaerts, Geert Brône and Robin De Ceukelaire
11 The Art of Teasing
A corpus study of teasing sequences in American sitcoms between 1990 and 1999

1 Introduction

It is a well-known fact that people who know each other very well, trust each other and share a lot of knowledge, ideas, beliefs and emotions do not necessarily communicate with each other in the most efficient and straightforward way. Instead, the high degree of mutual social confidence among group members enhances communication to take place on different layers of expression, be they serious or playful, involving such ubiquitous phenomena like irony, joint fantasies, pretend teasing etc. On the basis of their substantial and/or long-standing 'common ground' (Clark 1996), all members of a group are expected to anticipate and handle these different levels of communication, as a result of which social and communicative relations among in-group members are constantly (re)confirmed and reinforced.

In this contribution, we focus on humorous teasing as one prominent expression of such layered communication. Depending on the situational and contextual grounding of an interaction, teasing serves different communicational functions. It does make a difference, for instance, whether teasing takes place among long-time friends, relatives or among economic competitors, colleagues or even political enemies. Similarly, it makes a difference whether a teasing sequence occurs in the private setting of a household, in parliament, in a TV studio or as part of a screen play.

In the present study, we restrict our empirical focus to the occurrence of teasing sequences in four prominent American sitcoms of the nineties: *The Nanny*, *Friends*, *Married with Children* and *Spin City*. In this corpus, we observe how teasing can be used as a more or less subtle instrument to express certain feelings towards each other. A rich theatre producer teases his nanny to reveal his strong romantic feelings for her, and a shoe salesman teases his wife to reveal precisely the opposite. Teasing can thus be seen as an ideal means to "test the water", as Martin (2007) aptly remarks. It is therefore unmistakably part and parcel of human nature.

The general aim of this contribution is to gain a better insight in the socio-semantic characteristics of teasing as a multi-layered and multi-perspectival phenomenon. On the basis of corpus data, more specifically, we envisage an accurate empirical analysis of teasing as it is construed in the dialogue sequences of four famous American sitcoms. Through the identification of five parameters in the analysis of 402 teasing instances, we are able to derive an annotation grid for an integrated and adequate analysis of teasing as a multi-faceted phenomenon. Beyond the scope of this paper, we expect this annotation grid to be a valuable starting point for a similar analysis of teasing as it occurs in spontaneous everyday interactions.

The article is structured as follows. First, in section 2, we present a brief overview of the key notions of both the overall linguistic framework of this study and the phenomenon of teasing. Accordingly, section 2.1 elaborates on the socio-cognitive account of meaning, which serves as the linguistic background for this study, whereas section 2.2 provides a general overview of recent studies on different aspects of teasing. Section 3 deals with methodological aspects of the study, focusing on the specifics of the corpus. The empirical analysis in section 4 revolves around the identification of five parameters, the combination of which presents an integrated model, through which any given teasing instance can be defined and thoroughly described. Section 5, finally, derives a conclusion as well as some perspectives for future research on teasing.

2 Theoretical background

2.1 A socio-cognitive account of meaning

As the theoretical background for this analysis, we adopt a socio-cognitive, usage-based perspective on meaning, according to which meaning essentially resides in the intersubjective process of meaning coordination among interlocutors (Langacker 2001; Verhagen 2008; Brône 2010: 399; Langlotz 2011). In doing so, we move beyond the traditional cognitive linguistic, subject-centered account of meaning, in which aspects of mutual and joint interaction as described by, among others, Clark 1996 remain somewhat underfranchised.

Our account of *intersubjectivity* does not concern the interactive process of explicit meaning negotiation as it occurs among interlocutors and in which different opinions about a commonly focused topic are discussed. Instead, we define it as our cognitive ability to take other people's perspective and to model the mental states of our interlocutors. This view is very much in line with the *theory of mind* (Whiten 1991; Givón 2005), which revolves around our ability to identify and differentiate the mental from the physical world and, more specifically, the ability to conceptualize thoughts, ideas, emotions, attitudes, beliefs etc. in other people's mind (Brône 2010, 91–92). During interaction, both at the stage of interpretation and production, interlocutors imagine what they assume to be in the minds of their conversational partners and align their construal with it. Accordingly, conversation can be characterized as a process that requires constant alignment and negotiation among *intersubjective* viewpoints.

> Linguistic expressions are cues for making inferences, and understanding thus not primarily consists in decoding the precise content of the expression, but in making inferences that lead to adequate next (cognitive, conversational, behavioral) moves. (Verhagen 2005, 22)

With regard to the impact of these perspectival aspects of intersubjective meaning coordination on everyday language use, Clark (1996) identifies the notion of *layered meaning* as a key concept of his theory of language use as a joint activity. He points out that in many so called *staged communicative acts* (1996, 368) like sarcasm, irony, lying, teasing and many others, participants do not necessarily act and communicate in line with the expectations and norms of that specific situation. Clark links this observation to the crucial insight that the experience of common ground does not have the status of an independent or inherent value in communication. Instead, "when [we] act on the basis of our common ground, we are in fact acting on our individual beliefs or assumptions about what is in our common ground" (96). Indeed, interlocutors may always exploit common ground for humorous, ironic or other communicative purposes (Veale et al. 2006). Clark describes the meaning in staged communicative acts in terms of different meaning layers, where the primary or basic layer corresponds to the concrete situation of the communication between speaker(s) and hearer(s) (the *ground* as Langacker calls it).[1] On top of this primary layer, interlocutors may decide to create another, secondary layer of meaning, which can only operate relative to and hence dependent on the primary layer of interpretation.

In their analysis of adversarial humor, Veale et al. (2006), Brône (2008; 2010) and Brône and Oben (2013) identify prominent patterns of layered meaning, through which interlocutors achieve a *trump* over their opponents by pretending and then elaborating a misunderstanding, in which (parts of) the expressions used by a previous interlocutor are recycled and successfully turned against their original users, as illustrated in (1).

---

[1] With this distinction, Clark relates his model to the work of Russian linguist Mikhail Bakhtin, but also to Relevance theory, several discourse models and more cognitively oriented paradigms; for an overview, see Brône (2012).

(1) (our translation) Spectator shouting at Dutch politician H. Wiegel:
Son of a bitch!
H. Wiegel: *How nice of you to introduce yourself; my name is Hans Wiegel.*

In this brief dialogue, the second interlocutor creates a secondary layer of interpretation, involving a pretended misunderstanding, in which he activates an unanticipated alternative meaning, allowing him to achieve both verbal and social superiority over his opponent. On the basis of mutually assumed common ground, both speakers 'know' that the first speaker intended his utterance to be understood as an insult. Also on the basis of common ground, both speakers must conclude that the meaning construal in the reply of the second speaker will generally be regarded as superior compared to the initial insult by the first speaker.

2.2 Teasing

In line with a growing interest in several linguistic paradigms to focus attention on the interactive grounding of the language system and its function in shared cognition, modern humor research increasingly investigates aspects of interactional humor, such as teasing.[2] The following overview highlights which aspects of humorous teasing have been studied so far. In his early work on teasing in spontaneous conversation, Paul Drew (1987: 233) identifies three fundamental aspects of teasing:

> (i) the teases are not topic-initial utterances, (ii) they are all in some way a second, or a next, or a response to a prior turn, almost always the adjacent prior turn, and (iii) that prior turn is spoken by the person who is subsequently teased, in multiparty as well as two-part talk.

Although these insights are based on spontaneous conversation, they can be challenged by looking at our corpus data, which make clear that a) teasing *can* occur topic-initially, for instance when it is triggered by a tertiary trigger, i.e. when a non-animate object is the direct cause for a teasing instance; b) teasing can also be reactive to a previous *action* or to the *result* of a past action (see

---

2 Compare the interactional turn in models such as Cognitive Grammar (Langacker 2001, Verhagen 2005) and Construction Grammar (Goldberg 2006), or, in the field of psycholinguistics, the work by Clark (1996) on language as joint action as well as Pickering and Garrod's (2004) work on interactive alignment, which all have catalyzed research on cognition in interaction.

below) and c) a previous turn to a teasing instance need not be uttered by the ultimate target. In many cases it is a bystander who says or does something, for which a target is being teased by a teaser.

In her analysis of a data set of spontaneous interactions, Kotthoff (1998) builds on one of Drew's insights, namely the observation that no target immediately counters the teasing instance via a teasing instance of his or her own. While this might be a relevant observation for a corpus of spontaneous conversations, it certainly does not apply to teasing sequences in sitcoms, where an immediate teasing counter by the target is no exception, which can perfectly be explained in terms of *"competitive wordplay"* (Norrick 1993: 44). As will be demonstrated below, teasing instances are nearly always followed by a counter-teasing instance from the target.

In her conversation-analytical approach Günthner (2000: 156ff) provides a typological description of teasing, in which she identifies 6 components located in two dimensions. The first dimension concerns the different *interactional roles* ("Interaktionsrollen"), which may be involved in a teasing instance. Similarly, Kotthoff (1998: 158) identifies a) the producer of the teasing instance, b) the object of the teasing instance, and c) the public of the teasing instance. The second dimension of Günthner's analytical model concerns the three different *phases of a teasing sequence*, which she describes as a) the teasing utterance, b) the reaction by the target and c) the reaction by the public. With regard to the sequential organization, we mainly focus our attention on the first component, i.e. the teasing utterance itself. However, as apparent in our data, a teasing instance need not be an actual, verbal *utterance* as we will come across a number of non-prototypical forms of teasing, which feature non-actualized teasing instances or even actions instead of utterances.

In his extensive work on the *psychological and social dimensions* of humor, Martin (2007) categorizes teasing as a paradox, since it fulfills both aggressive and pro-social functions (Martin 2007: 124).[3] Amongst other aspects, Martin's main insights on teasing pertain to three psycho-social mechanisms: *group identity, affection* and *camouflage*.

When a group of teasers focuses a target, two indirect and subconscious messages are conveyed. On the one hand the teasers signal that they form a specific (but not necessarily named) group, affirming their *group identity* as they tease the target. On the other hand they emphasize the non-inclusion of the target in their group, which is verbalized by means of the teasing instance

---

[3] Compare in this respect Davies (1984: 362) who describes teasing in terms of the thematic principle of *contradiction*.

proper. "This type of humor enables members of an in-group to enhance their feelings of group identity and cohesiveness while excluding and emphasizing their differences from members of an out-group" (Martin 2007: 18). This aspect is also noted by Norrick (1993: 34): "spontaneous joking ends up more a matter of group cohesion than testing".

Closely related to the creation of group identity is the social function of what Martin calls "friendly teasing" (2007: 125). The idea is that two (or more) people tease each other and laugh at each other's teasing instance(s) to signal that their mutual friendship is located on a higher, *affective* level than the mutual friendship with less close friends. It is a way of "calling attention to the fact that they are close enough that they can say negative things and not take offense" (Martin 2007: 125). Consequently, friendly teasing is a possible way for the teaser to signal that he or she wishes to bring the mutual friendship with the target to a higher level. It can be seen as an 'initiation ritual' that implicitly allows the target to enter the select and intimate group of the teaser (cf. group identity). A closely related application is when two people wish to express their hidden romantic feelings for each other.

Dynel (2008) argues for a distinction between teasing and putdown humor depending on whether or not the target considers the utterance to be humorous. Apart from the difficulty in operationalizing this distinction, Dynel (2008: 248-249) identifies two concomitant problems herself. First, a target might experience the utterance as negative, but *pretend* to experience a positive effect. Second, extensive knowledge of the interpersonal context and background of the participants is needed in order to make a reliable distinction between the two humor types under discussion:

> "In some cases the differentiation between aggressive teasing and putdown humour can only be conducted on the basis of case study, which may even entail ethnomethodological analysis of the relation between conversationalists and the attitudes they hold for one another. (...) It is thus only each individual concerned that can honestly assess whether an ostensibly aggressive proposition is jocular, and hence categorise it as a tease, or whether it is hurtful, coinciding with a putdown." (ib.)

It may not be easy to utter criticism without causing a fight, hurting the recipient's feelings, or even without causing loss of face ("face threat", Keltner et al. 2001, cited in Martin 2007). However, when criticism is *camouflaged* in a teasing instance, it becomes less conversationally 'dangerous', since one can always claim "I was just kidding" when the recipient reacts to the criticism in an unexpected way. A similar view on this social function of teasing is developed by Norrick (1993), who states that criticism through teasing is "the least threatening of various parallel forms (...) and the exchange as a whole conduces more to bonding between the two participants than to face loss or gain for either one" (Norrick 1993: 34).

In terms of semantic analysis, this characteristic of *camouflage* pertains to the observation that the meaning of a teasing instance is essentially an intersubjective process of meaning coordination, in which on the basis of mutually assumed common ground among interlocutors, different layers of interaction are established (Clark 1996). Brône (2010: 283ff) observes that in most studies on teasing, few attention is paid to the analysis of socio-cognitive mechanisms, which allow a better insight in the discourse-semantic and interactional aspects of teasing utterances. He therefore presents a cognitive-inspired model for the analysis of interactional humor, in which the traditional, subject-oriented semantic construal mechanisms (*figure-ground reversal, metaphor, metonymy, subjective vs. objective construal* etc.) are enriched by intersubjective factors such as (*embedded*) *perspectivization* and *layering*, which aim at capturing the complex, i.e. multifocal and multilayered semantics of humorous teasing as a staged communicative act (Clark 1996). For the analysis of our data, we take Brône's integrated account as a starting point.

3 The corpus

The empirical base for this study consists of a corpus of teasing sequences collected from four American sitcoms, which all played in the same decade (1990–1999): *The Nanny, Spin City, Friends* and *Married with Children*). This resulted in a corpus of 402 teasing instances taken from 115 episodes (De Ceukelaire 2009).

The first sitcom, **The Nanny**, is set in New York and features a Jewish beauty consultant (Fran Fine) who is hired as a nanny by a rich English theatre producer and widower (Maxwell Sheffield) to take care of his three children (Maggie, Brighton and Grace). Fran rapidly wins the hearts of everyone in the household, except for Maxwell's business associate (C.C.), who genuinely dislikes Fran, regarding her as a rival. Her aversion towards Fran peaks when Fran and Maxwell gradually fall in love with each other. These developments are all very much to the liking of the butler (Niles), who finds great pleasure in regularly teasing C.C. The two have developed a customary teasing relationship (cf. Norrick 1993) based on mutual dislike.

The second sitcom, ***Spin City***, is also set in New York and provides us with an (exaggerated) inside look of the events at the City Hall. The mayoral team consists of the mayor himself (Randall Winston), his popular deputy mayor (Mike Flaherty), his personal assistant (Janelle), a young and introverted speech writer from Wisconsin (James), a single and desperate accountant (Nikki), a loquacious and bold secretary (Stacy), a black homosexual in charge of minority affairs (Carter), a stingy and overweight press attaché (Paul), and finally the somewhat oversexed Stuart, who will regularly tease anyone but the mayor himself.

Thirdly, the widely popular sitcom **Friends** is about six friends who face both professional and interpersonal issues on a daily basis. To some extent, the global popularity of the sitcom seems partly due to the diversity of the characters: the intelligent college professor/archeologist Ross, the dim-witted actor Joey, the astute but weird masseuse Phoebe, the beautiful fashion saleswoman Rachel, the highly competitive chef Monica, and the unconfident data analyst Chandler.

Finally, ***Married with Children*** is about a weary and drained shoe salesman (Al Bundy), who despises his dim and shallow wife (Peggy) and who is indifferent to his two children: Kelly, a hyperbolically unintelligent but beautiful high school senior, and Bud, whose intelligence makes up for his lack of sex-appeal. It is a disgruntled family, in which aggressive teasing between the members is more rule than exception.

4 Analysing teasing in 5 parameters

Teasing is a complex socio-semantic phenomenon, involving many different aspects such as the interplay between different levels of semantic organization, the exploitation of common ground among interlocutors by adopting different perspectives as well as the general process of intersubjective meaning coordination, in which attitudes, emotions, knowledge, judgments etc. are being anticipated and reacted upon. In order to capture this socio-semantic complexity as much as possible, this study aims for the construction of an integrated annotation grid, consisting of multiple parameters, five to be exact, which pertain to all relevant aspects of teasing. Adopting this annotation grid will allow highlighting in which dimensions teasing may vary across different instances, thus leading up to the identification of a prototypically organized category of teasing. In this section, we describe the variation for the following parameters: the teaser, the target, the trigger, the presence of a layered meaning structure and finally the type of relation among interlocutors.

4.1 Parameter 1: The teaser

It may seem self-evident that in every teasing sequence a teaser can be identified as illustrated in example (2), taken from *Married with Children*, in which Al and his family are stranded due to a broken axle on their car somewhere on 'Route 666'. Desperately seeking help in the deserted scenery, they find themselves suddenly alighted on a small town and some queer old inhabitants.

(2) MWC/005/023/0275
```
01 Peg      LOOK gentlemen;
02          (-) there's a COO:L twenty five cents in it for you if you can
            HAUL our CAR to a STAtion;
03 Zeke 2   we::ll,
04          N:ORMALLY it'd be (.) FOUR hundred ↑dolla:rs;
05 Zeke 1   but we'll do it for TWO hundred,
06          if you let us take OUR PICture with you (-)LEOPARD WOMAN,
07 Peg      ohehohohohoho: .h ↑o:w al-
08          the RUBES think I'm SEXY;=
09 Al       = <<p> hnh yea{hea}:;>
10          yea I would too peg if I drank WHISKEY for BREAKfast,
```

Al's teasing instance in line 10 is a prime example of a default conversational scheme: he is the obvious teaser, Peg is the obvious target. Subsequently, the entire sequence complies with the conversational default deictic system, which is anchored in the values 'I-you-now-here' as personal, temporal and local reference points, through which the roles of teaser, the teasing victim as well as the actual teasing message are identified.

How straightforward the identification of a teaser in this sequence may be, our data show that it may not always be unambiguously clear who the teaser in a teasing instance is. As a matter of fact, we distinguish three subtypes of teasing instances, all of them featuring a covert or indistinct teaser, which can be derived from a specific shift in the default deictic system. In what follows, we present a qualitative description of a single example for each subtype in order to demonstrate the different pathways, along which this deictic shift can be achieved.

4.1.1 A shift in the receiver

Consider the following teasing instance from *Spin City*, in which Mike and Ashley are confronted with annoying and boring neighbors (Yale and his wife Marie), who find joy in sharing their vacation videos with Mike and Ashley. At the beginning of the teasing instance Yale is on the verge of 'popping in' a new video, when Mike aptly reacts by comparing the degree of boredom to the stopping of time.

(3)   SPC/001/005/0203
     01 Marie   you ↑know we have a whole ↑BAG of ↑TAPES,
     02 Ashley I'm just going to the bathroom real ↑quick,
     03   you know just splash some WATER in my fa{ha}ce;
     04 Yale   so we'll just POP one in then huh,
     05 Mike   o yeah y you go ahead yale let's euh-
     06   (-) <<p> let's see if we can actually make time STOP;>

The interesting aspect about Mike's teasing instance is that it is not meant to be heard by Yale, but instead to be directed at Mike himself and, most of all, to the audience, which of course is omnipresent as well, albeit on another level of narrative organization. With regard to the participant roles involved in teasing (see section 2.2, Kotthoff 1998, Günthner 2000), this sequence demonstrates that at least in sitcoms, the target of a teasing instance need not be addressed directly by the teaser. What is striking in this case, particularly, is the non-coincidence of the communicative role of receiver (addressee) and the participant role of target of the teasing sequence. Indeed, Mike is both the sender and – together with the audience – the receiver of the communicative message, but obviously not the target of the teasing instance.

4.1.2 A shift in the message: non-actualized teasing

The second deictic shift, featuring an alteration in the message, is more complicated than the previous one. In order to fully comprehend the mechanism behind these teasing instances, we first look at a prime example from *The Nanny*. The excerpt starts with a grateful Mr. Sheffield (Maxwell), who thanks Fran for convincing him to hire the infamous actor Jack (lines 01 and 02). Unfortunately, the plan to hire Jack was entirely CC's idea, who now is enraged from frustration. She furiously asks what she has to do to please anyone (line 05), at which point Niles is on the verge of teasing her for this rather suggestive utterance. Mr. Sheffield, however, but also the audience, knows Niles well enough (based on *personal common ground*) to see in advance that a teasing instance is coming, and inhibits Niles from uttering it. Niles metaphorically argues against Maxwell's reprimand (lines 08 and 09), but Maxwell sticks to his guns. The fragment ends with Niles squirting lemon juice into CC's eyes.

(4) TNN/002/012/GAMMA-001
```
01 Mr. Sheffield   <<f> no miss fine i want to THANK you;
02                 (-) for CONVINCING ME to HIRE JACK;>
03 CC              <<ff> ↑maxwell?
04                 THAT was MY ID↑EA;
05                 WHAT do I have to do to ↑PLEASE anyone around this
                   house,>
06 Niles           ((opens mouth, on the verge of saying something))
07 Mr. Sheffield   niles-
08 Niles           but sir;
09                 FISH gotta ↑SWIM;
10 Mr. Sheffield   conTROL yourself man,=
11 Niles           =o very well sir;
12 CC              (-) hehehehehe::
13 Niles           lemon,
14                 ((squirts lemon in CC's eye))
```

The core of teasing instances like (4) is the observation that the *planned* teasing instance is being prohibited from becoming an *actual* teasing instance. Because CC's set-up in line 05 is remarkably suggestive and Niles and CC have a typical, deeply-rooted customary teasing relationship (Norrick 1993), Maxwell is perfectly able to both predict Niles' teasing instance and stop him in advance. In other words, Maxwell 'saw him coming', but chose to protect CC from again being the target of Niles' teasing instance.

Although Niles does not verbally express his teasing line, the intended teasing instance would have hinged on the exploitation of the illocutionary value of CC's question in line 5. Whereas CC intends this question as a rhetorical question, Niles is signaling that he would very much like to answer this as if it were a sincere informative question. The fact that the teasing instance remains unsaid but nevertheless is identified and appreciated as such demonstrates the impact of mutually assumed common ground among interlocutors, characters, audience etc.

Of particular interest in the present context is the question whether it is correct to speak of a genuine *teaser*, even a vaguely present one, when there is no verbally coded teasing taking place. Even without an explicit teasing instance, the intended teasing can be safely inferred by characters or an audience on the basis of the well-established common ground about the customary teasing relationship between Niles and CC. Additionally, the contextual fact that Maxwell stops Niles and the fact that Niles defends himself both yield the conclusion that Niles was on the verge of uttering a teasing instance. This observation supports that we are not dealing with an overt teaser, but rather with an *intended* teaser.

4.1.3 A shift in the teaser: indirect teasing

A third variant of atypical teasing instances with respect to the parameter 'teaser' are those instances which feature more of an off-screen director or choreographer, rather than an actual teaser. The teaser thus appears as a manipulator, who makes use of a medium to perform the teasing for him or her. An example of this is the following sequence from *The Nanny*. Fran has just been erroneously arrested for kidnapping a baby, when Mr. Sheffield and CC enter the police office to set things straight. After a brief conversation with the head police officer, a woman appears who is unmistakably a prostitute, claiming to recognize CC as her former colleague. Naturally, both Maxwell and CC are utterly startled; the former because he can't believe his business partner is a former prostitute, the latter because she indeed has never seen the woman in her life. It is not until the very end of the scene (lines 14–17), that everything becomes clear: Niles paid the prostitute to act as if CC was a former colleague.

(5) TNN/002/006/GAMMA-006
```
01 CC       before NANNY FINE entered our lives we never had to step
            FOOT in a place like this.
02 Hooker   ((arrives))
03          <<f> CC,>
04          GIRLfrie:nd;
05          GOT you again eh,
06 CC       you must have me confused with someone else;
07          <<p> ((at Maxwell)) I've never seen this person before IN MY
            LIFE;>
08 Hooker   oo: is THAT your game;
09          ↑is ↑cool;
10          just stay of second AVEnue;
11          EON is looking for you;
12          ((exit))>
13 CC       (–) <<p> ↑maxwell I ↑SWEAR;>
14 Niles    ((gives the hooker money))
15          here you ↑go:::;
16 Hooker   (–) how'd you LIKE it sugar, =
17 Niles    = o:w it was so GOOD I could do it again and again and
            again;
```

This teasing instance constitutes an illustration of layering and 'teasership'. With regard to allocating communication on different layers, it should be noted that Niles paid the prostitute to play the implied prostitute, who apparently recognizes (implied) CC as her former colleague. The perspective of these two roles – the real and the implied prostitute – is held together on the basis of common ground. In the base space, the real prostitute has never met CC, which is a true fact. The implied prostitute, however, is identical to the real prostitute, with the addition of a shared past with implied CC. In other words: she knows implied CC, and she knows that implied CC should know this too. This is the layered communication Niles wants the prostitute to participate in.

With regard to the teaser, it has already been stated that this teasing instance features some sort of director, choreographer or puppeteer, rather than an actual (visible) teaser. During the entire teasing instance (more specifically lines 3–13), Maxwell and the audience do not realize that the prostitute is actually playing a role. As mentioned, it is only from line 14 onwards that we realize that the prostitute's utterances were *staged* by the 'director' Niles. On the one hand, it thus becomes clear that Niles is not a prototypical teaser, since he does not do anything in the teasing instance proper. He merely set the stage, literally hired an actress and devised a story line, but this set-up had been arranged entirely before the actual teasing instance. On the other hand, it is clear that Niles is the one who initiated the diminishment of CC. She is the target of a staged communicative act (Clark 1996), and there is only one possible 'culprit', namely Niles.

It is important to note that the prostitute is *not* the teaser since she has never met CC and most certainly would have never met her, if it had not been for Niles. It is Niles, and Niles only, who creates the brief connection in both women's lives. Also, the prostitute is merely completing an 'assignment' as she is not teasing CC, but instead doing what Niles said in exchange for money. Finally, there is a complete lack of intention (with regard to teasing) on the prostitute's part. She is not pretending to know CC because she wants to tease her, but because she receives money for it.

In sum, Niles made use of a 'medium' (the prostitute) to indirectly tease CC, hence the categorization of this group of teasing instances as indirect teasing. Subsequently, there are three deictic anchor points that remain unchanged: there is still a certain message, a definite receiver (CC) and it all happens in the immediate present time zone. The shift is located in the sender (the teaser, Niles), which makes use of a medium to deliver the message.

4.2 Parameter 2: The target

For an accurate characterization of the target of a teasing instance, we take two dimensions into account. A first dimension concerns the relative position of the target to the teaser. In a default teasing instance, both teaser and target are part of the same conversational setting, in which the teaser directs their utterance at the target. In this case, we speak of a *present* target. There are, however, also cases in which the target does not form part of the same conversational setting as the teaser. He or she might be in the same room, but talking to someone else, or he or she might be on a remote location. Either way, the target is *absent*.

The second dimension concerns the number of targets that are being simultaneously[5] teased by the teaser. Again, the default teasing instance features a single teaser and a single target, but there are cases in which the teaser aims at multiple targets.

The combination of these two subparameters logically gives rise to four possible configurations:
A. A singular and present target
B. A singular and absent target
C. A compound and present target
D. A compound and absent target

Applied to the corpus, these configurations occur with the following frequencies:

Table 1: Absolute frequency of the parameter 'target'.

	A	B	C	D
The Nanny	167	34	6	4
Spin City	41	2	1	1
Married w. Children	84	16	2	0
Friends	44	0	0	0
Total	336	52	9	5

Firstly, the results clearly show that the default teasing instance in these American sitcoms indeed features a singular and present target (83,582% of the teasing instances in the corpus). On the other hand, however, these results also show that the other three configurations are also represented: 12,9% of the teasing instances of the corpus feature a singular but absent target, 2,2% form

---

4 We are not considering cases, in which the teaser rapidly teases one target after another. In that case, the result would be several successive single teasing instances directed each time at a singular target.

the mirrored configuration of a compound and present target, and 1,2% even feature a compound but absent target. The sequence in (6) illustrates the constellation with a singular but absent target. Mr. Sheffield is hosting a business diner for a rich investor, and is anxiously concerned about CC's tardiness.

(6) TNN/002/008/0067
01 Mr. Sheffield   where the devil's Cc;
02 Niles   well it is RAIning outside sir perhaps she MELTED;
03   (-) shall I see if there's a POINTY hat and chaNEL suit lying in the street,
04 Fran   ↑ahaa:-

Secondly, it is striking that apart from *Friends*, the relative occurrence of configuration B (a singular and absent target) is significantly higher than that of configurations C and D (12,9% versus 2,2% or 1,2%). What a priori might have been expected is that the three non-default configurations would have been evenly spread over the remaining 16,4%. Instead, the results show more of a 'secondary default' configuration B, and two real non-default ones (C and D). A possible explanation might be that people are more reluctant to tease an entire group (for fear of mass retribution, maybe, should the teasing instance be ill-received), and more willing to tease an absent target, since he or she is not able to immediately tease back. In other words: it is safer to tease a singular and absent target than multiple present targets.

4.3 Parameter 3: The trigger

Every teasing instance presupposes some sort of trigger, from which the teasing may be derived. This, however, does not imply that a trigger always needs to be clear-cut, or excessively 'marked'; it is very likely that some teasers only require minor (non)verbal elements in a given situation to construe a teasing instance.

With this in mind, we distinguish five possible triggers for subsequent teasing instances:

A. A **primary** and **verbal** trigger. The target verbally communicates something, for which he or she is subsequently teased.
B. A **primary** and **performative** trigger. The target acts in such a way, that he or she is subsequently teased.
C. A **secondary** and **verbal** trigger. A bystander, not the target, verbally communicates something, for which the target is subsequently teased. The bystander can thus be seen as an 'instigator'. If the utterance made by this

instigator is realized *consciously*, we interpret the subsequent teasing instance as a *joint* teasing instance, in which both the teaser and the instigator strive towards teasing the target.

D. A **secondary** and **performative** trigger. A bystander acts in such a way that the target is teased for the action of this bystander.
E. A **tertiary** trigger. A non-animate object is the cause of a subsequent teasing instance. Consequently, no distinction in a verbal, performative or passive component is possible.

In order to further illustrate this categorization, consider the following excerpts from the corpus. Example 8 (from *Friends*) corresponds with a primary and performative trigger, example 9 (from *The Nanny*) with a tertiary trigger. In example 8, Joey is convinced that a purse for men (the so-called 'man bag') is the rage in Europe, whereas everyone else thinks that he looks rather feminine wearing it. It is Chandler who eloquently points out Joey's fashion gaffe, by acting as if he is not talking to Joey, but to Joey's mother instead (Mrs. Tribiani, line 06).

(8)   FRS/005/013/0295
      01 Joey   ((enters))
      02   <<all> hey;>
      03 Chandler   hey;
      04 Chandler+Ross   ((looking at Joey's 'man bag', then at each other in amazement, then back at Joey))
      05 Chandler   wa:w you look just like your ↑SON;
      06   misses tribiani,
      07 Joey   (-) ↑what;
      08   are you referring to my MAN's BAG,

Prima facie, it seems that the trigger in this fragment is the man bag itself, which would result in a tertiary trigger. This conclusion, however, would be incorrect, since it is not the object that causes Chandler's teasing instance, but *Joey's wearing it* instead. It is, in other words, the odd combination of the manly Joey and the girly man bag that provokes Chandler's teasing, and not the man bag on its own.

In example 9, Fran has taken the children (Brighton, Maggie and Grace) on a trip to the bridal shop where she used to work. While she is chatting with the owner, Brighton and Maggie discover a naked shop-window dummy.

(9) TNN/001/021/0102a
01 Brighton ((standing next to shop-window dummy))
02 maggie LOOK;
03 it's your new BOYfriend;
04 ((knocks on its head))
05 uh it's got your persoNAlity TOO;
06 Maggie (–) and your EQUIPMENT;

As it is clear from this example, it is the non-animate shop-window dummy that causes Brighton to tease Maggie, and vice versa. The first teasing instance, uttered by Brighton, falls under category E because of a tertiary trigger, whereas the subsequent utterance by Maggie, who reacts to what Brighton just said, falls under category A.

The following table presents an overview of the quantitative results for this parameter, which clearly show that the default trigger of a teasing instance is primary and verbal (category A).

Table 2: Absolute and relative frequencies for the parameter 'trigger'.

	A	B	C	D	E
The Nanny	131	16	52	2	10
Spin City	37	6	2	0	0
Married w. Children	62	11	19	2	8
Friends	21	14	5	2	2
Total	**251**	**47**	**78**	**6**	**20**
	(62,4 %)	(11,6 %)	(19,4 %)	(1,4 %)	(4,9 %)

With regard to the question through which specific semantic features or operations verbal utterances are preferably turned into triggers that ignite a teasing instance, we point to the use of hyperunderstanding (Veale et al. 2006; Brône 2008, 2010) as one particular and popular process of intersubjective meaning coordination. In hyperunderstanding, a second speaker recycles verbal elements of a previous speaker in an unexpected, non-salient way in order to gain the rhetorical and intellectual upper hand over their opponent. The verbal element, which is picked up and reinterpreted by the second speaker is referred to as the 'key element' (Brône 2008). In applying this strategy, speakers present themselves as masters of verbal expression and manipulation, capable of successfully exploiting the semantic potential of their opponent's utterance.

Example 10 from *The Nanny* is set around the dinner table, when Fran's mother remarks that CC seems to be reluctant to eat her tongue. It is the ambiguous value of the word *tongue*, meaning either the organ or the fish, that triggers Niles' teasing instance in line 04, after CC's excuse why she isn't eating her tongue. At first sight, Niles' utterance seems fully incongruous in a food-related conversation, until we realize the exploitation of the aforementioned ambiguity.

(10) TNN/001/016/0049
    01 Sylvia   miss babcock;
    02   you've hardly touched your ↑tongue;
    03 CC   actually I'm on a no tongue DIET;
    04 Niles   <<p> o the senator will be so disappointed;>

A more sophisticated example of teasing on the basis of hyperunderstanding is the following sequence in (11) from *Married with children*, in which two key-elements are in play. Al opens up with a first hyperunderstanding of Peg's question 'did you miss me' in the sense of "aiming (with a weapon) at somebody". Peg, however, manages to overpower Al by suggesting that he might need 'a bigger gun' then. Although the word 'gun' has not been used by Al before, it does perfectly match the domain of weaponry, which was introduced by Al's hyperunderstanding. In her sublime reply, Peg stays within Al's conceptual domain and manages to set up yet another hyperunderstanding, which trumps her opponent's initial hyperunderstanding. In her suggestion of him needing 'a bigger gun', she metaphorically refers to Al's allegedly small penis, thus snatching victory from under his nose in this teasing battle.

(11) MWC/005/001/0246
    01 Peg   ((enters))
    02   <<f> ↑hi honey->
    03   he↑he,
    04   did you MISS me;
    05 Al   with every BULLET so fa:r
    06 Peg   (–) we:ll-
    07   maybe you need a bigger GUN sweetheart;
    08   (-) not that i don't LOVE your ITTY BITTY one

With regard to the entire corpus, it turns out that in 67 instances (16,6 %), the realization of teasing hinges on the hyperunderstanding of some key-element, thus indicating its relative importance as a socio-semantic strategy in the realization of interactional humor.

4.4 Parameter 4: Layering

In section 2.1, we introduced the concept of layered meaning, as it was developed by Herbert Clark (1996). In the analysis of teasing, layering plays a crucial role as it appears to be present in most – if not all – teasing instances. We shall illustrate this vital mechanism by means of the following teasing instance from *Spin City*. Stuart does not like the idea that James idolizes the new public schools chancellor: he believes James is merely trying to get a better and more lucrative job by working for this new chancellor. James, on the other hand, does not concur: he explains that the chancellor was his former dean at the University of Columbia, which explains his rather close relationship with him. James further relates how he was a "totally unsophisticated geek" when he started college, at which point Stuart teases him.

(12) SPC/001/006/0205
      01 Stuart   jumping ship,
      02   (-) EGGBOY,
      03 James   (–) ↑what?
      04 Stuart   KISSING up to the new public schools chancellor,
      05   go work under him;
      06   maybe LEAP frog a few positions;
      07   gamble he's a candidate DOWN THE LINE.
      08 James   ↑stuart he was the dean of students at Columbia;
      09   when I showed up freshman year I was this (-) TOTALLY UNSOPHISTICATED GEEK;
      10 Stuart   and he told you it was okay to be that way for ever,

With regard to layering in this fragment, the following movements/actions happen: the first 9 lines all happen on the first layer, which is the layer of bona-fide communication (cf. Kotthoff 1998) commonly referred to as the base space. The main purpose of this first layer is the exchange of information, preferably in the most efficient way. In this case, Stuart verbalizes his complaint and the speculation that the new chancellor has a very good chance of climbing high on the political ladder. James' exchange of information is the aforementioned fact that the chancellor was the former dean of students at the University of Columbia.

In line 10, however, the conversation takes a new direction. Stuart teases James by pretending to have understood that the chancellor told James that it was okay to remain a totally unsophisticated geek. The purpose of this utterance is no longer the efficient exchange of information, but rather the teasing of a target (James) instead. It is a shift from a serious interaction to a more playful interaction. This shift can be seen as the activation of a second layer, created on top of the first layer (Clark 1996). More technically, the entire mechanism consists of the following:

LAYER 2   Implied Stuart thinks implied James is still a geek.
LAYER 1   Stuart pretends that the content of layer 2 is real/true[6].

The notion 'implied' is used to denote those participants that feature on the second layer. It is a role that is played by each first-layer participant, similar to children who pretend to be their favorite superheroes. Yet, Stuart does not pretend to be someone completely different, but instead to be a slightly different *version* of himself.

Two problems arise when analyzing the parameter of layering. The first one is the empirical observation that the layering in a teasing instance is not always as clear-cut as in excerpt 12. The second problem is concomitant to the first: it is even harder to conjure up a common factor which unites the atypical instances (which was the case with the parameter of teaser). The following example from *Friends*, for instance, features a rather vague instance of layering. The context is fairly straightforward: Rachel dreads the sight of someone touching their eye, which gives rise to numerous teasing instances by the entire group of friends.

(13)   FRS/005/022/0304a
       01 Rachel   I'm sorry I'm NOT going to an EYE doctor;
       02 Ross   <<len> o god;
       03   ↑here ↑we go:->
       04 Chandler   what;
       05 Ross   ANY time ANYthing comes close to TOUCHING her eye,
       06   or ANYone else's,
       07   she like (.) FREAKS out;
       08   <<dim> watch watch->
       09   ((moves finger close to his eye))
       10 Rachel   <<f> ross> come on;
       11   that's-
       12   alright;
       13   fine;
       14   okay I have a ↑WEIRD ↑thing with my eye-

---

5 The representation is read from the bottom up. Note that we omitted a third layer, namely the layer of the sitcom itself: it is actually the actor Alan Ruck (layer one) who pretends to be Stuart Bondek (layer two) who pretends to be implied Stuart, who thinks implied James is still a geek (layer three). We consciously chose not to incorporate this layer, since it does not affect the teasing instances proper. Nevertheless, it should always be kept in mind that this layer is present, and that sitcoms are always 'scripted'.

15		can we just not TALK about it plea:se-
16	Monica	[<<p>↑ALright->
17	Ross	[<<p>↑ALright->
18	Joey	[<<p> <incomprehensible>>
19	Chandler	<<p>↑ALright->
20	Monica	<<all> hey rache->
21		you know that GREAT song ehm-
22		(.) me myself and-
23		((moves her finger close to her eye))
24		[<<f> EYE->
25	Rachel	[<<ff> aw> monica;
26		come o:n;
27	Ross	hey does anyone wanna get some lunch,
28		<ollie's and favors>
29		((moves his finger close to his eye))
30		<<f> SAY EYE,>
31	Rachel	<<ff+dim> ross stop it-
32		come on;>
33	Chandler	HOW much (.) did I LOVE (.) the king and-
34		((moves his finger close to his eye))
35		<<f> EYE->=
36	Rachel	Chandler-
37		<<p> alright [okay:,>
38	Joey	((rubs his eye))
39		[<<f> me too me too me too;>

Consider Monica's teasing instance in lines 21–24. The instance proper consists of Monica barely touching her eye, right in front of Rachel. She anchors this action in the homophonic relationship between 'eye' and 'I', referring to Joan Armatrading's hit song *Me, Myself, I*. It may be not so easy to determine whether this teasing sequence involves layered meaning, but ultimately it cannot be ignored. Obviously, Monica is making fun at Rachel because of her absurd phobia and she pretends to genuinely ask Rachel about the song under concern, as if it were a simple exchange of information. On the basis of cultural common ground (almost) everybody knows how the title of the song is completed and therefore it does not need to be explicated in order for the humor to work. As a matter of fact, the humorous mechanism which is at stake here is hyperunderstanding, but not in the prototypical way as in this sequence, the reinterpretation of a first utterance is made by the same speaker of that first utterance (intra-speaker hyperunderstanding). In our example, Monica exploits the homophonic relation between the expected word (*I*) and its homophonic counterpart (*eye*), which is realized in combination with a disambiguating deictic gesture in lines 23 and 24. In these lines, Rachel is directly teased by Monica, who also indulges in basically positive, in-group *schadenfreude* (Feyaerts & Oben 2014).

4.5 Parameter 5: Relation

The final parameter, relation, is a social parameter which has a special status in comparison to the other four parameters of teasing. It is the only one that can be determined prior to any teasing instance. At any given moment in time one should be able to determine the relation between any given two or more people, provided one shares the necessary common ground about the people involved as well as about their context and situation.

The analysis of our data has rendered seven types of interpersonal relation, which are represented and illustrated in table 3. The first vertical axis expresses whether the relation under concern is strong, weak or absent. The selection of either of these three values depends on two aspects which characterize the relationship: duration and frequency. Accordingly, for every teasing instance, it can be determined how long teaser and target know (duration) and how often they meet each other (frequency). The second axis determines the polarity of the relation: is the strong or weak relation positive, neutral or negative? A closer look at the relations between the characters in *The Nanny* may illustrate our point.

Fran and Maxwell have known each other for quite some time and they interact with each other on a daily basis, which leads to a strong relation. At the same time they have also grown very fond of each other (it is arguable that they are starting to fall in love), which results in a positive strong relation. Niles and CC are also supposed to know each other for quite a long time, but they can't stand each other's presence. We thus claim that they share a mutually close, but negative relation. Finally, CC and Gracie, one of Maxwell's children, hardly ever interact and therefore their (weak) relation is neither straightforwardly positive nor negative, which results in a neutral weak relation.

Our data did not yield any example of a strong and neutral relation, as this characterization may be typical, for example, for non-fictitious, long-standing professional relationships among colleagues.

Table 3: The types of interpersonal relationships

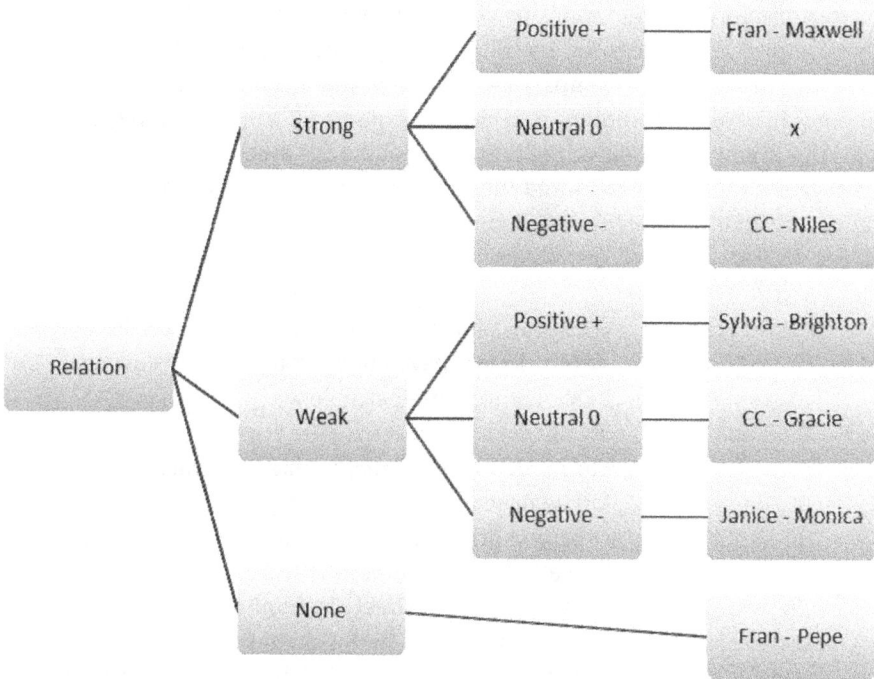

4.6 Two final examples

By way of summarizing our overview of the relevant parameters that allow to determine and characterize teasing sequences, we shall now consider two final excerpts – one prototypical case of teasing and one which is more peripheral – and subsequently analyze these fragments in terms of the five aforementioned parameters.

The first excerpt, example (14) from *The Nanny*, represents a prototypical teasing instance as every parameter can be easily identified and straightforwardly determined. The fragment is set in Mr. Sheffield's office, where he and CC are doing some paperwork while Niles is cleaning Maxwell's desk. Suddenly Fran barges in, subtly trying to tell Maxwell something in private, without Niles hearing it. Based on a mutual trust between long-time friends Maxwell and Niles, the former deems the secrecy unnecessary and invites Fran to speak freely (line 09). CC replies to Maxwell's statement by using a hyper-understanding, thus setting up a first teasing instance in which she targets Niles (line 10). More specifically, CC offers an unexpected causal explanation for

Maxwell's statement as it identifies Niles as the person who violates the elementary house rule of secrecy by listening at the door. In giving this explanation, CC metonymically turns Maxwell's positively intended utterance into a rather negative complaint, thus altering the illocutionary status of Maxwell's utterance. In line 11, Niles in turn trumps this initial teasing instance by construing yet another hyperunderstanding, in which he exploits CC's allegation by specifying the reason why he listens at the door. He realizes the second teasing instance as he suggests CC being a cat – and thus inferior to him – by referring to the typical feline behavior of scratching at doors.

(14) TNN/002/005/0063b
```
01 Mr. Sheffield   <<all> miss fine we're in a bit of a CRUNCH here->
02                 <<rall> do you have anything to say that's even (.)
                   REMOTELY comprehensible;>
03 Fran            ow alright alright;
04                 but I ↑DID wanna tell you this in private;
05                 follow my eyes,
06 Mr. Sheffield   what you don't want to talk in front of the lamp,
07                 (-) wa o ↑niles;
08                 o ↓you can speak freely in front of ↑hi:m,
09                 we have no secrets in this ↑house,
10 CC              <<len> that's because he listens at the DOOR;>
11 Niles           how else would I hear you SCRATCHing to get back IN;
```

The following table represents the analysis of this second teasing instance based on the five parameters.

Table 4: The parametrical analysis of example (14).

Teaser	Niles is the obvious teaser in line 11.
Target	CC is the obvious target of Niles' teasing instance. Like in the majority of teasing instances in the corpus, the target is singular and present.
Trigger	CC's rather hostile teasing instance in line 10 is the ultimate trigger for Niles' teasing instance in line 11. It is a prototypical primary and verbal trigger, as in 62,4 % of the corpus data, involving hyperunderstanding of the key-element 'he listens at doors'.
Relation	CC and Niles represent the textbook-example of a strong but extremely negative relationship.
Layering	The theatrical stage (layer 2) built on top of the bona-fide interaction consists of implied Niles claiming that implied CC is a cat.

The final excerpt, also taken from *The Nanny*, features a more peripheral teasing instance, in which some parameters are more complex and less easy to determine. The fragment is another example of non-actualized teasing, a subphenomenon of teasing which we discussed previously in section 4.1.2.

(15) TNN/002/006/GAMMA-005
    01 Fran   o:w I can't BE↑LIEVE I'm holding a BABY;
    02   if only you came with a HUSband and a house in GREATneck;
    03   (–) okay we gotta act FAST here;
    04   gracie go bring down your pink blanket;
    05 Gracie   ↑not my ↑blanke:y,
    06 Brighton o GOD-
    07   I can't believe you still HAVE that thing;
    08 Fran   and brighton;
    09   bring down the snoopy up in your closet;
    10 Brighton WHAT snoopy in my closet;
    11 Fran   <<p> <<all> you know->>
    12   you're just like my MOther;
    13   WHAT nestle's crunch bar under my nordic track;
    14   (-) GO;
    15 Niles   ((arrives, coming from living room))
    16 Fran   o:w what a DA:Y I had toDA:Y-
    17 Niles   mm let me guess-
    18   YARD SALE at mia farrow's, =
    19 Fran   = <<p> oh> o::ho:w,
    20   Maggie go see if you can find some bottles,
    21   niles do we have any old NIPPLES around the house? =
    22 CC   = ((enters))
    23   hello ↑hello,
    26 Niles   ((bites fran's jacket, as to restrain himself from teasing cc))

Fran enters the Sheffield mansion holding an abandoned baby, and urges Maggie, Brighton and Gracie to find essentials for the child. Niles is asked for some old nipples to place on the bottles mentioned in line 22, at which exact point CC enters and thus triggers a second, metonymically motivated part/whole-interpretation, which refers to CC in a rather unflattering way. The values of the different parameters in this sequence can be determined as follows:

Table 5: The parametrical analysis of example (15).

Teaser	As it is an example of non-actualized teasing, there is no real, prototypical teaser. The fact that Niles bites Fran's coat as a sign of fighting the temptation to tease, shows that he could and would most certainly tease CC, but that he for some reason restrains himself. Concomitantly, we can neither say that there *is* a teaser, nor that there *isn't*. The teaser lies somewhere between absolute presence and absolute absence.
Target	The same analysis holds for the target, which is somewhere between absolute presence and absence as well.
Trigger	The non-actualized teasing sequence is triggered by hyperunderstanding of the key-element 'old nipples' in line 23.
Relation	CC and Niles share a strong but extremely negative relationship.
Layering	Layering is quite a complex parameter in non-actualized teasing: since the teasing instance is not realized, it is impossible to determine a priori how the layering would be manifested. However, through the (potential) trigger 'old nipples' and especially on the basis of expectations and other types of common ground viewers share about the genre, the series, the characters etc. viewers are well-equipped to make safe *predictions* about the hypothetical layering of meaning in this sequence.

In this final subsection we have shown that the five parameters of teasing are not always unambiguously present in a teasing instance. There are indeed many types of teasing that feature rather complex parametrical structures, as pointed out in excerpt (15).

5 Conclusion and future research

In this article we presented an empirical analysis of the phenomenon of teasing as it occurs in four American sitcoms during the nineties. On the basis of a corpus of 402 teasing sequences we have identified five parameters, the combination of which results in an integrated annotation grid. These parameters focus on the specifics of 1) the teaser, 2) the target, 3) the trigger, 4) the interpersonal relation, and 5) the presence of a layered meaning structure. The application of this analytical model allows for a nuanced typological description of teasing as a prototypically structured category of interactional humor. Compared to existing studies of teasing, our corpus-based empirical approach allows for an encompassing, more fine-grained analysis of teasing as an intersubjective process of meaning coordination, in which both cognitive-semantic and social aspects need to be taken into account.

The present study still leaves plenty of room for future research. The first and most obvious elaboration of our model lies in the analysis of larger corpora as well as other types of corpora. The parameters of our annotation grid are determined by the analysis of teasing instances in American sitcoms, but it would be interesting to see to what extent this model can be successfully applied to the analysis of teasing in European or present-day sitcoms. Another interesting perspective would be to investigate instances of teasing in spontaneous conversation among friends, where in-group teasing is commonly expressed as a staged communicative act and thus operated as a positive strategy of social strengthening among the members of a community.

In our study, second, we have mainly adopted a qualitative perspective in an attempt to identify and illustrate every parameter as a component of an integrated analytical model. In this qualitative approach, some quantitative aspects in the interpretation of our data are awaiting further analysis. Pursuing this line of research may reveal additional insights, for instance, about the relative weight of different subtypes of teasing across different data sets.

References

Brône, Geert. 2008. Hyper- and misunderstanding in interactional humor. *Journal of Pragmatics*, 40 (12), 2027–2061.
Brône, Geert. 2010. *Bedeutungskonstitution in verbalem Humor: ein kognitivlinguistischer und diskurssemantischer Ansatz*. Frankfurt/Main: Peter Lang.
Brône, Geert and Bert Oben. 2013. Resonating humor: a corpus-based approach to creative parallelism in discourse. In Tony Veale, Kurt Feyaerts and Charles Forceville (eds.), *Creativity and The Agile Mind: A Multidisciplinary Approach to a Multifaceted Phenomenon*, Berlin: Mouton de Gruyter, 181–203.
Clark, Herbert. 1996. *Using Language*. Cambridge/New York: Cambridge University Press.
Davies, Catherine E. 1984. Joint joking. Improvisational humorous episodes in conversation. In C. Brugman et al. (eds.), *Proceedings of the 10th Annual Meeting of the Berkeley Linguistics Society*; Berkeley: University of Berkeley Press, 360–371.
De Ceukelaire, Robin. 2009. *The art of teasing. Een empirisch-theoretische benadering van teasing in vier Noord-Amerikaanse sitcoms van 1990 tot 1999*. MA thesis University of Leuven (KU Leuven).
Dolitsky, Marlene. 1992. Aspects of the unsaid in humour. *Humor. International Journal of Humor Research*. 5(1–2), 33–43.
Drew, Paul. 1987. Po-faced receipts of teases. *Linguistics*, 25, 219–253;
Dynel, Marta. 2008. No aggression, only teasing: The pragmatics of teasing and banter. *Lodz Papers in Pragmatics*. 4(2), 241–261.
Feyaerts, Kurt and Bert Oben. 2014. Tracing down schadenfreude in spontaneous interaction. Evidence from corpus linguistics. In Wilco van Dijk & Jaap W. Ouwerkerk (eds.) *'Schadenfreude': Understanding Pleasure at the Misfortune of Others*. Cambridge University Press, 275–291.

Givón, Talmy. 2005. *Context as Other Minds. The Pragmatics of Sociality, Cognition and Communication*. Amsterdam/Philadelphia: John Benjamins.

Goldberg, Adele. 2006. *Constructions at Work*. Oxford: Oxford University Press.

Günthner, Susanne. 2000. *Vorwurfsaktivitäten in der Alltagsinteraktion. Grammatische, prosodische, rhetorisch-stilistische und interaktive Verfahren bei der Konstitution kommunikativer Muster und Gattungen*. Tübingen: Max Niemeyer.

Keltner, Dacher, Lisa Capps, Ann M. Kring, Randall C. Young and Erin A. Heerey. 2001. Just Teasing: A Conceptual Analysis and Empirical Review. *Psychological Bulletin*, 127 (2), 229–248.

Kotthoff, Helga. 1998. *Spaß verstehen: zur Pragmatik von konversationellem Humor*. Tübingen: Niemeyer.

Langacker, Ronald W. 2001. 'Discourse in Cognitive Grammar', *Cognitive linguistics*, 12–2, 143–188.

Langlotz, Andreas. 2011. *Creating Social Orientation through Language: A Socio-Cognitive Theory of Situated Social Meaning*. Habilitation. University of Basel.

Martin, Rod A. 2007. *The Psychology of Humor; An Integrative Approach*. Elsevier Academic Press.

Norrick, Neal. 1993. *Conversational joking: Humor in everyday talk*. Bloomington: Inidiana University Press.

Pickering, Martin and Simon Garrod. 2004. Toward a mechanistic psychology of dialogue. *Behavioral and Brain Sciences* 27: 169–226.

Veale, Tony, Kurt Feyaerts and Geert Brône. 2006. The Cognitive Mechanisms of Adversarial Humor. *Humor: The International Journal of Humor Research*, 19 (3): 305–338.

Verhagen, Arie. 2005. *Constructions of Intersubjectivity. Discourse, Syntax and Cognition*. Oxford: Oxford University Press.

Verhagen, Arie. 2008. Intersubjectivity and the architecture of the language system. In Jordan Zlatev, Timothy P. Racine, Chris Sinha, and Esa Itkonen (eds.), *The shared mind: perspectives on intersubjectivity*. Amsterdam: John Benjamins, 307–331.

Whiten, Andrew. 1991. *Natural Theories of Mind: Evolution, Development and Simulation of Everyday Mindreading*. Oxford: Blackwell.

Index

amplitude 160, 161, 176
analogy 112, 121, 122, 123, 124, 125, 126, 127, 142, 144
antanaclasis 104, 105, 106
Antonopoulou, Eleni 2, 4, 6, 18, 26, 41, 199–200
appropriateness 95, 96, 200, 201
Aristotle 73, 74, 82, 112, 127
assumptions 31, 59, 80, 81, 113, 114, 140, 168, 170, 183, 217
Attardo, Salvatore 2, 3, 4, 6, 9, 31, 70, 76, 91, 92, 95, 101, 105–108, 112, 113, 114, 116, 123, 148, 149, 191, 192, 198, 199, 200, 201, 204, 206, 210

Bachorowski, Jo-Anne 156, 157, 158, 159
background knowledge 8, 154, 167, 168, 169, 171, 172, 185, 198, 211
Barsalou, Lawrence 167, 185, 186, 187
Bergen, Benjamin K. 1, 4, 5, 50, 52, 54, 55, 59, 185, 186
Berlyne Daniel 134, 140
Bihrle, Amy 179
Binsted, Kim 1, 4, 5, 52, 59,
bisociation 6, 70, 88, 114
blend 28, 91, 93, 94, 95, 96, 97, 100, 108, 116, 192, 194, 196, 205, 210
Blending Theory (see BT)
boundaries, category 69, 72, 87, 88, 94, 115
brain response 151, 175, 176, 177
Brône, Geert 2, 3, 4, 10, 11, 13, 18, 31, 41, 42, 111, 116, 117, 133, 150, 191, 201, 216, 217, 221, 231
Bryant, Gregory A. 4, 7, 8, 153, 156, 158-161
BT (Blending Theory), 8, 9, 28, 70, 93, 94, 113, 115, 116, 191, 193–94, 196, 197–98, 201, 212
Bybee, Joan 16, 17, 19, 31
bystander 219, 229, 230

cartoons 27, 28, 29, 30, 31, 42, 93, 179
categorization 11, 76, 227, 230
category subversion 78, 80
characterisation 193, 198, 211, 225, 240

Chomsky, Noam 49, 65
CL (see Cognitive Linguistics)
Clark, Herbert H. 153, 169, 215, 216, 217, 218, 221, 227, 233
clause structure 26, 41, 43, 52–53, 57–61, 183
cloze probability 173, 174, 176
CMT (Conceptual Metaphor Theory) 9, 113, 114, 191, 192, 193, 196, 197, 201–2, 205, 207, 211–12
cognition in interaction 218
Cognitive Linguistics (CL) 1, 2, 3–4, 7, 33, 62, 168, 191, 192, 198, 200
cognitive mechanisms 3, 13, 49, 111, 114
cognitive models 8, 169, 170–71, 182, 186, 194
coherence 7, 38, 133, 135, 138, 179
– scale 136, 137
Colston, Herbert L. 151, 152, 153
common ground 9, 215, 217, 218, 221, 222, 225, 227, 236
Conceptual Blending (see BT (Blending Theory))
conceptual domains 5, 6, 63, 93, 94, 95, 99, 100, 106, 194, 195, 196, 197, 205, 232
– source 62, 96, 100, 113, 126, 193, 194, 203, 204, 205, 208, 209, 210
– target 62, 113, 126, 192, 194, 195, 197, 203, 205, 208, 209, 210
Conceptual integration (see BT (Blending Theory))
conceptualisation 120, 121, 208, 210, 212
conceptual mapping 79, 95, 99
Conceptual Metaphor Theory (see CMT)
connections 28, 79, 95, 96, 99, 105, 184, 194
constituents 59, 60
constructional pragmatics 5, 37, 59, 60, 64–65
Construction Grammar (CxG) 4, 5, 13, 14, 15, 17, 19, 27, 28–29, 31, 37, 41, 42, 43, 50
constructions 13, 14, 15, 16, 20, 21, 25, 31–32, 36, 38, 40–43, 51, 52, 53, 59–61
– discourse-based 15, 16, 42

- grammatical 3, 4, 14, 55, 58
- schematic 14, 22, 25, 41, 43
- semi-schematic 16, 25, 28, 30, 39
- semi-substantive 22, 28, 39, 40
- sentence-level 5, 41
- substantive 14, 23, 25, 41
contexts 1, 2, 17, 19, 32, 33, 42, 43, 129, 130, 131, 168, 169, 170, 173
- biasing 130, 131, 136, 138
- supportive 132, 143
contextual information 8, 129, 130, 131, 168, 185, 186
conventionality 16, 17, 32, 34, 39, 77, 117, 122, 131
conventions 5, 15, 17, 19, 20
conversation, spontaneous 153, 156, 159, 218, 219, 241
corpus linguistics 21, 34, 42
Coulson, Seana 1, 4, 8, 9, 13, 21, 64, 70, 93, 94, 96, 113, 115, 116, 133, 150, 168, 170, 171, 173–175, 177–181, 183, 185, 186, 191, 196
Coulthard, Malcolm 22, 26
creativity 4, 6, 15, 65, 70, 89, 111, 117, 118, 125
Cruse, Alan 13, 14, 15, 19
CxG (*see* Construction Grammar)

De Ceukelaire, Robin 10, 221,
direct access view (*see* irony)
Discoursal incongruity (*see* incongruity)
discourse 2, 5, 8, 13, 14, 16, 17, 18–19, 42, 43, 115, 116, 151, 179, 180
- classroom 17, 19, 22–23, 26
- features 42
- legal 107
discourse patterns 4, 13, 14, 16, 18, 31
discourse settings 8, 31, 32, 33, 34, 36, 170, 171, 181
discourse space 28, 31, 38
discourse types 17, 18, 20, 25, 26, 33, 36, 42
distance theory 6, 91, 92, 94, 95, 108, 200
domains (*see* conceptual domains)
Dore, Margherita 4, 9, 91
duality 112, 113, 114, 115, 123

embodied grammar 49, 51, 53, 55, 57, 59, 61, 63, 65, 67
entailments, shared 101, 102
ERPs 8, 175, 176, 177, 178, 180, 181
exaggeration 104, 105
experiments (*see* thought experiments)
expressions
- familiar 134, 142
- fixed 16, 132
- truncated 32, 33

Fauconnier, Gilles 1, 70, 77, 93, 170, 194, 210
Fein, Ofer 4, 7, 130–132, 135, 136, 139, 140, 142
Feyaerts, Kurt 1–4, 10, 13, 16, 18, 31, 41, 42, 111, 116, 150, 191, 201, 236
figurative language 115, 129, 133, 151
figurativeness 7, 121, 132, 133, 135, 136, 138, 139, 140, 142
Fillmore, Charles 14, 16, 17, 19, 26, 33, 37, 50, 52, 64, 167
Fónagy, Ivan 91, 114
frames 8, 16, 42, 64, 95, 167, 170–72, 182, 183, 184, 185, 186, 187, 194, 198
discoursal 29–30
frame semantics 62, 167, 169, 171, 173, 175, 177, 179, 181, 183, 185, 187
frame-shifting 8, 9, 70, 149–51, 171, 172, 173, 174, 177, 178, 179, 181, 182, 183, 186
Freud, Sigmund 88, 111, 124, 134, 142

Galileo 73, 74, 82, 89
Generalized Theory of Verbal Humour (*see* GTVH)
genres 5, 13, 15, 16, 17, 19, 21, 22, 25, 26, 28, 32, 36, 40, 42
- established 19, 20, 22, 31
Gibbs, Raymond W. Jr. 4, 7, 8, 80, 129–132, 142, 143, 147, 148, 150–153, 196
Giora, Rachel 1, 2, 4, 7, 31, 70, 82, 85, 114, 129–136, 138–140, 142, 143, 151, 181, 191
Glenberg Arthur 54, 186
Glucksberg, Sam 129, 130, 152

Goldberg, Adele 13, 17, 18, 31, 33, 37, 50, 51, 218
Graded Salience Hypothesis 7, 114, 130, 131, 132, 137, 138, 142
Grady, Joseph 93, 94, 96, 103, 106, 194, 195, 196–97
Graesser, Arthur 112, 114, 200, 206
grammar 4, 14, 31, 50, 57, 58, 181
Gries, Stefan 34, 47
GTVH (Generalized Theory of Verbal Humour), 3, 8, 9, 70, 76, 77, 85, 113, 114, 191, 198, 199, 200, 201, 212

humor 2, 5, 6–7, 10–11, 49, 58–59, 64–65, 70, 89, 90–91, 112, 114, 116–28, 149, 212
– computational 199
– interactional 4, 10, 218, 221, 232, 240
– linguistic 55, 59, 61, 63, 64, 65, 149, 150
– metaphorical perspective on 111, 113, 115, 117, 119, 121, 123, 125, 127
– satirical 124
– verbal 3, 70, 71, 76, 77, 88, 113, 114, 150, 187, 191, 198, 199
humor and characterisation 191, 193, 195, 197, 199, 201, 203, 205, 207, 209, 211, 213
humor comprehension 59
humorous language 1, 2, 3, 49, 55, 58, 64, 65, 150, 163
humorous non sequitur endings 179
humorous teasing 10, 215, 218, 221
humour (see humor)
hyperunderstanding 231, 232, 235–36, 238, 240

idioms 17, 27, 31, 80, 81, 83, 130, 132, 142
imagery 5, 53, 59, 60, 61–62, 64–65
incongruity 42, 43, 91, 92, 93, 94, 95, 97, 107, 108, 116, 148, 149, 199, 201
– appropriate 2, 3, 71, 75, 79, 81, 83, 101, 116, 200, 201
– discoursal 13, 15, 17, 19, 21, 23, 25, 27, 29, 31, 33, 35, 37, 39, 41
incongruity resolution 2, 3, 95, 106, 114, 116, 149, 150
incongruity theories 112, 113

inferences 52, 53, 62, 65, 184, 185, 191, 194, 197, 203, 205, 208, 210, 211, 217
inferential structure 57–58, 62
innovation, optimal 4, 7, 133, 134, 135, 139, 140, 142
input spaces 28, 93, 103, 113, 115, 116, 117, 194–95, 209
intersubjectivity 216
irony 7, 8, 40, 84, 85, 86, 97, 147, 148, 152, 153, 155, 159, 163, 217
– Direct Access View of 130, 131, 132, 135, 138, 142
– verbal 152, 160, 161
irony and humor 147, 149, 150, 151, 153, 155, 157, 159, 161, 162–63, 165
irony and simile 84, 85, 86

Johnson, Mark 62, 63, 64, 72, 77, 90, 93, 101, 192
joke comprehension 167, 168, 169, 171, 173, 175, 177, 178, 179, 180, 181, 183, 185, 187, 189
joke effects 178, 180
jokes
– narrative 9, 76, 180, 181, 182
– one-line 9, 173, 174, 179
– philosophical 6, 70
– self-standing 204, 211

Katz, Albert 130, 152
Kay, Paul 14, 16, 17, 19, 37, 50, 52
key-element 232, 238, 240
knowledge 1, 8, 51, 53, 63, 80, 154, 183, 222
– contextual 167, 169, 173
– frame-based 64
– linguistic 5, 43, 50, 51, 55, 59, 64, 65, 168
Knowledge Resources (KRs), 199, 202
Kotler, Nurit 4, 7,
Kövecses, Zoltan 113, 192–94, 197
Kutas, Marta 8, 10, 11, 21, 64, 66, 164, 173, 174, 175, 176, 177, 178, 187, 188–89
Kyratzis, Sakis 115, 116, 117, 191, 200

Lakoff, George 49, 53, 62, 63, 74, 77, 93, 101, 123, 192, 207
Langacker, Ronald W., 13, 15, 17, 19, 21, 28, 31, 38, 49, 50, 51, 53, 78, 216, 218

Language
- embodiment of 5, 50
- everyday 197, 205
- literal 131
- natural 55, 58
- non-humorous 58
- nonliteral 130, 131
language comprehension 7, 129, 167, 168, 170, 182
language exposure 51, 58
language processing 54, 167, 176, 177, 186
language structure 19, 49
language use 5, 49, 51, 63, 65, 129, 132, 217
laughter 7, 88, 114, 115, 119–21, 124, 125, 147, 148, 149, 152, 153–59, 161, 162, 163
- antiphonal 156, 157–58, 166
- provoke 88
layering 31, 153, 215, 217, 221, 227, 232, 233, 234, 235, 240
left hemisphere (see LH (left hemisphere))
lexical 15, 16, 25, 32, 56, 76, 78, 186
LH (left hemisphere) 178, 179, 180, 181
linguistic structures 49, 50, 55, 59
listeners 37, 83, 85, 86, 148, 149, 151, 152, 153, 155, 157, 170, 171, 172, 173
literal interpretations 62, 63, 107, 125, 126, 129–33, 135, 136, 137, 138, 139, 140, 142–43, 205, 211
LM (see logical mechanism)
logical mechanism (LM) 76–77, 98, 107, 108, 114, 116, 199, 201

mapping 92, 93, 94, 95, 96, 99, 100, 101, 105, 106, 108, 123–24, 194, 197, 201
Martin, Rod 3, 95, 215, 219, 220
McCarthy, Michael 22, 27–28
meaning construction 9, 162, 167, 169, 170, 182, 186
memory 167, 176, 182, 185, 194
mental spaces 3, 8, 70, 77, 87, 93, 94, 113, 116, 192, 194, 195–96
metaphor 92, 94, 95, 101, 103–8, 111, 112, 114, 115, 116, 124, 126, 140–43, 192–97, 200–207
- conceptual 9, 62, 63, 114, 118, 120, 121, 124, 191, 192, 193, 197, 211
- conventional 102, 104, 115, 118, 121, 124, 197
- creative 117–18, 122, 126
- dead 121
- entrenched 196, 197, 205
- failed 6, 92, 99, 101, 105
- humorous 6, 91, 92–97, 99, 100, 101, 103, 105–9, 115, 116, 117, 192, 200, 201, 202
- mixed 101, 103, 105, 106
- novel 7, 9, 93, 115, 116, 135, 136, 139, 140, 142, 196, 197, 201, 208, 211
- overdone 103, 104, 105, 106
- primary 104
- sensory 122, 124
- unfamiliar 136, 137, 138, 139
- universal 192–93
metaphor and humor 6, 7, 9, 111, 112, 114, 115, 116, 192, 200, 211
metaphor comprehension 114
metaphor humorous 96
metaphorical expressions 9, 91, 98, 113, 117, 118, 119, 122, 193, 200, 202, 204, 207, 212
metaphorical mappings 6, 7, 111, 121
metaphorical meaning 112, 116, 136, 142, 205, 211
metaphorical puns 117, 125
metonymy 13, 34, 80, 83, 91, 102, 108, 116, 121, 201, 221
models, mental 51, 171, 189
motor imagery 54, 55, 61
Müller, Ralph 4, 6, 7, 9, 112, 117, 124, 200
Mukařovský, Jan 117, 134

Nikiforidou, Kiki 2, 4, 6, 16, 26, 28, 41
non sequitur endings 178, 179
Norrick, Neal 205, 219, 220–21, 225

Oakley, Todd 93, 94, 96, 113
O'Connor, Mary Catherine 17, 19
Optimal Innovation Hypothesis 7, 129, 138, 139, 140
Oring, Elliott 71, 95, 96, 98, 101, 114, 116, 200, 201
Östman, Jan-Ola 13, 14, 16, 21, 26, 41

Paul, Jean 111, 112, 118, 122, 123, 124, 126
Peleg, Orna 130, 131
perceptual symbols 185–87
performative 229, 230
pitch 156, 159, 160, 162
pleasure/pleasurability 7, 129, 131, 133, 135, 137, 139, 140–43, 145
Pollio, Howard 91, 94, 114–16
pragmatics 4, 13, 38, 50, 51, 58, 59, 62, 167, 168–70, 172
pretense 153, 217, 227, 233
processing 7, 49, 95, 129, 132, 143, 151, 173, 175, 177, 179, 180
– higher-level 9, 178
processing differences 130, 132, 180
processing difficulties 132, 174, 180
properties, discoursal 19, 21, 32, 36, 40, 42
prosody 160, 161, 162
Provine, Robert 154, 159
punch line 161, 162, 178, 181, 199, 204, 207, 211

Raskin, Victor 2, 3, 8, 64, 70, 76, 113, 128, 198, 213
reading times 8, 135, 136, 151, 174, 175, 177, 178
– increased 174
– self-paced 173
representation
– message-level 8, 170, 171, 173, 178
– schematic 51, 52, 185, 187
RH (right hemisphere), 178, 179, 180, 181
right hemisphere (see RH (right hemisphere))
role, participant 224
Rumelhart, David 184, 198

salience 7, 19, 32, 41, 42, 76, 129, 131, 132, 133, 134, 135, 136, 140, 142
sarcasm 88, 130, 147, 148, 151, 152, 153, 163, 217
scalar humor 59
script opposition 9, 41, 103, 107, 108, 198, 199, 202, 212
scripts 6, 36, 42, 64, 70, 76, 78, 85, 87, 88, 107, 114, 182, 184, 198–99

Searle, John 73, 82, 130
semantic activation 176, 179, 180
Semino, Elena 34, 94, 103, 191, 193, 196, 197, 207
sentence meaning 168, 170
sentence pattern 50, 51, 52, 57
sentence type 50, 57, 137, 139
Shuval, Noa 4, 7
Simpson, Paul 18, 31
Sinclair, John 22, 37
sitcoms 39, 219, 222, 224, 234
Smoski, Moria 156, 159
source domains (see conceptual domains)
spaces (see mental spaces)
– blended 93, 116, 196, 209
space structuring model 8, 167, 168, 170, 186
Sperber, Dan 142, 153
Spivey-Knowlton, Michael 168
SSTH (Semantic Script Theory of Humour), 3, 8, 76, 198, 199
staged communicative acts 4, 8, 153, 163, 217, 221, 227, 241
Standard Pragmatic Model 130, 131, 132, 135, 138, 142
Stefanowitsch, Anatol 16, 34, 52
stereotype 85, 86, 87, 97
subversion 6, 71, 73, 74, 75, 78, 79, 80, 81, 82, 83, 85–89, 210

target domains (see conceptual domains)
teaser 206, 219, 220, 222–23, 226, 227–30, 234, 240
teasing 10, 215–225, 6, 69, 70, 71–73, 75, 77, 79, 82, 87, 88
– compressed 69, 71, 224, 226, 227, 229, 230, 232, 233, 236, 237, 238, 239, 240, 241
thought experiments 73, 75, 77, 79, 81, 83, 85, 87, 89
trumping 71, 80, 81, 87
Tsakona Villy 2, 4, 6, 28, 199, 200
Tsur, Reuven 94, 200
Turner, Mark 49, 70, 77, 79, 93, 94, 123, 170, 193, 194, 196, 210

understanding 14, 51, 59, 61, 65, 80, 96, 114, 129, 180, 181, 182, 192, 194, 217
Ur-jokes 77
utterances 13, 19, 31, 49, 53, 61, 117, 133, 142, 149, 163, 172
– contexts of 168, 169
– ironic 153, 160
– nonliteral 129, 130

validity 32, 34, 196, 200
Veale, Tony 1–6, 13, 18, 41, 42, 76, 79, 80, 88, 91, 100, 110, 111, 113, 116, 150, 201, 231
Verhagen, Arie 216, 217, 218

Wilson, Deirdre 142, 153

Zwaan, Rolf 54, 186

www.ingramcontent.com/pod-product-compliance
Lightning Source LLC
Chambersburg PA
CBHW070610170426
43200CB00012B/2641